Canadian Protestant
and Catholic Missions,
1820s–1960s

Toronto Studies in Religion

Donald Wiebe, General Editor
Trinity College
University of Toronto

Vol. 3

Published in association with
the Centre for Religious Studies
at the University of Toronto

PETER LANG
New York · Bern · Frankfurt am Main · Paris

Canadian Protestant and Catholic Missions, 1820s–1960s

Historical Essays in Honour of John Webster Grant

Edited by
John S. Moir
C. T. McIntire

Foreword by
Robert T. Handy

PETER LANG
New York · Bern · Frankfurt am Main · Paris

Library of Congress Cataloging-in-Publication Data

Canadian protestant and Catholic missions, 1820s–1960s.
(Toronto studies in religion ; vol. 3)
1. Missions—Canada.   2. Missions, Canadian.
3. Grant, John Webster.   I. Grant, John Webster.
II. Moir, John S.   III. McIntire, C. T.   IV. Series.
BV2810.C29   1987   266′.00971   87-22612
ISBN 0-8204-0465-9
ISSN 8756-7385

CIP-Kurztitelaufnahme der Deutschen Bibliothek

Canadian prostestant and catholic missions,
1820s [eighteen hundred and twenties] −
1960s : histor. essays in honour of John Webster
Grant / ed. by John S. Moir; C.T. McIntire. −
New York; Bern; Frankfurt am Main; Paris:
Lang 1988.
  (Toronto Studies in Religion; Vol. 3)
  ISBN 0-8204-0465-9

NE: Moir, John S. [Hrsg.] ; Grant, John Webster:
Festschrift; GT

Printed by Weihert-Druck GmbH, Darmstadt, West Germany

THE SERIES EDITOR'S PREFACE

Toronto Studies in Religion, published in association with the Centre for Religious Studies in the University of Toronto, is concerned primarily with the empirical, analytical, and theoretical study of religions. It aims to publish original research in the historical, phenomenological, and social-scientific study of the world's religious traditions, as well as new structural and theoretical interpretations of religion in general. Philosophical, and even speculative approaches to understanding religious phenomena, carried within a generally historical/empirical framework, will also be given consideration. The series will also include works on methodological problems in the academic study of religions, translations of works that deserve a wider readership and that will encourage international scholarly discussion and debate, symposia, and other appropriate projects.

This volume is of particular interest to the series because its authors continue the transformation of the study of a religious phenomenon that has, until recently, been almost entirely hagiographical and edifying. The history of missions, to be sure, became an academic discipline in the European context in the latter half of the nineteenth century. And that new discipline had expected of its practitioners possession of the same intellectual qualities and commitments that characterized the scholars in other fields of study in the university setting; they, like the others, that is, were expected to submit themselves to the same morality of knowledge. Nevertheless, missiology, as that historical study of missions came to be called, was still conceived to be an essentially religious/theological enterprise concerned, as one of its champions put it, with "the story of the way of God among the nations of the earth." Stephen Neill's plea in 1970 for a serious consideration of "The History of Missions [As] An Academic Discipline," consequently, distinguishes between the church historian and the secular historian in making the task of the former the understanding of the world "in the light of a divine purpose." No such distinction is assumed here and the editors and authors quite consciously transcend this theological intention, although they do not deny that their work may hold some import for theology. This new history of missions, therefore, stands squarely within the pale of the academic/scientific study of religions as an historical-cum-sociological enterprise which is focussed on an immensely important aspect of the history of our culture that has for far too long been ignored outside religious and theological circles.

Donald Wiebe
Centre for Religious Studies
University of Toronto

TABLE OF CONTENTS

FOREWORD

Robert T. Handy

The publication of a volume of historical essays in honour of John Webster Grant is a welcomed event. Grant first became known to me some thirty years ago when he was professor of church history in Vancouver. Since then our professional responsibilities have brought us together on many occasions, for as this American became deeply interested in Canadian church history, Grant gave generously of his time to help me understand it better. In his writings he has offered helpful comparisons between Canadian and American church history which have been particularly useful to us south of the border.

Widely known over the past three decades through many books written and edited and through many published chapters and articles, Grant has rightly been considered as the dean of Canadian church historians. I share the judgment of that reviewer of his pioneering *Moon of Wintertime: Missionaries and the Indians of Canada in Encounter since 1534* (1984) who said, "His appreciation for historical accuracy, theological flexibility, cultural diversity, and human empathy with every concrete situation will make this work endure as a benchmark for its genre."

The fruits of his scholarship have also been shared generously with his students at Emmanuel College and the University of Toronto. I have had the privilege of seeing him in action on several doctoral examining committees, and have appreciated not only the way that the breadth of his knowledge is displayed on such occasions, but also the thoughtful manner in which he guides candidates to do the best work of which they are capable in putting their dissertations in final form.

Throughout Grant's impressive career he consistently showed qualities of mind and spirit that have endeared him to generations of students, colleagues, and others in Canada and beyond, and they in relatively brief contacts have learned to respect not only his scholarship but his personal warmth and genuine concern for people. Many persons near and far have reason to be grateful to him for his wisdom and patience, and will rejoice in this tribute to his leadership in the field of Canadian religious history.

ACKNOWLEDGEMENTS

This volume of essays presents the results of new research in the history of Canadian Christian missions since the 1820s. The editors and the authors dedicate them to Professor John Webster Grant who retired in 1984 from his position as Professor of Church History at Emmanuel College in the University of Toronto and the Toronto School of Theology. Missions history is an important topic in his writings, and all of us are prepared to acknowledge that on this topic, as on others, we have learned much from him.

By way of introduction the editors provide two items. The first reviews Grant's career and appends a list of his major writings, and the second offers a discussion of the approaches and themes of the essays. Professor Robert T. Handy writes the foreword which indicates something of the international influence Grant has enjoyed.

The volume began at the initiative of the Canadian Society of Church History and has proceeded with the support of several institutions. In particular, we wish to acknowledge with thanks grants and other assistance toward publication received from: the Canadian Society of Church History; Emmanuel College and Victoria University, Toronto; the Committee on Theological Education for Ministry and the Book Publishing Fund of the United Church of Canada; The Humanities and Social Sciences Committee of the Research Board of the University of Toronto; Trinity College, Toronto; and the Centre for Religious Studies of the University of Toronto.

We express our thanks also to Professor Donald Wiebe, editor of the series Toronto Studies in Religion, to Ms. Siobhan Jones, staff assistant, and to the staff of Peter Lang Publishers.

The joint meeting of the American Society of Church History and the Canadian Society of Church History at McMaster University, April 1987, provided a fitting occasion for the presentation of these essays to Professor Grant.

John S. Moir and C. T. McIntire
University of Toronto
April 1987

CONTRIBUTORS
in order of appearance

John S. Moir is Professor of History at Scarborough College, University of Toronto.

C. T. McIntire is Associate Professor of History at Trinity College, University of Toronto.

Robert T. Handy is Henry Sloane Coffin Professor Emeritus of Church History, Union Theological Seminary, New York.

Elizabeth Muir is completing a Ph.D. at McGill University's Faculty of Religious Studies, working on a thesis on the role of women in early Canadian Methodism.

Robert Merrill Black is finishing a Th.D. at Trinity College, University of Toronto, with a dissertation on Protestant missions in French Canada.

Brian P. Clarke, a Research Reader at the Centre for Religious Studies, University of Toronto, holds a Ph.D. from the University of Chicago where he wrote a thesis on Irish Catholics in Victorian Toronto.

Geoffrey Johnston received a Th.D. from Knox College, Toronto, after writing a thesis on Presbyterian missions in Trinidad. He is currently Director of Studies at The Presbyterian College in Montreal.

Ruth Compton Brouwer has a Ph.D. in history from York University and completed a thesis on Canadian women and foreign missions, especially in India.

Ronald G. Sawatsky graduated with a Ph.D. from the Centre for Religious Studies, University of Toronto, where he wrote a dissertation on evangelicals in Canada before the first world war.

Alison Kemper holds a Th.M. from Trinity College, University of Toronto and has a research interest in women and religion in Canada.

Brian J. Fraser was awarded a Ph.D. in history by York University where he completed a thesis on Presbyterian religious and social thought around the turn of the century. He now teaches at the Vancouver School of Theology.

Mark George McGowan is completing a Ph.D. in history at the University of Toronto with a thesis on Roman Catholics in Toronto from the 1890s to the 1920s.

Paul R. Dekar has a Ph.D. from the University of Chicago and currently teaches church history at the Divinity College, McMaster University.

A BIOGRAPHICAL SKETCH OF JOHN WEBSTER GRANT, WITH A LIST OF HIS MAJOR WRITINGS

John S. Moir

Biographical Sketch

Born 27 June 1919 at Truro, Nova Scotia, John Webster Grant matriculated from historic Pictou Academy in 1935 and entered Dalhousie University in Halifax. Three years later he graduated with a B.A. *magna cum distinctione* and the Prince of Wales Medal, and entered Princeton University on a junior fellowship to study politics. A year later John declined a senior fellowship from Princeton to return to Halifax to begin theological studies at the United Church of Canada's Pine Hill Divinity Hall. While a student at Pine Hill John completed his M.A. at Dalhousie in 1941 and that same year won Nova Scotia's Rhodes Scholarship. Because of the war he postponed his entry into Oxford University and instead finished working for his certificate in Theology in 1943 when he was ordained as minister of the United Church in West Bay, Nova Scotia.

John's stay in the pastorate was short, for in 1943 he joined the Wartime Information Board in Ottawa as Director of Information to Non-Roman Catholic Churches. Two years later, in the closing months of the war, he was appointed a chaplain in the Royal Canadian Navy, a position he also held in the Naval Reserve from 1952 to 1959. When the war ended John and his wife Gwen, whom he had married in 1944, took up residence in Oxford to complete his tenure of the Rhodes Scholarship. In 1949 he received the D. Phil. degree, and his dissertation was published in 1959 as *Free Churchmanship in England, 1870-1940*. Two years earlier his book on ecumenism, *World Church: Achievement or Hope?*, had already been produced in Canada.

Returning to Canada after John's graduation the Grants settled in Vancouver where John had been appointed Woodward Professor of Church

History at Union College of British Columbia. He remained there for the next decade except for 1957-8 when he was Visiting Professor at the United Theological College of South India and Ceylon in Bangalore, India. That visit led to the publication one year later of *God's People in India*. John left teaching in 1959 to join the editorial staff of Ryerson Press, and one year later succeeded Dr. Lorne Pierce as its editor-in-chief. Even while filling the editorial chair, however, his writing continued, with *The Ship under the Cross* being published in 1960 and *George Pidgeon: A Biography* appearing just two years later.

The call of the classroom was, however, still strong and in 1963 John resigned from Ryerson Press to become professor of church history in the United Church of Canada's Emmanuel College, Toronto. The academic life provided further incentives and opportunities for writing, and in addition to numerous articles he produced four more monographs -- *God Speaks . . . We Answer* in 1965, *The Canadian Experience of Church Union* in 1967, *The Church in the Canadian Era* in 1972, and finally *Moon of Wintertime: Missionaries and the Indians of Canada in Encounter since 1534* in 1984, the year of his retirement from Emmanuel College. Even in retirement he has continued to write and as this volume of essays is going to press John's next study, a history of religion in Ontario, is in its final stages of publication.

The range of John's interests and writing during these years is displayed in the bibliography appended to this sketch. His academic achievements as author and teacher are attested to by the four honorary degrees conferred on him over the space of a quarter century by Union College of British Columbia, by his alma mater Pine Hill Divinity Hall, and by Trinity and Victoria universities in the University of Toronto. As well as the Rhodes Scholarship he has received two travelling awards and in 1976-7 held a Canada Council Leave Fellowship to assist his research into the history of missions to native Canadians. He has over the years been much in demand, both in Canada and abroad, as a lecturer, and among the invitations he has accepted were those of Kerr Lecturer at McMaster Divinity College in 1967 and Vanier Lecturer at the University of Ottawa in 1973.

In addition to his regular teaching duties as professor of church history at Emmanuel College in the Toronto School of Theology, including the offering of advance degree courses and supervising the theses of graduate students in the School, John served as chairman of the School's Historical Department from 1969 to 1972. He was also a member of the University of Toronto's Department of Religious Studies, and after being cross-appointed to the School of Graduate Studies in the University of Toronto he became in 1977 one of the original faculty members of the University's graduate Centre for Religious Studies. These latter appointments meant that he was frequently involved in the supervision and examination of theses in various graduate departments of the University including History, Sociology, and the Ontario Institute for Studies in Education, as well as in the Toronto School of Theology.

As a member of Emmanuel College in Victoria University, John served for several years during the 1970s on Victoria's Board of Regents and Finance Committee and on the Victoria Commission on University Government, and from 1964 to 1979 was Associate Director of Victoria's Centre for Reformation and Renaissance Studies. From 1972, when the quarterly *Studies in Religion/Sciences Religieuses* was founded, until 1976 he was the managing editor of that journal. His memberships in scholarly historical societies included the American Society of Church History, the Canadian Society of Church History of which he was president in 1967-8, the Canadian Society of Presbyterian History, the Canadian Methodist Historical Society of which he was elected president in 1983, and the Canadian Historical Association. On the theological side John was secretary of the organizing committee of the North American Academy of Ecumenists from 1965 to 1967 and later an executive of the Academy, a member of the Council on Theological Research and Scholarship of the Association of Theological Schools, and president of the Pacific Coast Theological Conference in 1953-4.

This brief recital of John's busy academic career does not take account of his many active years as a churchman. He has had five hymns, four of them translations from the Latin, published in various hymnbooks in Canada, the United States, Britain, and Australia, and he prepared the lectionary in the Service Book of the United Church of Canada. As a professorclergyman without the responsibilities of a parish, he has inevitably been asked -- and has accepted -- to fill church pulpits on innumerable occasions. His most extended and intensive service to his church, however, involved the five years, 1967 to 1971, that he served as chairman of the executive committee of the United Church's commission on the proposed union with the Anglican Church of Canada.

When, in 1984, John retired from teaching -- but not from research, writing, lecturing, preaching and church responsibilities -- friends and colleagues organized a day-long conference on a theme that had often engaged John's own talents and time, namely, the relationship of religion to Canadian national identity. The four papers read that day in May to a large audience at Emmanuel College were subsequently published as part of the proceedings of the Conference of the Association for Canadian Studies in *Religion/Culture: Comparative Canadian Studies -- Etudes canadiennes comparées*. In introducing that volume the editors, Bill Westfall and Louis Rousseau, expressed concisely the same feelings that motivated the production of this Festschrift: "Professor Grant is without doubt one of the leading scholars in the history of religion in Canada, a man whose teaching and writing have done so much to enliven what for so long has remained a neglected field of study."

Monographs

World Church: Achievement or Hope? (Toronto: Ryerson, 1956)

Free Churchmanship in England, 1870-1940 (London: Independent Press, 1958)

God's People in India (Toronto: Ryerson, 1959; London: Highway, 1960; Madras: CLS, 1960)

The Ship under the Cross (Toronto: Ryerson, 1960)

George Pidgeon: A Biography (Toronto: Ryerson, 1962)

God Speaks ... We Answer (Toronto: Ryerson, 1965)

The Canadian Experience of Church Union (London: Lutterworth, 1967)

The Church in the Canadian Era (Toronto: McGraw-Hill Ryerson, 1972; 2nd ed., Burlington, Ont.: G.R. Welch, 1987)

Moon of Wintertime: Missionaries and the Indians of Canada in Encounter since 1534 (Toronto: University of Toronto Press, 1984)

A Profusion of Spires: Religion in Ontario until 1900 (Ontario Historical Society, Ontario Historical Studies Series, forthcoming)

Books edited
The Churches and the Canadian Experience (Toronto: Ryerson, 1963)

Salvation! O the Joyful Sound: The Selected Writings of John Carroll (Toronto: Oxford, 1967)

General editor, *A History of the Christian Church in Canada* by H.H. Walsh, John S. Moir, and John Webster Grant, 3 vols. (Toronto: Ryerson and McGraw-Hill Ryerson, 1966-72)

Die Unierten Kirchen (Stuttgart: Evangelishes Verlagswerk, 1973), English text

Articles and Contributed Chapters
"Population Shifts in the Maritime Provinces," *Dalhousie Review*, 17:3 (1937-38), 282-94

"Conflicting Interests in the Far East," *Dalhousie Review*, 18 (1938-39), 315-27

"Asking Questions of the Canadian Past," *Canadian Journal of Theology*, 1:2 (July 1955), 98-104

"Christianity and Contemporary Societal Thought," in R.C. Chalmers and J.A. Irving, eds., *The Light and the Flame* (Toronto: Ryerson, 1956), 105-18

"Blending Traditions: The United Church of Canada," *The Canadian Journal of Theology*, 9:1 (January 1963), 50-9

"Liturgical Revision in the United Church of Canada," *Studia Liturgica*, 3:1 (Winter 1964), 189-90

"Blending Traditions: The United Church of Canada," in John Webster Grant, ed., *The Churches and the Canadian Experience* (Toronto: Ryerson, 1963), 133-44

"Principles of Union in Canada," *Journal of Ecumenical Studies*, 3:1 (Winter 1966), 250-3

"Introduction" to John S. Moir, ed., *The Cross in Canada* (Toronto: Ryerson, 1966), vii-xv

"The Church and Canada's Self-Awareness," *Canadian Journal of Theology*, 13:3 (July 1967), 155-64

"The Impact of Christianity on Canadian Culture and Society, 1867 to the Present," *Theological Bulletin*, McMaster Divinity College, 3 (January 1968), 39-50

"The Reaction of WASP Churches to non-WASP Immigrants," Canadian Society of Church History, *Papers* (1968), Part I, 1-15

"Canadian Confederation and the Protestant Churches," *Church History*, 38:3 (September 1969), 327-37

"Trends in der Kongregationalisten Theologie," (English original) in Norman Goodall, ed., *Der Kongregationalismus* (Stuttgart: Evangelishes Verlagswerk, 1972), 156-71

"'At least you knew where you stood with them': Reflections on religious pluralism in Canada and the United States," *Studies in Religion/Sciences Religieuses*, 2:4 (Spring 1973), 340-51

"Die Entstehung der unierten Kirchen der Gegenwart" and "Die Bedeutung der Kirchenunionen" (English originals), in *Die unierten Kirchen* (Stuttgart: Evangelishes Verlagswerk, 1973), 7-28, 321-40

"Christianity in Canada," in Robert Choquette, ed., *L'homme, les religions et la liberte / Man, Religion and Freedom* (Ottawa: University of Ottawa Press, 1974), 9-37

"Canada, Christianity in," in F.L. Cross, ed., *The Oxford Dictionary of the Christian Church* (London: Oxford University Press, 1974), 228-9

"The Methodist Church (Canada)," in Nolan B. Harmon, ed., *Encyclopedia of World Methodism* (Nashville: United Methodist Publishing House, 1974), 385-401

"Pioneer of Union: Fifty Years of the United Church," *Chelsea Journal*, 1:5 (September-October 1975), 245-9

"A Moratorium on Canadian Church Union Talks," *Mid-Stream*, 15:3 (June 1976), 256-62

"Religious and Theological Writings," in Carl F. Klinck, ed., *A Literary History of Canada*, 2nd ed. (Toronto: University of Toronto Press, 1976), 2:75-94; 3:104-10

"A Decade of Ferment: Canadian Churches in the 1960's," in Stewart Crysdale and Les Wheatcroft, eds., *Religion in Canadian Society* (Toronto: Macmillan/McLean-Hunter, 1976), 207-18

"Religion and the Quest for a National Identity: The Background in Canadian History," in Peter Slater, ed., *Religion and Culture in Canada* (Waterloo: Wilfrid Laurier University Press, 1977), 7-22

"Indian Missions as European Enclaves," *Studies in Religion/Sciences Religieuses*, 7:3 (1978), 263-76

"The United Church as Context of Ministry," *Theological Education in the 80's* (Summer 1978), 3-7

"The United Church of Canada: Its Way of Experiencing and Expressing the Ultimate Reality and Meaning," in section on "History," *Ultimate Reality and Meaning*, 1:2 (1978), 100-6

"Rendezvous at Manitowaning: The Scramble for Indian Souls," *Bulletin of the Archives Committee of the United Church of Canada*, 28 (1979), 22-34

"Missionaries and Messiahs in the Northwest," *Studies in Religion/Sciences Religieuses*, 9:2 (1980), 125-36

"Response to Robert T. Handy, 'Trends in Canadian and American Theological Education, 1880-1980': Some Comparisons," *Theological Education*, 18:2 (Spring 1982), 226-33

"Carroll, John Saltkill," in *Dictionary of Canadian Biography*, 11 (Toronto: University of Toronto Press, 1982), 143-4

"Leading a Horse to Water: Reflections on Church Union Conversations in Canada," in Horton Davies, ed., *Studies of the Church in History: Essays honoring Robert S. Paul on his Sixty-fifth Birthday* (Allison Park, Pa.: Pickwick, 1983), 163-81

"Pierce, Lorne," and "Ryerson Press, The," in *The Oxford Companion to Canadian Literature* (Toronto: Oxford University Press, 1983), 648-9, 721-2

"The Churches in Canadian Space and Time," *Mid-Stream*, 22: 3,4 (July/October 1983), 354-62

"The United Church: Its Heritage in Evangelism," *Touchstone*, 1:3 (October 1983), 6-13

"Religion and Life in Upper Canada," in Nick and Helma Mika, *The Shaping of Ontario* (Belleville: Mika, 1985), 134-9

"United Church of Canada," in *The Canadian Encyclopedia*, 3 (Edmonton: Hurtig, 1985), 1869-70

"Holmes, Elkanah," and "Hubbard, Hester Ann," in *Dictionary of Canadian Biography*, 6 (Toronto: University of Toronto Press, 1987), 324-5, 335-6

"Lois Wilson," in *The Canadian Encyclopedia* (2nd ed.; Edmonton: Hurtig, forthcoming)

"Ketchum, Seneca," in *Dictionary of Canadian Biography*, 7 (Toronto: University of Toronto Press, forthcoming)

"Evans, Ephraim," in *Dictionary of Canadian Biography*, 12 (Toronto: University of Toronto Press, forthcoming)

APPROACHES AND THEMES

IN THE HISTORY OF MISSIONS

C. T. McIntire

Multifactoral History

The essays in this volume are historical studies of various people and their activities in Christian missions in Canada and abroad between the 1820s and the 1960s. The studies are intended to illuminate a type of activity which has exercised considerable influence in Canadian religious history. They are published in the hope that what they uncover will be useful both to Canadian historical study and to the comparative history of missions.

Most of the essays study events in the narrower period between the 1870s and the 1920s. This may be called the second of two periods of extensive missionary activity in Canadian history. The first came in the seventeenth century when the French settled New France and evangelized the Indians. The second period was dominated by English-language missions undertaken by both Protestants and Roman Catholics within Canada and around the world. Canadians became senders of missionaries even as simultaneously they continued to be the subjects of missions by others.

The volume is not a continuous and comprehensive history of Canadian missions, but a chronologically arranged series of investigations into that history. We may read them as ten case studies in missions history. The subject is almost exclusively English-language missions. One essay does take a look at French-speaking Protestant missions in French Canada, but even here much of the initiative for the missions came from English-speaking sources. Regionally most of the essays pertain to central Canada, especially Toronto, while three essays relate to other regions -- the Maritimes, French Canada, and the Prairies. Overseas the essays take us to two lands -- Trinidad and India -- and by immigration and the flow of money and missionaries we make contact with the Ukraine, Ireland, Switzerland, France, the Vatican, England, Scotland, and the United States. In terms of denominational identities the missions include work by Methodists, Presbyterians, the Church of England in Canada, Roman Catholics, and members of these traditions co-operating in non-denominational evangelical work. These essays analyze a wide variety of missions, including foreign missions, urban missions, missions among non-English immigrants, missions among Jews, missions among Indians, and social missions. It must be admitted from the outset that all the essays focus on the missionaries and their senders, and none examine the reception of the missionaries or the impact of the missionaries on the peoples missionized. Thus, while the essays are in some ways wide ranging, they are in other ways greatly restricted in what they attempt to study. Nonetheless, through these ten doorways, they open our senses to a vast and complex world of Christian missions.

The volume is a contribution to the current efforts to define new attitudes and new approaches to the historical study of missions. It is possible to distinguish an older historiography of missions from a newer one to which these essays belong. The older historical studies were written to tell the "story of missions" and to recount the "deeds of the missionaries." Those histories followed with pious respect the triumphs and the accomplishments of the missionaries and of the societies and agencies which supported them. They most often took the form of missionary biographies or of histories of denominational missions and other missions agencies. The very best of these, like the incomparable work of Kenneth Scott Latourette, told the story in a wide context, even a global context, and made us aware of many of the complexities of missions undertakings. While they no longer presented missions in explicitly theological terms as the handiwork of God and they no longer depicted missionaries in simple hagiographic colours, they continued to think of missions as strictly theological and evangelistic movements to spread the Gospel, driven by motives of bringing glory to God and of extending the church of Christ, the company of the redeemed. This older missions history was designed to serve as a branch of theology or missiology.[1]

The essays in this volume belong to a new missions historiography. They certainly retain a clear sense of respect for the missionaries and their work, and they continue to regard Christian missions as primarily religious in character. Hence they discuss readily the Christian dedication of the missionaries and identify the theological ideas and spiritual motivations of the senders and the goers. The essays move dramatically beyond such matters, however. They seek as a conscious matter of method to analyze the multifactoral complexity of the missions and with a sense of critical fairness to identify the ambiguities of the work and the motivations of the people involved. At the same time they attempt to distinguish between, on the one hand, the intentions and actual work of the missionaries and, on the other, the unintended results of their work which often in retrospect accentuated both the complexities and the ambiguities of the work. Consequently, these essays do present the work of missions as religious in character, but at the same time they treat them also as social, political, and economic. They do interpret missions as acts of spiritual devotion, but at the same time they analyze them as relations of social classes, as relations between women and men, as encounters between cultures, as immigration, as modes of conflict, and much more. This new approach to missions history treats life as a whole, even when focussing upon only this or that activity or moment of life. Like the older missions history these essays tell us about individual missionaries and mission societies, and they teach us about the course of events and how things happened. But these essays understand the missionaries to be involved in more complicated relationships than we knew them to be engaged in before, and they endeavour by analysis to disclose this multiplex character of the events. The essays introduce us to a multiplicity of factors as they seek to identify and explain the course of events. This missions history aims to enlarge our historical understanding of missions and by so doing to contribute to our understanding of religion, human culture as well as theology.

Missions History in Abundance

The history of missions has burgeoned into a genuine area of research all its own. It has become an exciting field which conjoins world history, regional history, social history, intercultural history, women's history, ethnic and immigration history, demography, political and economic history as well as religious history. Perhaps it is fair to say that historians studying missions history wish to share in making religious history the global and multifactoral history that it ought to become.

John Webster Grant himself has contributed to the transformation of missions history. His book *Moon of Wintertime: Missionaries and the Indians of Canada in Encounter since 1534*, published in 1984, exemplifies the characteristics of the new missions history. Because of its topic and approach, it appears as exceptionally inclusive history. It studies a full-dressed encounter of cultures, of whole ways of life. Most volumes on missions history published these days manifest only some of the elements of the new missions history, but taken altogether they too contribute to the expansion of our understanding of the multiplex world of missions. The sheer scope of scholarship now appearing is impressive. A few examples will indicate the character of the work. In Canadian missions history, noteworthy are Elizabeth Jones' *Gentlemen and Jesuits: Quest for Glory and Adventure in the Early Days of New France* on the French Christians and the Indians in the 1600s,[2] and two books on missions in China, Alvyn J. Austin's *Canadian Missionaries in the Middle Kingdom, 1888-1959*,[3] and Stephen Endicott's *James G. Endicott: Rebel out of China*.[4] On American missions, William R. Hutchison has contributed *Errand to the World: American Protestant Thought and Foreign Missions*,[5] and joined with Torben Christensen to publish a volume of studies of Americans, British, and others in *Missionary Ideologies in the Imperialist Era, 1880-1920*.[6] Kenton J. Cylmer examines missions and foreign policy in *Protestant Missionaries in the Philippines, 1898-1916: an Inquiry into the American Colonial Mentality*.[7] Other important studies look at the world of missions from the other side around, from the experience of those who received the impact of the missionaries. Two of these are Jacques Gernet's *China and the Christian Impact: A Conflict of Cultures*, on the response of the

Chinese elite to the Jesuits between the 1580s and the 1660s,[8] and William G. McLouglin's *Cherokee Renascence, 1794-1833*, on how the Cherokee Indian Nation incorporated some and rejected some of what the missionaries brought them.[9] These are only a few of the many studies now appearing. Many more are on the way. For example, at the 1986 meetings of the American Historical Association in Chicago four sessions were devoted to papers on missions history.

Equally important, the archives which contain the resources necessary for missions history are now becoming well organized and enabling scholars to reach into vast stores of new material. In Canada, chief among these are the archives of the Presbyterian Church in Canada, of the United Church of Canada, of the Anglican Church of Canada, and of the various Roman Catholic Church dioceses. These are the archives on which the research for these essays has depended to a large degree. Similar archival organization is occuring in the United States, Italy, the Vatican, Great Britain, France, and the other sending nations of Europe. In the United States, besides ecclesiastical archives, noteworthy is the archive of the Billy Graham Center in Wheaton, Illinois, which is rapidly becoming the largest missions archive in North America. Numerous projects to publish missions sources are underway or completed, like the microfilm reproduction of *The Chinese Recorder*, a newspaper produced in China between 1867 and 1941. Kathleen L. Lodwick has created a complete two volume index to this extraordinary source.[10] Sustained missions research projects are underway on the Oblates in Western Canada, the Maryknoll Fathers in various parts of the world, and, at the University of Kansas, on missionaries to China.

As if to top off the new interest in missions history, the film *The Mission* dramatized the experiences of the Jesuits and the Indians in the 1760s and 1770s near Iguacu Falls where the Spanish and Portugese empires met in the wilderness. The film has given wide and sympathetic publicity to missions history by winning both the Palme d'Or for best film at the 1986 Cannes Film Festival and an Oscar nomination for best picture by the American Academy of Motion Pictures in 1987.

Five Themes

As we read through this volume we discover several themes which appear in all or nearly all of the essays. Five themes receive particular attention. First, all the essays disclose the religious devotion of the missionaries and reflect movements of renewal in both Protestant and Roman Catholic circles. They all show the presence of other concerns and motivations as well -- adventure, opportunities not available at home, control over people who might threaten those in authority, class condescension, extension of respectability, Canadianization of newcomers, civilizing those considered primitive or heathen, and much more. We cannot fail to be struck by the ambiguity of missions.

Secondly, all the essays reveal that missions brought about an encounter of cultures, the creation of complex relationships among two or more ways of life of different peoples. The peoples we meet in these essays are many, and they manifest many different religious-cultural identities. There are English and Scottish Canadian Protestants, French Canadian Catholics, Irish Catholics, Swiss Protestants, Ukrainian Byzantine Catholics, non-Christian Canadian Indians, non-Christian Africans, Hindus in India and Hindus from India in Trinidad, American Protestants and Catholics, and East European Jews. It becomes clear to us that we cannot understand the religious encounters that missions precipitated without also comprehending the many other aspects of the life of those missionized. To say it in other words, the religions we study in this volume are cultural, and the cultures we find discussed here are religious. Consequently, the work of religious conversion did not proceed in any case here before us without involving in some fundamental way the attempt to bring those converted into different expressions of culture. This induced conflicts of culture among those converted as well as between the missionaries and those they missionized.

The specifically Canadian content of the religious-cultural encounters we learn about in these essays appears in the conviction, referred to directly or indirectly in every essay, that Canadian society was a Christian society, at least until the 1930s. In the earliest essay about the period when Upper Canada was still thought of as British, to Christianize included to civilize as part of its meaning. Later on, as a sense of Canadian identity was emerging, to Christianize partly meant to Canadianize. Overseas, in relation to those considered heathen, to Christianize continued to include within its meaning to civilize, and even, as in Trinidad, to Canadianize.

It is noteworthy that both Catholics and Protestants agreed that Canadian society was Christian, and members of each group considered their religion to be the only one suitable for advancing the Christian society of Canada. In these pages, with a few exceptions like the Church of England bishop of Montreal in the second essay, Catholics and Protestants agreed in counting each other to be not really Christians. Church of England, Wesleyan Methodist, and Presbyterian missionaries in French Canada tried to convert French Catholics to Christianity. The English-speaking Catholic hierarchy in Toronto strove to prevent the Presbyterian wolves from stealing their Ukrainian Catholic sheep. Catholics were not even sure about other Catholics when ethnic-cultural identities intervened. The English-speaking hierarchy in Toronto intended to tame the Irish Catholic immigrants and to integrate them properly into the Roman version of Catholicism, and the French and English Catholic bishops competed against each other to control the Byzantine Ukrainian Catholics. As for the Protestants, after an early non-denominational start in French Canada, each denomination went on to create its own missions societies, and thereafter denominational societies remained the norm. Nondenominational evangelical societies continued to be the exceptions into the 1920s.

The work among Jewish immigrants in Toronto which the last essay discusses was an anomaly on at least two counts. The mission went against the trend toward denominationalism as well as the practice of eliminating where possible "foreign" expressions of culture. The leaders of the mission sought to Christianize the Jews and to turn East European Jewish immigrants into Canadians in some sense. Yet, they finally broke with the Presbyterians who sponsored the work in order to turn the mission into a non-denominational one. Earlier they spontaneously sought ways for the Jews to become Christians while retaining their Jewish identity and continuing to practice as Jews as much as possible. For a time before the mid-1920s they came up with what they called a Christian synagogue. Back in the years before the first World War, it was a Presbyterian minister, James A. MacDonald, about whom we read in the eighth essay, who urged people to try to untangle the preaching of the spirit of Christ from the preaching of a British version of culture when the missionaries took their work overseas.

A third theme which appears in some way in all the essays is the union of evangelism with some form of a social expression of Christianity. This point is really another way of looking at the issue of the encounter of cultures when missionaries do their work. All those before the 1920s who believed that Canada was a Christian society believed that Christian religion had social consequences. On the whole, in that period both Catholics and Protestants in English Canada concurred in approving the general character of society as it then existed, minus, of course, any elements which were detrimental to themselves. The question of how evangelism and social work related arose when people began to notice that some things were wrong in the society whose general Christian character they nonetheless approved. In particular, the dawning recognition that poverty existed in the wilderness or in the urban centres and that immigrants experienced basic human hardship led people to work expressly for social relief and social reform. This evoked statements about missions and programmes of missions which included, as part of what was understood by evangelism, working to eliminate harmful social conditions. We see this union of evangelism and social action in the very first essay when the missionaries became concerned about the poverty of the Indians. In the third essay, we learn that Toronto Catholics created the local unit of the Saint Vincent de Paul Society in order to combat both the material and spiritual poverty of the Irish immigrants. In the sixth and seventh essays we find evangelicals in the Church of England in Toronto and in other churches devising ways to meet the spiritual and the social needs of the sick, the poor, and the outcast of the city. In the last essay we follow the extraordinary history of the antecedents of the Scott Mission in Toronto as the original mission to meet the spiritual and social needs of Jews became a social service mission which sought to fill the spiritual and social needs of anyone who came their way. These essays demonstrate that as people became aware of poverty and social problems, they undertook new missions or recast old ones in order to ensure that social action was part of what they meant explicitly by missions. When we couple these experiences of the need for social missions with the general appreciation that Canadian society until the 1930s was Christian, we can conclude, judging from these cases, that the question to ask is not whether to relate evangelism and society, but what social consequences and social message did people want their evangelistic missions to have.

A fourth theme running through all the essays is innovation. The missionaries and their senders whom we come across in this volume were avid creators of new organizations and new means of missions in Canada. They recognized new needs in new situations and freely borrowed from outside Canada or devised their own spontaneous solutions. In any case, what they established was their own and the process of creativity was constant. The missionaries in essay one built missions stations, hospitals, and bark schoolhouses in the wilderness, and began teaching, preaching, providing medical care, and training in domestic economy among the Indians. As we read through the essays we find the missionaries and missionary senders establishing one institution, social structure, and programme after another -- missions societies, churches, schools, benevolent societies, hospitals, health care centres, girls' homes, women's circles, governing boards, mission stations, homes for the aged, day nurseries, savings banks, clothing centres, sewing societies, missions halls, Bible classes, Sunday schools, prisoners' aid, half-way houses for released prisoners, organizing committees, a deaconess training home, newspapers, a publishing house, student organizations, a Christian synagogue, and on and on. There seemed to be no end to their initiative and innovation. They were activists who had a sense that they could set to work to meet whatever need came their way. And all of this they comprehended within their understanding of missions.

All this activity and organizing brought with it ample conflict, and conflict of many kinds. The conflicts that receive special attention in these pages are the struggles between the missionaries on one side and the controlling authorities of the missions on the other. Among the Roman Catholics there were the efforts by the bishops to keep the mission priests and the missions committees under the regulations of the church. Among Protestants there were parallel attempts by the Toronto Presbytery to control the Christian Synagogue, or by the Presbyterian missions board to control their innovative missionary in central India. We only get glimpses in these essays of the conflicts between missionaries and those whom they sought to missionize, whether they be the wilderness Indians in the 1820s and 1830s, the Irish poor in Toronto, the Hindu upper caste in central India, the Byzantine Rite Ukrainians in the Prairies, or the East European Jews in central Toronto. The signs of such conflicts are there, and a missions historiography which gave full attention to those affected by the missionaries would bring the conflicts out into the open. As these essays stand, however, they show us enough about the results of the creative work of the missionaries to make us realize that ambiguity often reigned there as elsewhere in life. The results of the missions were, to say the least, mixed. These essays do not tell a tale of straightforward triumph.

A fifth theme which we can trace through almost all of the essays is gender. We learn much about the roles of women in missions and the effect on missions of the relations between women and men. Paying attention to gender roles as part of the multifactoral study of missions is one of the marks of the newer missions history. Four of the essays are devoted primarily to discovering and understanding women's roles, and three others include the discussion of women's roles as an important part of their study. The remaining essays allow us to detect women's roles within their treatment of other topics. What emerges from the volume is an awareness that women's roles in missions may no longer be overlooked or taken for granted. These roles were surprisingly varied. In these pages women appear in the roles we commonly know about -- as wives of missionary husbands and as the members of the Women's Missionary Societies. In Protestant circles women as wives made up close to half of the missionary work force, and as WMS members they created a significant share of the funding, the spiritual support, and the publicity for missions. Much could be learned by further new style studies of these traditional roles. These essays show that women are also the subjects of missions. Missionaries met them as members of the tribal Indian villages in the Canadian wilderness, as heads of target households among the Irish immigrants to Toronto, as members of the Presbyterian girl's homes and high school in Trinidad, as high-caste Hindu inhabitants of the enclosures called zenanas, as criminals in Toronto, or as Jewish mothers. These essays disclose further that women were leaders and innovators in their own right, whether as missionaries in the field, as members of the organizing committees and boards, or as the head of the institution to train deaconesses to be leaders at home. We learn that women found opportunities in missions to exercise their abilities that were not available to them at the same time in the traditional society. Indeed women sometimes got into trouble with their male counterparts in the field or on the controlling committees who were not ready to accept leadership from women. Moreover, we note in at least two cases that women were free to exercise leadership in the early pioneering stages of a mission which they were prevented from exercising in later more established stages. The women who were leaders were usually, but not always, unmarried in those days. If we add the numbers of unmarried women to the numbers of missionary wives, we find that women made up a clear majority of the workers in missions at home and overseas.

Further Research

These five themes are large ones. They cannot be handled merely by means of these ten essays, and we cannot reach solid conclusions about them from this volume alone. Nevertheless, while we wait for further research and for a look at more cases we can benefit from the understanding of these themes that the essays permit us to achieve even now.

A desire for more research on missions history is an appropriate response to a volume like this. It was one of the organizing considerations in planning the volume to include mostly newer scholars, the bulk of whose productivity would lie ahead. The actual topics included in this volume derive entirely from their current research and were not the result of assignments by the editors. The fact that the volume is as comprehensive as it is in terms of religious traditions, cultures, types of missions, and time span is due wholly to the wide range of interests of those conducting research in missions history. Further investigations can aim to fill in the gaps, and can employ additional research techniques -- like quantification, time-series analysis, and systematic factor analysis. We may expect more publications on Canadian missions history in the coming years, and this future for missions history will be due in no small part to the example and influence of Grant himself.

Notes

1. Latourette, who was Sterling Professor of Missions and Oriental History at Yale University, produced an extraordinary number of books on missions history. They are not hagiographic but they are triumphalist, and partly due to his desire to be utterly all inclusive in his naming of missions and missionaries, they tend toward monofactoral religious explanation and to simplify the complexities and ambiguities of missionary work. Because of his pioneering global perspective and the encyclopedic character of his books, however, they continue to be essential reading. Notable among the long list of his writings on missions history are: *A History of the Expansion of Christianity*, 7 vols. (New York: Harper, 1937-1945); *Christianity in a Revolutionary Age*, 5 vols. (New York: Harper, 1958-1962); and *A History of Christian Missions in China* (New York: Macmillan, 1929).
2. Jones: (Toronto: University of Toronto Press, 1986).
3. Austin: (Toronto: University of Toronto Press, 1986).
4. Endicott: (Toronto: University of Toronto Press, 1982).
5. Hutchison: (Chicago: University of Chicago Press, 1987).
6. Christensen and Hutchison: (Aarhus: Aros Publishers, 1982).
7. Cylmer: (Champaign: University of Illinois Press, 1987).
8. Gernet: (Cambridge: Cambridge University Press, 1985).
9. McLoughlin: (Princeton: Princeton University Press, 1987).
10. Lodwick: (Wilmington: Scholarly Resources, 1986).

I

THE BARK SCHOOLHOUSE:

METHODIST EPISCOPAL MISSIONARY WOMEN

IN UPPER CANADA, 1827-1833

Elizabeth Muir

Historians have paid scant attention to the contribution of women in the development of the Canadian Methodist Indian missions in the early nineteenth century. Yet for a brief period in the 1820s and 1830s, more than two dozen energetic Methodist Episcopal missionary women held leadership positions on at least six of the missions in Upper Canada. They taught school, led worship, and initiated and supervised women's groups -- at the River Credit, nineteen miles west of York; at Grape Island in the Bay of Quinte, six miles from Belleville; at Rice Lake, twelve miles north of Cobourg; at the Lake Simcoe Mission; on the south side of Lake Huron at the Sah-geeng; and at the Muncey Mission on the River Thames. Scattered throughout record books, newspapers and journal accounts from 1827 to 1833 are references to the work of twenty-five of these women: Sally Ash (Mrs. Sabine Frazer); Eliza Barnes (the second Mrs. William Case); Miss Bayles; Mrs. John B. Benham; Miss Brink; Sophia Cook; Margaret Dulmage (Mrs. Sylvester Hurlburt); Phoebe [Phebe] Edmonds [Edwards]; Susannah Farley (Mrs. Solomon Waldron); a sister Miss Farley; Miss French; Hester Ann (Hetty) Hubbard (the first Mrs. William Case); Miss Huntingdon; Miss Kunze; Sarah Lancaster (Mrs. Thomas Ross); Miss Manwaring; Mrs. McMullen; Miss Pinny; Miss E. Rolph; Sarah Rolph (Mrs. George Ryerson); Miss Sealy; Eliza Sellicks [Sillick, Scelec]; Miss Stockton; Miss Verplanck; and S. Yeomans.[1] Undoubtedly other women were actively involved whose names are lost, perhaps forever.

The Work

One woman stands apart from all the others -- the dynamic American missionary teacher and preacher, Eliza Barnes. She was more widely known than the other women, and her exploits recorded in greater detail. The Methodist historian John Carroll compares her to three of the most respected women in early Methodism: Mary Bosanquet Fletcher, one of the great eighteenth century Wesleyan preachers in England; Alice Cambridge, who defied the ban against women preaching in Ireland in 1802 and was expelled but later re-admitted into the Methodist fellowship; and Mary Barritt Taft, who travelled as much, if not more, than the other English Wesleyan itinerants.[2] That Eliza was considered different from the other teachers is evident from the fact that the Missionary Society recorded her salary under the special heading "Miss Barnes" rather than the usual designation "female teacher," even though she received a female school teacher's wage.[3]

Eliza was born in Boston, Massachusetts, in 1796. Nothing is known of her life until 1827 when her name appears in reports from the Canadian missions. Her first years as a missionary were a whirlwind of activity. She travelled from mission to mission supervising Indian women, organizing benevolent societies, teaching children and adults, not unlike the flamboyant Grace Murray who rode on horseback, often alone, throughout England and Ireland, organizing and supervising women's classes for John Wesley.[4] Much of her time Eliza went back and forth between missions and urban centres, bringing raw materials to Indian women and returning to city bazaars with the finished products for sale: moccasins, gloves, straw hats, and brooms. she accompanied male missionaries on exploratory trips in Upper Canada to assess new sites for Indian missions. At least once a year, she toured the eastern United States raising funds by speaking to large groups about her missionary work, and some of the mission buildings were constructed as a result of her success.

According to John Carroll, Eliza had been "tolerated" as a preacher for some time previously to 1828; at one time she created a "sensation" preaching in York. She was responsible for a great revival near Belleville in June, 1828, such as was not seen again in the area for thirty years;[5] and the next year her preaching caused a mild "Pentecost" at Yellowhead's Island in Lake Simcoe. The Indian missionary Peter Jones wrote of that occasion:

> We joined in prayer and praise, and it seems as if the very gates of heaven were opened to our souls, and the spirit of God descending upon our hearts . . . the path appeared like a blaze of fire . . . and everything was glorious and heavenly. the whole encampment manifested the presence of God.[6]

Peter's journals refer to a number of occasions when Eliza "addressed," "preached" or "exhorted" on the Indian missions in Canada in 1828 and 1829, and on her American tours in 1829 and 1830.

Eliza appears to have been more aggressive than most of the other women, but no more daring. Women who chose a missionary career in that era needed courage and a spirit of adventure, for they had to endure great hardships, and often risked their lives. Travel was hazardous, and the work demanded frequent trips by land and water between the missions. Margaret Dulmage Hurlburt worked for twenty-one years as a missionary; at times in the late fall she was so drenched by water on canoe trips that gloves would freeze to her hands.[7] Eliza Barnes and Miss Verplanck were thrown from a wagon travelling between Rice Lake and Credit Mission; Eliza and Phoebe Edmonds had a terrifying moment when a sudden gale almost capsized their schooner on "Lake Koochecheeng" [sic] en route to visit mission sites.[8]

Housing was often primitive, supplies were scarce, and loneliness was a part of many of the women's daily existence. Susannah Farley Waldron was often short of food. Once she was unable to offer a visiting clergyman anything at all to eat.[9] She lived on Indian missions for twelve years, and on one trip from Whitby to the Muncey Mission she travelled with two children by canoe and on horseback through mire and bush and over logs, harrassed continually by mosquitoes, only to reach a vermin-infested mission house which had to be turpentined completely to be made livable.[10] Mrs. John B. Benham taught school in a bark "wigwaum" at the Sah-geeng Mission on Lake Huron in 1831, sixty miles from the closest white settlement, without seeing another white woman for a year. The New Yorker, Miss Bayles, was isolated at her school half the year in 1833 because of ice.[11] Sally Ash and Eliza Barnes taught in a seventeen-foot square school house on Rice Lake in 1828. The six-foot high sides and roof were made of ash and cedar bark fastened to upright posts. Indian women wove bark carpeting and the men built a clay oven. Sally and Eliza not only taught twenty-five girls "domestic economy," and how to read, sew, knit, and braid straw in the tiny building, but they lived in it as well. Shortly after it was built, the house caught fire, and the women had a narrow escape. That summer, Eliza lived in a wigwam on an island because of virulent fever on the mainland.[12]

Health care was inadequate. Infant mortality was high and women often died in childbirth or suffered ill health as a result of the rigours of their existence. The Grape Island Mission near Belleville boasted a log hospital for women as early as 1828 and the River Credit settlement had a hospital building twenty feet by forty feet at least by 1829.[13] Generally, however, physicians were distant -- forty miles from the Mission on Yellowhead's Island in 1820.[14] Missionary women who became ill, or those who married and became pregnant might be bundled off to in-laws, friends or relatives. Often, however, the missions took their toll. Credit missionary Sarah Rolph Ryerson, the daughter of the prominent Canadian physician and politician John Rolph, was the first woman to die exhausted from her work.[15] Three years later, her husband, the Rev. George Ryerson, still devastated by the loss, wrote his brother Egerton on the death of Egerton's wife:

> I assure you I sympathize with you in your afflictions. I know how to feel for you, and you as yet know but a small part of your trials. Years will not heal the wound. I am even now quite overwhelmed when I allow myself to dwell upon the past. I need to suggest to you the common place topics of comfort and resignation.[16]

Hetty Hubbard Case, the gentle American missionary who became the first wife of the General Superintendent of Indian Missions, became seriously ill after the birth of their daughter. After a long illness, she died on the Grape Island Mission, a bride of little more than two years. Sophia Cook taught for two years at the Credit Mission when ill health forced her to return to her home in Rochester, New York, in 1834, although she did return to the Alderville Mission to spend the last eight years of her life there in the 1840s. Eliza Barnes' only child, Caroline Hetty Case, died shortly before she would have been a year old.[17] Susannah Farley Waldron was left alone on a remote mission with a three-day old baby in convulsions while her husband, Solomon, began a week's tour of missions.[18] Missionary husbands had little time to devote to family crises.

The classroom work, itself, was demanding. Classes were large and the work hours long. Sophia Cook taught reading, writing, arithmetic, geography, and grammar to almost fifty children at the Credit. Both Miss Huntingdon and Miss Pinny taught thirty. There were thirty-eight girls in the school at the Lake Simcoe Mission in 1832, and Hetty Hubbard had thirty in her class on Grape Island four years earlier.[19] The women were in charge not only of week-day schools, but also instructed adults in the evening and organized a full program for Sunday. Their days began at five o'clock in the morning in winter-time, four in summer. On Sundays there could be as many as six sessions -- prayer meetings, preaching services, and classes.[20]

Although newspaper accounts and missionary reports described the North American Indian as wild, savage, barbarian, and dangerous, these stories were no doubt highly exaggerated, and in fact the missionaries faced greater danger from travelling and the hardships of overwork. There was some concern, however, at one time for the safety of the teacher at the Muncey Mission because of an initial resistance to the school by the Indians who were afraid that "white" schooling would prevent their children from learning how to hunt.[21] Miss Farley was assaulted there by a drunken half-breed who came to the school, "stove in the door," seized her and tore her dress to shreds, and her brother-in-law, Solomon

Waldron, faced a knife-wielding man in the church.[22] but these appear to
have been isolated instances.

It seems patently obvious that only those missionaries who were
physically fit would be able to tolerate the conditions the mission field
imposed, and there were moral and spiritual demands as well. Methodism
was a 'serious' business, and missionaries were expected to be paradigms of
piety and sobriety. Indian children were praised for their serious and
prayerful deportment. Women, especially, were called upon to be exemplary,
and Methodist hagiography portrays the female teachers as living up to the
stereotype. Phoebe Edmonds was a "pious girl:" Sarah Rolph Ryerson was
an "accomplished, amiable lady, meek, kind, and generous:" Sophia Cook
was actively and zealously "engaged in works of faith and labours of
love."[23] Eliza Barnes' diary displays an emotionally controlled formality.
Three weeks after she married William Case, she was still referring to him
as "Mr. Case." Not until a month after her wedding does she refer to him
as "my dear husband." Her sister teachers, with whom she had worked for
several months, are mentioned as "Miss Verplanck" and "Miss Cook."[24]

Order, stability, and diligence were also external marks of internal
grace. Bells, horns, and regular meal times were part of an extremely
structures, rigid missionary existence. Neatness was supremely important. A
high ranking visitor to the school at Grape Island in 1828 reported that
the operations were in perfect order. "There was a place for everything,
and everything was in its place," he wrote.[25] Two years later, Peter Jones
made a detailed inspection of all the houses there and found Margaret
Dulmage Hurlburt's house "all neat like a white squaw's house, except that
the tea kettle was out of place." The fact that she was sick in bed was no
excuse.[26] The Canada Conference of the Missionary Society noted the
importance of setting a example of industrious labour for the Indians. Only
in displaying "settled habits of industry" could this trait be encouraged in
the Indians, and the accepted missionary theory was that settled tribes
were more easily taught Christian precepts, educated, and civilized. "A
roving life" exposed the Indians to temptations, and reduced the chances
of the "indolent savage" becoming an "industrious Christian."[27] For all
Methodists, however, settled habits were part of godliness. The denomina-

tional newspaper, the *Christian Guardian*, urged all men to stay at home as much as possible: "as a bird wandereth from her nest, so is a man that wandereth from his place."[28]

Minister's wives, as many of the missionary teachers became, were enjoined to be the holiest, most spiritual women in the congregation in habits, conversation, and in their whole deportment.[29] An early London Methodist Conference had spelled out the requirement that they be patterns of cleanliness and industry as well:

> Let nothing slatternly be seen about her; no rags; no dirt; no litter. And she should be a pattern of industry: always at work, either for herself, her husband or the poor.[30]

Missionaries were not allowed human frailty, although occasionally there is a glimpse of something less than perfection. In his autobiography, Solomon Waldron mentions disagreements between some of the missionaries and particularly between Eliza Barnes and Hester Ann Hubbard, both of who were "passionately fond" of William Case, and both in turn his wife. Only when Hester Ann died, he notes, did the "painful struggles" between the women cease. Susannah Farley gave up tea, tobacco, and alcohol in 1835 -- evidently she had been using these stimulants for some time previously.[31]

Nor were the women permitted discontent. Public reports emphasized over and over again that they were "happy in their employment." Mrs. Benham was "healthy and happy" in her isolation surrounded only "by 150 Indian souls."[32] The women, however, can no longer speak for themselves, and we do not know if this was indeed the case; their letters and diaries are not extant except for a brief extract from Eliza Barnes' journal in August, 1833, the month she married William Case. In terse, short sentences, she mentions her marriage, and refers to some problems:

> 6th Tuesday., I returned with Mr. Case to the Island. I stopped here until the next Tuesday. My trials were neither few nor small.

13th Tuesday., I went in company with Mr. Case to Belleville, where I stopped until the 28th. There we were married.[33]

Three years earlier, when she had spoken at the John Street Church in New York City, it was reported that she talked about "her trials and sufferings" while "labouring on our Indian missions."[34] Most of the women stayed only a short time at their station, but it was a Methodist tradition to move clergy regularly from circuit to circuit, and this may have been a factor in their frequent moves. In addition, ill health often forced them to leave a mission after a short stay.

The Changing Roles
Even with the harsh working conditions, however, it should not be surprising that these women were in the forefront of this new missionary endeavour, "civilizing" the Canadian Indians. From its beginning, Methodist polity ensured that women would have a leadership role outside the home in the operations of the church. John Wesley had insisted on the segregation of men and women when he first organized his followers into small bands and classes in 1742, immediately thrusting women into positions of authority as leaders of the women's groups. It was not long before burgeoning classes forced many of these capable women to become public speakers and preachers, and Wesley encouraged them to develop their talents to the utmost. Congregations, too, were segregated, with separate church entrances and seating for men and women, and even thought there was some resistance, this separation of sexes became the norm for Methodist worship.[35] American and Canadian societies adopted the practice, although in sparsely settled pioneer communities it could not always be enforced and gradually disappeared. When, however, the Canada Conference of the Methodist Episcopal Church set up Indian schools in 1825 to "tame the savages and Christianize the heathen," the authorities thought it 'proper' that female missionaries be sought to teach the women and girls apart from the men and boys.

It is interesting to note that the first two women to arrive at the missions were Americans -- Eliza Barnes and Hetty Hubbard. Many of those who followed had either lived in the United States for a number of years, or had been born there and emigrated as young children to Canada. Susannah Farley, Sophia Cook, and Mrs. John Benham were New Englanders by birth; Sophia and Mrs. Benham had lived there for some time. Women had been active in the church in that country since the seventeenth century. In the early nineteenth century, there were a number of women who were well-known and who attracted multitudes to hear their sermons -- in Vermont, New Hampshire, Massachusetts, New York, Ohio, and other northern States -- in several denominations.[36] Dorothy Ripley, claimed by the Methodists although she never actually joined a society, had a reputation as an international preacher, and crossed the Atlantic nineteen times between 1825 and 1831. Dorothy often preached to the Indians, and in 1806 had addressed Congress from the speaker's chair with the permission of Thomas Jefferson.[37] Miss Miller was preaching on the western frontier in the 1820s, encouraged by a Methodist Episcopal clergyman, although opposed by her bishop. Methodist Episcopal churches were opened to accomodate the Primitive Methodist preacher Sister H. M. Knowles in 1831 in Ohio, and Ann Wearing, a Primitive Methodist itinerant in New York and Philadelphia, was warmly welcomed by Methodist Episcopal clergy there in 1830.[38]

In Upper Canada, women were extremely active during that same period of time in the same geographical area as the missions in some Methodist denominations. For example, Elizabeth Peters, Betsy Henwood, and Maria Hoskings, all preachers with the Bible Christian Church, had emigrated from England in 1830 with their husbands, spending the days on board the brig *Friends* preaching, sewing, cooking, knitting, and caring for their children much as they would do afterwards on shore. Elizabeth Dart Eynon sailed later on the brig *Dalusia*, endured a stormy forty-two day ocean crossing in the summer of 1833, and became one of the best-loved and best-known Bible Christian itinerants in the Cobourg-Peterborough area. She had been preaching since 1815 when she became the first itinerant in that Church. Ruth Watkins' brother and sister-in-law were preaching in York for the Primitive Methodists; Ruth had been the first

Primitive Methodist missionary to come to North America, arriving in New York in 1829.[39]

The Canadian Methodist Episcopal Church was not as progressive in its attitude to careers for women outside the home, and it was becoming increasingly more conservative. Many of the women who were attracted to the missions had been nurtured in the liberal American atmosphere, and were called to serve not far from where the Bible Christian and Primitive Methodist women were preaching. They found severe limitations on their activity. Preaching was clearly out-of-bounds. Records show that Ellen Bangs Gatchell was speaking in the Methodist pulpit in the Niagara area in 1810 "to the satisfaction of the people" and she "exhorted like a streak of red-hot lightning." Ellen's brother, the historian and itinerant Nathan Bangs, was a childhood friend and supporter of the American feminist evangelist Phoebe Palmer.[40] Two decades later, however, this sort of behaviour was not acceptable. Women were to promote Christianity by the "eloquence which flows from subjection," noted the *Christian Guardian* in 1829. A woman preaching was considered to be an "eccentric effort," out of her sphere. Even leading family devotions in the absence of one's husband was a privilege for women, the paper pointed out.[41] Ladies preach the precious gospel by sewing gloves and moccasins, knitting mittens, making baskets and brooms, George Ryerson explained to the Dorcas Society in New York at its Anniversary service in 1831.[42] But the women did preach -- at first. Eliza Barnes appears to have been the most eloquent, but Hetty Hubbard and Susannah Farley were also described as gifted speakers, and Hetty spoke both in Canada and in the United States when she and Eliza went on tour. It is reported that Eliza "settled down" soon after she arrived in Canada, and it is noteworthy that there are no more references to any of the women preaching or speaking in this tradition after 1830.[43]

Other boundaries were imposed on the women. Most of the female missionaries were restricted to a teaching role and within that profession to a clearly defined area: instructing women and children in elementary education and "domestic economy" or how to keep house. At Grape Island in 1830, Miss French taught the girls to make their own clothing; the boys learned arithmetic, English grammar, writing, and geography under a male teacher. Miss Manwaring had the care of the younger boys as well as the girls there in 1833 during the summer months while the male teacher took the boys into the field to teach them agriculture. At the River Credit in 1828, Miss Lancaster, "a pious young lady from York," taught her pupils to read, write, sew, and knit.[44] Much of the women's time was taken up in supervising the activities of the Dorcas Societies -- groups of women who gathered together to make hand-crafted goods for sale. The money raised was used at the missions for school supplies and other expenses. Some of the women did have other responsibilities, and were not as limited. Margaret Dulmage taught classes of men as well as women and travelled with her husband Sylvester on pastoral visits. In 1829, a woman, Miss Stockton, was hired to introduce the Pestalozzian method of instruction at Grape Island, a system which would be used by both male and female teachers.[45]

For the most part, however, as the nineteenth century progressed, Episcopal Methodists became more inclined to define for women a role of submissive virtuous housewife and benevolent charity bazaar lady. Woman's proper sphere is in the home, the *Christian Guardian* assured its readers in 1829. Housework is a woman's "peculiar and appropriate employment" and demands her full attention, the paper noted. Week after week, the denominational newspaper hammered home the role of woman in Christian society:

> The wife is not expected to go into the field, the workshop or the counting house.

> To the middling class of life there is no female accomplishment more valuable than housewifery.[46]

God had placed women in the home to serve and submit, the newspaper pointed out, in order to eliminate the perpetual strife which would result from equality, but in any case, they were not strong enough emotionally or physically for the 'more rigorous' outside jobs. Women are "subjected to

the trials and weakness of a feeble constitution" wrote the editor of the
Methodist *Christian Advocate*.[47] And in the opinion of the *Christian
Guardian*, a "Good Wife" makes it her business to serve and her pleasure
to oblige her husband, whereas a "Good Husband" attributes his wife's
follies to her weakness.[48]

Not all women were willing to fit this stereotype and to accept the
advice offered by the "Ladies Department" of Canada's best known
religious journal. One woman in 1829 who found the *Christian Guardian*'s
view of women offensive summarized it in these words:

> Honour us; deal kindly with us. From many of the opportunities,
> and means by which you procure favourable notice, we are
> excluded. Doomed to the shades, few of the high places of the
> earth are open to us. Alternately we are adored, and oppressed.
> From our slaves, you become our tyrants. You feel our beauty,
> and avail yourselves of our weakness. You complain of our
> inferiority, but none of your behaviour bids us rise. Sensibility
> has given us a thousand feelings, which nature has kindly denied
> you. Always under restraints, we have little liberty of choice.
> Providence seems to have been more attentive to enable us to
> confer happiness than to enjoy it. Every condition has for us
> fresh mortifications; every relation new sorrows. We enter social
> bonds; it is a system of perpetual sacrifice. We cannot give life
> to others without hazarding our own. We have sufferings which
> you do not share, cannot share . . . .[49]

Much to the amusement of the editor, another woman wrote "a spirited
letter of reproof" to the *Advocate* for publishing so many degrading
lectures for wives and ladies and none for husbands and gentlemen.[50] In
1833, two women wrote that women in other countries had much greater
opportunities:

> Women in this country are not sufficiently considered, they who

in every other land have attracted to themselves the consideration of all, have here been neglected and left in oblivion.[51]

Given this climate, the Indian missions offered exciting opportunities for
women to step beyond the commonly accepted mould. A salaried teaching
career outside the home would be an appealing possibility -- not only for
disatisfied women within the church, but in society as well. In her studies
of Canadian schools in the nineteenth century, Alison Prentice points out
that it was not until 1871 that an equal number of men and women were
teaching in public or common schools in Upper Canada. By 1851, only
twenty per cent of all teachers were female. Although women were considered to be more suitable for nurturing infants and very young children,
there was a question as to how effective they would be in "governing"
school-aged children. Indeed, before 1840, Prentice notes, there were very
few schools at all, and most education took place at home with voluntary
instructors.[52] Some women advertised in the *Christian Guardian*: the Misses
McCord had a Day and Boarding School in York in 1831, and Miss Sarah
Foster a similar establishment.[53] But these situations, even in secular
society, were few.

The salaries paid the female missionary teachers were lower than
those paid to the male teachers on the missions; this was the usual social
practice. And Prentice notes that as more women entered the profession,
their salaries declined as a percentage of men's. In 1851 in Toronto, a
woman was paid sixty-nine per cent of a man's salary; by 1861, she was
paid only forty-one per cent of his salary. It has been suggested that in
the latter part of the century, school trustees discovered that they could
have two female teachers for the price of one male, and they began hiring
more women, and paying them less proportionately.[54] Something similar
may have happened at the Mission Schools. In 1832, white male school
teachers were paid between £37.10.0 and £40.0.0 per year; females were
paid on the average £29.5.0 or approximately seventy-five percent of the
male salary. In 1850, a female teacher at the Grand River received £15.0.0
per year, whereas the male teacher was paid £50.0.0. The woman received
only thirty per cent of the man's salary. There is, however, the example

of Sophia Cook who was paid £46.0.0 to teach at the Alderville Mission in 1844, and this compares favourable with the male teacher's salary of £50.0.0 per year. In any event, in 1832, the women at the missions were paid more than the Indian missionary teachers. Both Peter Jones and John Sunday who were acclaimed internationally were paid only £25.0.0 a year to do the same work as their white brothers and sisters.[55] Moreover, the

Table 1
*Comparison of Selected Male and Female Salaries
in Upper Canada*[56]

	Female	Male
Average salary, 1851 School teacher, Toronto	£73.2.0	£105.0.0
Average salary, 1851 School teacher, province	£33.10.0	£55.2.0
White school teacher, Methodist Episcopal Indian Missions, 1832	£29.5.0	£37.10.0 to £40.0.0
White missionary Methodist Episcopal Indian Missions, 1832		£50.0.0
Itinerant preacher, 1832 Primitive Methodist Church	£10.0.0	£16.16.0 to £21.8.0
	(plus room and board)	
Indian teacher/missionary Methodist Episcopal Missions, 1832		£25.0.0

female missionary teachers received a considerably higher wage than the female itinerants travelling in the same territory for the Primitive Methodist Church. These latter women received only £10.0.0 a year although they were given free room and board in addition to their stipend (see Table 1).[57]

It is not possible to tell if all the female missionary teachers were paid, but it is probable only the single women were. Many of the year-end statements list only "female teacher" beside the wage with no name. The first women to teach were single; working on the missions provided an option, at least for a few years, to the norm of marriage. Generally, singleness was not well-thought of. Celibacy, the *Christian Guardian* noted, is like a fly in the heart of the apple; it is confined and "dies in singularity." On the other hand, marriage is like a "useful bee"; it feeds the world "with delicacies" and "promotes the virtues of mankind."[58] Most of the women did marry on the mission field, although some like Sophia Cook remained single, a respected career woman all her life. Many of those women who did marry, married missionaries or ministers, and it is likely that they would be expected to continue their work without pay, as part of the duty of a missionary's wife.

While it is true that teaching school at least permitted a career, it is also the case that in society at large in Upper Canada, it was not a prestigious position. Some considered teachers to be on the same level as household servants.[59] This does not appear to have been the situation at the missions. In a society where only men had access to "the high places of the earth," where women were excluded from the "opportunities and means" to "procure favourable notice,"[60] missionary teachers were highly regarded and experienced adulation in the workplace denied most women. Indians flocked to greet them when they arrived at missions; Indian women patterned their lives after them; Indian children and other missionaries' children bore their names; and Missionary Society members revered them. Their obituaries depict them as without fault; indeed they became part of a Methodist missionary hagiography while still alive. In 1832, an anonymous donor who gave twenty dollars to make Eliza Barnes a life member of the Missionary Society described her as the "lady who is living among the Indians teaching their little ones to read the good book."[61] Peter Jones' diaries sing their praises and his prayers are full of gratitude for his "devoted" white sisters.

But while the women were accorded such high status in one context, they were often publicly referred to elsewhere anonymously as "the female teacher" or "a pious lady." Mission accounts tantalize with the paucity of detail about the women's work; there are passing references to faceless spinsters known only by their father's last name or missionary wives identified by their husband's name. Male teachers and missionaries by contrast generally rated an initial or a first name. In 1832, when Sylvester Hurlburt wrote to William Case from Grape Island on the progress of the mission, he noted:

> the female school was never doing better; the girls love and respect their teacher, and so they should, for she feels deeply interested for them, and takes much pains to instruct them and improve their manners.[62]

Typically, the teacher's name is not mentioned by Case, and might have been Miss Verplanck or his wife, Margaret Dulmage. The *Christian Guardian* paid tribute in 1830 to an "anonymous pious lady" who laboured at several mission stations and travelled extensively to aid the society, in all probability referring to Eliza Barnes.[63] The lives of some of these women can be pieced together; but many are known only as Miss French, Miss Manwaring, Miss Huntingdon.

There were other rewards for women who worked on the missions besides the more tangible benefits of a career, a salary, and high praise. Devout Christians of that day had seized upon the idea of rescuing the "perishing" Indian as a romantic and glorious notion. After they heard the Indian convert Peter Jones speak, women as far away as Great Britain were caught up in the excitement of shepherding the Indians into the Christian fold. Several English ladies wanted to go to America, he wrote from England, and "teach the Indians to be good and how to make nice work."[64]

The Women's Missionary Societies were especially concerned with ameliorating the conditions of Indian women "exposed to the barbarism of savage life," and they firmly believed that a transformation could be effected after a short exposure to Christian examples. Women's support could help turn "squalid wretchedness" to "prosperity," "loathsome drunkeness" to "exemplary temperance and sobriety." "Wasting diseases," extreme poverty, and misery could be eradicated, the women were convinced, and instead there would be fervent and "decent" devotion, industry and clean houses.[65]

The Indians themselves reinforced the concept of immediate metamorphosis. Peter Jones wrote that the Sah-geeng Indians on Lake Huron had been

> slaves to their carnal appetites, and would strip themselves almost naked in order to obtain strong drink; they were indolent; but now they are sober, warmly clad, and in their right minds.[66]

Mary Crow at Grape Island told a visitor:

> It is very little while the Lord bless my soul, and give me a white heart.[67]

They depicted their transformation, it should be noted, as a conversion from a life alien, vicious, and primitive to one that was peace-loving, white, and by implication English. A Rice Lake Indian wrote:

> My tomahawk away I throw;
> My broog-koo-mon [scalping knife] I need not now.
> Like white man in my house I'll dwell,
> So bark wigkewaum, farewell, farewell.[68]

Missionaries often exhibited Indian children to awe-struck assemblies who marvelled at their ability to learn, and at their change. In the fall of

1827, at the third anniversary gathering of the Canada Conference
Missionary Society of the Methodist Episcopal Church, fourteen children
from the River Credit school displayed samples of their writing, read from
both the New Testament and the English Reader, spelled words of four
syllables, repeated the Lord's Prayer and Ten Commandments in English
and in Indian, and sang hymns in both languages.[69] The next year Hetty
Hubbard "examined" twenty Grape Island school children in the Kingston
chapel before a large, interested audience. A newspaper report of the
event noted that the clean, well-behaved children were very recently part
of a tribe of Indians who had been "grasping at the intoxicating bowl" and
"wallowing in filth about our streets."[70] In the early spring of 1829, Eliza
Barnes and Hetty took six of their charges with them to New England and
then to New York where two thousand Sabbath School teachers and pupils
listened to these Canadian eight-year old Indian boys and teen-aged Indian
girls read from the New Testament, answer catechetical questions, and
spell. One child spoke to the whole assembly.[71]

Christianizing Canada's "child killers" and "idol worshippers" was not
only a thrilling idea,[72] it was a moral imperative. The Methodists believed
that it was a matter of justice that those people who had inhabited the
country first should be shown the way of salvation. Even more than that,
converting the Indians assured the missionaries of rewards in heaven, for
on the "great day of retribution" all those who had saved even one soul
would be acknowledged.[73] The women missionaries would be amply repaid
later for any sacrifices they had to make now.

Not all women, of course, were able to do God's work on the battle
front. Those who could not become missionaries encouraged those who
could; and groups of city church women organized themselves into Female
Missionary and Dorcas Societies. They held fund-raising bazaars, and
provided the missionary women with emotional and spiritual support,
money, and material goods.

Some women continued to work on the missions after 1833, although
their numbers were substantially reduced. After 1833, the Canadian
Methodist Episcopal Church merged with the British Wesleyans, a conservative stream of Methodism which had passed legislation in 1803 prohibiting

women from speaking in the pulpit in the London Conference. The union disrupted the publication of the Missionary Society Reports, and when they appeared again, there were few references to salaries for women school teachers. Reports from the missions published in newspapers rarely mentioned women, and the extant journals indicate that most of the women who taught after 1833 were supportive wives of missionary husbands. Even Eliza Barnes restricted her activities after her marriage to the widower William Case in 1833. Described as a woman "possessed of a powerful mind," she, nevertheless, appears to have adjusted to the expected model of a Methodist minister's wife, quietly teaching household and domestic science at the missions where they lived.[74] The schools, as well, changed. The day schools had not been as successful as the denomination had hoped, and they were gradually replaced by a few residential industrial schools for young children apart from the Indian communities. The first one began in Cobourg in 1844. Separate programmes were offered for boys and girls, presenting only a few opportunities for women as teachers.

The Devolution

By 1834, it seems that the brief period of heady activity for women in the Canadian Methodist Episcopal Church was over. Methodist women settled into a more conventional Victorian existence. The evidence indicates that the same devolution also took place, a couple of decades later, in the more radical Methodist denominations in Canada as well. By 1847, at least, Bible Christians were objecting to women preaching in their pulpits; and in the second half of the century Primitive Methodist women were more often invited to speak on special occasions such as church openings, rather than included on regular preaching schedules.[75]

However brief their heyday, the women teachers had made a significant contribution to Methodist missions. They had been co-workers in a missionary endeavour, which, although it may be questioned today, was believed to be one of the most important Christian activities at the time. They displayed their willingness and ability to live in primitive conditions in spite of the socially accepted theory that women were not emotionally or physically strong enough. They served as a role model for other women who felt suffocated by the conditions and limitations imposed by contemporary mores, and they helped to carve out a place for women in the teaching profession outside the home. Probably the women who benefitted most were those who were single. Because of the salary, they could sustain themselves financially and be independent; and their profession gave them some validity as a person apart from that given to women in marriage. Married women teachers also had the advantage of a career, but they were almost certainly expected to undertake conventional work as well -- bringing up children, household duties -- in addition to teaching, but for all the women missionaries, the missions provided an opportunity not available to many women in Upper Canadian society at that time.

Notes

1.   The names in square brackets are assumed to be alternate spellings, and not additional teachers.

2.   John Carroll, *Case and His Cotemporaries or, The Canadian Itinerants' Memorial*, 5 vols. (Toronto: Methodist Conference Office, 1867-1877), 3:169. Details of the preaching careers of Fletcher, Cambridge, and Taft may be found in Z. Taft, *Biographical Sketches of the Lives and Public Ministry of Various Holy Women* (London: Kershaw, 1825), 19 *ff.*, 269 *ff.*; in L. F. Church, *More About the Early Methodist People* (London: The Epworth Press, 1949), especially chapter 4; and in C. H. Crookshank, *History of Methodism in Ireland*, 3 vols. (London: T. Woolmer, 1885-1888), *passim*.

3.   See United Church of Canada Archives [hereafter UCA], *Reports of the Methodist Episcopal Church, Canada Conference Missionary Society*, 1825-1832, *passim*.

4.   W. W. Stamp, *The Orphan-House of Wesley* (London: John Mason, 1863), 47 *ff.*

5.   Carroll, *Case*, 3: especially 169, 177, 184.

6.   Peter Jones, *Life and Journals of Kah-ke-wa-quo-na-by* (Toronto: Anson Green, 1860), 256. For fuller details of Eliza's activities, see Elizabeth Muir, "Woman as Preacher: Early 19th Century Canadians"

in *Women: Images, Role-Models* (CRIAW Conference Proceedings, 1984), 195-201, and "Petticoats in the Pulpit: Three Early Canadian Women," in Canadian Society of Church History, *Papers* (1984); and Carroll, *Case*, 3: *passim*.

7.	*Christian Guardian*, 29 October 1873, 351, c. 2, obituary.

8.	Jones, *Life and Journals*, 289, 229.

9.	*Christian Guardian*, 3 December 1890, 779, c. 2, obituary.

10.	UCA, Solomon Waldron, "A Sketch of the Life, Travels and Labors of Solomon Waldron, A Wesleyan Methodist Preacher, Written By Himself."

11.	For details of Mrs. Benham, see *Christian Guardian*, 14 August 1833, 158, c. 3, letter from William Case; *Christian Advocate*, 12 July 1833, 182, c.4, letter from William Case; and also 1 March 1833, 106, c. 3. The latter reference states that the distance was seventy miles. J. E. Sanderson, *The First Century of Methodism in Canada* (Toronto: Wm Briggs, 1908-1910), 2:293, notes that she was two years without seeing another white woman. For information on Miss Bayles, *Christian Advocate*, 13 December 1833, 62, c. 3, letter from J. Clark.

12.	*Christian Advocate*, 19 September 1828, 10, c. 2, 3. Also, George F. Playter, *The History of Methodism in Canada* (Toronto: Anson Green, 1862), 358 *ff*; and Carroll, *Case*, 3:193.

13.	*Christian Advocate*, 24 October 1828, 30, c. 1, report from Francis Hall; and 3 July 1829, 173, c. 5, letter from G. Ryerson as quoted by William Case,

14.	*Christian Advocate*, 26 March 1830, 118, c. 2, letter from William Case.

15.	*Christian Guardian*, 21 November 1829, 8, c. 1, 2, obituary.

16.	UCA, Egerton Ryerson Papers, letter from George Ryerson to Egerton Ryerson, London, England, 29 March 1932.

17.	For details of Hetty Hubbard, see *Christian Guardian*, 1 October 1831, 187, obituary; for Sophia Cook, see 19 December 1849, 240, obituary; for Caroline Case, see 15 October 1834, 195, c. 5, and 9 September 1835, 175, c. 3.

18.	Waldron, "A Sketch," 32.

19. *Christian Advocate*, 1 March 1833, 106, c. 3; 13 April 1832, 130, c. 3, letter from Gilbert Miller; 24 October 1828, 30, c. 1, letter from Francis Hall.

20. *Christian Guardian*, 13 February 1930, 98, c. 3, and 99, c. 1, 2, report from John Benham, Grape Island.

21. *Christian Advocate*, 12 May 1827, 141, c. 4.

22. Waldron, "A Sketch," 21.

23. Peter Jones, *Life and Journals*, 151; *Christian Guardian*, 21 November 1829, 8, obituary of Sarah Ryerson; and 19 December 1849, obituary of Sophia Cook.

24. UCA, Extract from Eliza Barnes diary.

25. *Christian Advocate*, 5 September 1828, 2, c. 3, Francis Hall writing from Trafalgar.

26. Jones, *Life and Journals*, 284.

27. *Christian Advocate*, 26 March 1830, 108, c. 2, report from William Case. See also John Webster Grant, *Moon of Wintertime: Missionaries and the Indians of Canada in Encounter since 1534* (Toronto: University of Toronto Press, 1984), *passim*.

28. *Christian Guardian*, 12 December 1829, 12, c. 1, 2.

29. *Christian Guardian*, 5 November 1831, 208, c. 2.

30. UCA, *Methodist Minutes*, London Conference, 1780.

31. Waldron, "A Sketch," 14.

32. *Christian Advocate*, 1 March 1833, 106, c. 3.

33. Extract from her diary.

34. Jones, *Life and Journals*, 217.

35. *Methodist Minutes*, London, 1780, 1789.

36. Nancy Hardesty, *Great Women of Faith* (Nashville: Abingdon, 1982), *passim*; Barbara Brown Zikmund, "The Struggle for the Right To Preach", in Rosemary R. Ruether and R. R. Keller eds., *Women and Religion in America*, 1, *The Nineteenth Century* (San Francisco: Harper & Row, 1981), *passim*; G. A. Burgess and J. T. Ward, *Free Baptist Cyclopaedia* (N.p.: Free Baptist Cyclopaedia Co., 1889), *passim*, describing some of these women.

37. *Christian Advocate*, 10 February 1832, 95, c. 4, 5, obituary. See also Dorothy Ripley, *The Bank of Faith and Works United* (Whitby: G. Clark, 1822), *passim*; Lorenzo Dow and Peggy Dow, *The Dealings of God, Man and The Devil; as Exemplified in the Life, Experience and Travels of Lorenzo Dow*, 2 vols. (New York: Cornish, Lamport, 1851), *passim*, especially 1:189. Dorothy participated in Quaker and Methodist activities, although she never officially joined either denomination. She is, however, one of a few women in Nolan B. Harmon, *Encyclopedia of World Methodism*, 2 vols. (Nashville: United Methodist Publishing House, 1974).

38. George Brown, *Recollection of Itinerant Life: Including Early Reminiscences* (Cincinnati: R. W. Carroll, 1868), 183 *ff.*, describes Miss Miller's activities. See also *Primitive Methodist Magazine*, 1829-1832, *passim*; and John H. Acornley, *A History of the Primitive Methodist Church in the United States of America* (Fall River, Mass: Acornley, 1909), 16 *ff*. There was a great deal of co-operation and interchange of preaching places among the Methodist groups at that time in United States.

39. For details see: Muir, "Petticoats," and "Woman as Preacher," *passim*; also "Elizabeth Dart," in *Dictionary of Canadian Biography*, 8 (Toronto: University of Toronto Press, 1985), 200-1; *Primitive Methodist Magazine*, 1829-1831, *passim*; *Bible Christian Magazine*, 1833-1853, *passim*; Elizabeth Peters, "An Account of The Voyage From England to America in 1830," in Howard H. Finley, *The Diaries of William and Elizabeth Peters Recounting The Voyage to the New World on the Good Brig Friends in 1830*, 1942, Archives of Ontario.

40. Abel Stevens, *Life and Times of Nathan Bangs* (New York: Carlton & Porter, 1863), 350 *ff*; Carroll, *Case*, 1:224; *Methodist Episcopal Church in Canada - Ontario Conference Minutes*, 1863, obituary of J. Gatchell.

41. "Ladies Department," *Christian Guardian*, 5 December 1829, 21, c. 2; and "Gentlemen's Department," 12 December 1829, 29, c. 12.

42. *Christian Advocate*, 1 April 1831, 122, c. 5.

43. *Christian Advocate*, 5 May 1829, 145, c. 2; Carroll, *Case*, 3:171, 202, 169; Jones, *Life and Journals*, 140; Playter, *History*, 342.
44. *Christian Guardian*, 27 November 1830, 6, c. 3; 18 September 1833, 26; 5 September, 1828, c. 3.
45. *Christian Guardian*, 29 October 1873, 351, c. 2, obituary; *Canada Conference Missionary Society Report*, 1829, 17. J. H. Pestalozzi, a nineteenth century European philosopher, was in favour of natural-ness and opposed to discipline, a theory which seems out of line with the highly structured and regulated classes described in the mission reports.
46. *Christian Guardian*, "Ladies Department," 21 November 1829, 5, c. 2; 4 December, 1830, 10, c. 4; 5 June 1830, 230, c. 3.
47. *Christian Advocate*, "Ladies Department," 9 September 1826, 4, c. 4; *Christian Guardian*, 12 December 1829, 28, c. 3.
48. *Christian Guardian*, "Ladies Department," 28 November 1829, 13, c. 4.
49. *Christian Guardian*, "The Gentlemen's Department," 21 November 1829, 3, c. 2.
50. *Christian Advocate*, 21 March 1834, 119, c. 1.
51. *Christian Guardian*, 17 November 1833, 208.
52. Alison Prentice, "The Feminization of Teaching," in S. M. Trofi-menkoff and A. Prentice, *The Neglected Majority* (Toronto: McClel-land and Stewart, 1981), 49-65, and A. Prentice, *The School Promo-ters* (Toronto: McClelland and Stewart, 1977; 2nd ed., 1984), *passim*.
53. *Christian Guardian*, 9 July 1831, 139; 19 March 1831, 75.
54. Prentice, "The Feminization," 49-65.
55. *Missionary Society Reports*, 1825-1832, 1847-1851.
56. Salaries are found in: Prentice, "The Feminization," 60; *Missionary Society Report*; and *Primitive Methodist Disciplines*.
57. *Disciplines of the British Primitive Methodist Connexion* (York, Upper Canada: W. J. Coates, 1833), 40.
58. *Christian Guardian*, 12 June 1830, 236, c. 2.
59. Prentice, "The Feminization," 61.
60. See above, note 49.
61. *Christian Advocate*, 10 February 1832, 95, c. 3, 4.

62. *Christian Guardian*, 24 October 1832, 199.
63. *Christian Guardian*, 14 April 1830, 309.
64. *Christian Advocate*, 27 January 1832, 86, c. 3.
65. *Christian Guardian*, 14 August 1830, 309, c. 2, Second Annual Report of York Female Missionary Society.
66. *Christian Guardian*, 22 January 1831, 41, c. 5, in a letter from the River Credit mission.
67. *Christian Advocate*, 17 October 1828, 26, c. 1.
68. *Christian Guardian*, 13 March 1830, 131.
69. *Missionary Society Report*, 1827, 1.
70. *Christian Advocate*, 8 August 1828, 195, c. 3.
71. *Christian Advocate*, 6 March 1829, 106, c. 2.; 3 April 1829, 122, c. 5.
72. *Christian Guardian*, 10 September 1831, 174, c. 12, Fifth Annual Report of The Cramahe Female Missionary Society.
73. *Christian Advocate*, 18 November 1826, 41, c. 5.
74. Carroll, *Case*, 4:268; Sanderson, *The First Century*, 2:86, *Christian Guardian*, 11 May 1887, 299, c. 3, obituary.
75. See Muir, "Petticoats," and "Woman as Preacher."

2

DIFFERENT VISIONS: THE MULTIPLICATION OF

PROTESTANT MISSIONS TO FRENCH-CANADIAN

ROMAN CATHOLICS, 1834-1855

Robert Merrill Black

Between the years 1834 and 1855, individuals of Church of England, Congregationalist, Methodist, Presbyterian, and Swiss Calvinist backgrounds tried to work together to bring the perceived benefits of the Protestant Reformation -- "life and liberty and progress and happiness" -- to the French-Canadian people, and to assimilate them into the mainstream of North American life.[1] This study investigates the reasons for the failure of that cooperative attempt, showing it to be due to the lack of Protestant consensus about the basis of cooperation, and to the strength of the Ultramontanist Roman Catholic response. The complexity of the topic demands first a description of the Protestants concerned and an account of attempts after the Peace of 1763 to convert French-Canadian Roman Catholics to Protestantism. The body of the paper begins with the formation in 1834 of a nondenominational mission under Swiss auspices and the creation in 1839 of the nondenominational French-Canadian Missionary Society (FCMS) under local anglophone control. It continues with the birth for denominational reasons of separate Church of Scotland and Church of England missions in 1841 which initiated a period of rivalry, attempted reconciliations, and expansion. The story concludes with the beginning of a Wesleyan Methodist mission in 1855, which essentially terminated Protestant cooperation within the FCMS and among these missions generally.

In the two decades being studied, just under two thousand francophone Roman Catholics left their church for Protestantism as a result of these missions, and several hundred became convinced evangelical Protestants. Although limited in their results, these missions do offer a view of some of the earliest roots of Protestant ecumenism in Canada, even in that era of divisive controversy. The vision held by mission supporters was of a Protestant Canada, united in essentials and pluralistic in non-essentials. It failed in this instance because anti-Roman Catholicism proved to be an insufficient basis on which to build a lasting consensus, when no alternative basis as yet existed. Only in later years did practical cooperation among Protestants gain strength, the result of working together on less divisive, more positive matters. Roughly, from Confederation in 1867 until after the First World War, a Protestant vision of Canada as "His Dominion" flourished; the roots of that cooperation and dialogue are found as early as the period under study.[2]

A full account of the tensions between the denominations involved in the French-Canadian missions is beyond the scope of this study. Their fundamental differences were both doctrinal and philosophical. Fierce debate over the control of the income from the lands of the Clergy Reserve involved the thorny issue of church-state relations, and the thornier practical issue of denominational income. Other debates were Canadian versions of the longstanding Calvinist-Arminian conflict over free will and predestination. Still other points of conflict involved church government and baptism, all hinging on "proper interpretation" of the Bible. Most participants in these debates were British immigrants, well-versed in these controversies and deeply influenced by historic denominational animosities, so it was not surprising that different visions were retained in Canada.

The census returns of 1844, 1851/2, and 1861 for Lower Canada show that members of the Church of England formed the largest identifiable body within the non-Roman Catholic population, approximately 35% of that grouping, followed by the Presbyterian family of churches at about 26%. These percentages remain stable in the period studied, although in fact there may have been some leakage of both their numbers to the Methodist churches, which grew from 13% to 17%, and to the Baptist churches which increased from 3% to 5%. The Congregationalists had a changing membership which always retained about 3% of the total. All the denominations were concerned with laying their foundations in the colony and all, particularly the larger churches, had their internal divisions and "parties" to preoccupy them. Protestants exhibited a great deal of variety in practically every way.

In spite of differences, most Protestants were united in believing Roman Catholic French-Canadian society to be inferior to British Protestant society: they believed French Canadians had "primitive" agricultural practices which tended to exhaust the soil, widespread illiteracy which debilitated them, and embedded poverty born of a lack of thrift and industry and compounded by the "sanctified extortion" of the "Romish" tithe. The close identification between the Roman Catholic church and French-Canadian nationalism induced some Protestants to see a causal relationship between the two, and therefore to support remedial action against Roman Catholics by the Protestant population.[3] Whether the hindrances to the progress of Protestant business and civilization were in fact due to Roman Catholicism, and whether opposition to that church could provide a sufficient basis for such action, remained to be seen in the coming decades.

The Evangelical Impulse

The people active in the planning and direction of the missionary "crusade" against Roman Catholicism in Lower Canada were found in all the Protestant denominations. These evangelicals had an intense conviction of God's involvement in history, and were distinguished from the mainstream of Protestant orthodoxy not by theological difference but by "emphasis and a sense of urgency." They "professed conversion [often emotional and dramatic] and accepted forms of discipline designed to strengthen their faith and to shew forth its implications."[4] Often their influence within each of the denominations was significant because of their leadership in charitable causes and various forms of public service.

A forceful imperative for the evangelicals was the joint propagation of their faith. "Let us go and make mankind Christian first," they said, "and then discuss whether they shall be of our denomination or not."[5]

They also shared the conviction that Roman Catholics were not Christians, and hence were proper subjects for proselytism. They believed Roman Catholicism was a superstitious, corrupt system, and a caricature of truth. Because of such matters as the strong political influence of the Roman Catholic clergy, the Roman Catholic prohibition against individual perusal and interpretation of the Bible, and the absence of significant educational provisions for Roman Catholics -- all matters which evangelicals regarded as restrictions on the individual's "right of private judgment" -- Roman Catholicism was to evangelicals a system inimical to the liberties and responsibilities, and hence the prosperity and peace, of Anglo-American Protestant civilization. Protestants generally believed that the progressiveness of their civilization was a sign of God's blessing on it, and at least some French Canadians were inclined to agree with them.[6]

The missions which existed after 1834 were built upon sporadic earlier efforts to evangelize francophone Roman Catholics, and were stimulated by a growing concern about the expanding size of the French-Canadian population. An early attempt by the British imperial government after the Peace of 1763 to use three francophone clergy to attract French Canadians into the Church of England had quickly proved a dismal failure, and thereafter the government played no overt role in schemes to "Protestantize" the French Canadians. Protestants who settled in Canada in the eighteenth and early nineteenth centuries tended to cooperate well with Roman Catholics. Congregational minister Henry Wilkes reminisced in 1846 that most Montreal Protestants early in the nineteenth century were very comfortable with that cordial co-existence and mutual toleration, and criticized any proposed proselytism of Roman Catholics as "sedition against the body politic." In the face of this body of opinion, the few evangelicals at that time "had not the courage to make [a] stand."[7]

As the number of evangelicals increased, so did an uncompromising opposition to Roman Catholicism in Lower Canada. Sporadic Methodist efforts to make converts were begun in 1809 in Quebec City by Pierre Langlois, a Channel Island class leader. The results were as limited as those coming from a more purposeful mission sponsored by the British Wesleyans, when Guernsey evangelist Jean de Putron worked in the Quebec

City and Montreal areas from 1815 to 1821.[8] In the 1820s, several officers of the British forces stationed in Lower Canada, concerned with the growing radicalism of French-Canadian politics, began to use their influence to "disseminate the Gospel" amongst the French Canadians, probably in keeping with the view expressed some years later by the *Montreal Witness*, that "many a Christian missionary is . . . a British consul of the most unexpensive [*sic*] and efficient kind; and his congregation a society for the protection of British lives and property."[9] Captain Thomas Gummersall Anderson secured the services of a Swiss agent of the British Reformation Society who worked without success, and Major William Plenderleath Christie worked assiduously to find francophone Protestant schoolteachers and settlers for extensive holdings at L'Acadie which he administered for his late brother-in-law, Bristol merchant Alexander McGinnis.

Christie proposed a Swiss missionary for ordination to Bishop Charles James Stewart, who rejected this proposed assault on Roman Catholics within his diocese. Christie even suggested in 1830 that Protestants show their unity in a common mission to the French Canadians, if for no other reason than "to stop the mouth of the railing accusation, that 'Protestants cannot agree'."[10] These two military officers were joined gradually by other Protestants who took it upon themselves to purchase and distribute French-language religious materials supplied from overseas sources such as the British and Foreign Bible Society, the Society for Promotion Christian Knowledge, and the Religious Tract Society. This sowing of spiritual seed sometimes bore fruit later in the evangelical missions.[11]

Well-organized American evangelicals, reacting to the increasing emigration of French Canadians into the American border areas and the labour-hungry mill towns of New England, early took an interest in the evangelization of French Canadians. Protestants saw in the newcomers and their priests the seeds of eventual "Papal tyranny" in America. Border-area churches made revivalistic use of such French-speaking Protestant ministers as the Congregationalist Edward Kirk, then of Albany, New York, and long a supporter of the FCMS, and the Episcopalian Charles Henry Williamson of New York City, later agent of the Church of England mission at Sabrevois. Support was later channelled to the missions in Lower Canada itself by American evangelical missionary organizations. The French Association of New York, founded in 1835 to evangelize France, was broadened in 1839 to become the Foreign Evangelical Society of New York. It and its 1849 successor, the American and Foreign Christian Union, were early supporters of organized evangelical missions to French-Canadian Roman Catholics, finding them convenient sources of agents for American home missions.[12]

The Arrival of the Swiss

The first enduring mission to the French Canadians had a somewhat unplanned beginning in 1834. The Rev. Henri Olivier, his wife, and two students, Samuel Dentan and Daniel Gavin, were designated for work among the Sioux by their Swiss sponsors, the Société des Missions Evangéliques de Lausanne. At the port of New York, on their way to Lower Canada, the foursome was met by several Presbyterian ministers who asked them to enter instead the field of French-Canadian evangelism, and provided them with letters of introduction to the minister of the American Presbyterian Church in Montreal. After their arrival in Lower Canada, the Swiss were also encouraged by ministers of local Baptist, Congregational, and Methodist churches to undertake the evangelization of the French Canadians. The four agreed to refer the matter to their Swiss sponsors, and Olivier and his wife in the meantime accepted Methodist facilities for use as a base of operations and on Christie's behalf quietly secured colonies of francophone Swiss Protestants for the enormous holdings in the Upper Richelieu Valley which the Major inherited in 1835.[13] Their Swiss parent body told them to move on to the Sioux mission. Olivier and his wife declined, although Dentan and Gavin obediently went west. The Methodists briefly discussed creating their own missionary agency to assist the Swiss missionaries, but the reality of limited Methodist resources and the failure of the earlier efforts of Langlois and de Putron caused them to lean more to non-denominational evangelical co-operation.[14] The Oliviers were courted by a local Baptist pastor, John Gilmour, and eventually joined that denomination, a setback for co-operative efforts. The Swiss couple made no converts, but by continued correspondence with their friends in Lausanne they managed to convince Henriette Odin Feller and Louis Roussy to join them in 1835.

The non-Baptist evangelical community of Montreal kept its distance from the new Swiss arrivals, content instead to band together to support a francophone colporteur from the Bible Society for that city.[15] Feller and Roussy renewed their friendship with the Oliviers, who invited them into Baptist fellowship. The Oliviers soon returned to Europe and the new-comers continued to work but without any formal links with the Baptists. Roussy taught at a school at L'Acadie at Major Christie's request and with his support until resistance by Roman Catholic priests forced both Roussy and Feller, in May 1836, to move a few miles east into the more heavily anglophone Protestant area of St. Johns (now Saint-Jean-sur-Richelieu). No one attended the school the Swiss missionaries opened there in the Methodist chapel, and after a period of discouragement only the Baptist pastor Gilmour, showed sustained interest.[16]

The Swiss mission might have died but for a fortuitous event. Marie Lore of L'Acadie, the Massachusetts-born daughter of a French sailor, had married a French Canadian about 1816 and moved to Lower Canada. She had been a Protestant before conforming to Roman Catholicism after her marriage, and had retained her practice of Bible reading. Being terminally ill, she sought out the evangelical comfort offered by the francophone missionaries and became their first convert. When this "first fruits" of Protestant missionary effort died in August 1836, the anglophones of St. Johns turned out in force to give her an honoured burial. Lore's daughter then invited the Swiss to open a school near her home on the Grande Ligne, a long frontier road piercing Major Christie's unsettled holdings in the forest south of St. Johns. The missionaries moved there in September 1836, Feller as a teacher and Roussy as an itinerant preacher, and a year later they opened their first church. The Grande Ligne mission was launched.

For the first decade of its work, the Grande Ligne mission was funded by contributions from British, Swiss, and American individuals and by the Foreign Evangelical Society of New York. The mission was built on

an evangelical non-denominational and not a denominational basis. A little
money continued to come from the local Baptists, but even that little was
declined when the local Baptist missionary society attempted to exercise
too much control over the missionaries. For a decade the Swiss tried
sincerely to maintain this nondenominational basis, "being then of opinion
that they could labor more efficiently if they were independent of all
religious parties."[17] The intense individualism of Madame Feller revealed
itself in her determination to keep the mission in her hands and away
from the control of the anglophone community. For the rest of her life,
the Grande Ligne mission remained essentially a foreign francophone
mission in Lower Canada. Feller was unable to engage wide anglophone
support and commitment on her terms, and thus cooperative action was
prevented from the start.

The Beginnings of the French-Canadian Missionary Society

The Rebellions of 1837 and 1838 in Lower Canada were not supported
or encouraged by the Roman Catholic Church, but many Protestants
interpreted the radicalism and assertive nationalism demonstrated in those
limited uprisings as the fruit of lives formed under the influence of
unreformed religion. Evangelicals underscored their longstanding identification of Roman Catholicism with French-Canadian nationalism, and
believed that to undermine the former was to address the problem of the
latter. Concerned laity and clergy of all Protestant denominations held a
series of "earnest conferences" in Montreal during the winter of 1838/9,
out of which arose the anglophone-controlled French-Canadian Missionary
Society.[18]

The FCMS was formed on 13 February 1839 at a public meeting timed
to coincide with the public discussion of the famous report by Lord
Durham recommending the assimilation of the French Canadians into
British imperial culture. An observer recorded "the excited state of feeling
at the time,"[19] but the meeting took place despite the apprehensions many
evangelicals felt for their own safety. The guiding spirit behind the FCMS
was a Congregational minister, Henry Wilkes, a leader of the evangelicals
of Lower Canada. He was a committed advocate of interdenominational

cooperation, in spite of the lack of success of previous experiments in Lower Canada. "[W]hile catholic expressions may be used freely on the platform, and in conversing as private individuals," Wilkes wrote later, "yet each *ism* will assert itself as united work begins." This same phenomenon was noted by other observers.[20] The "isms" or denominational systems were still more powerful than the ideals of evangelical cooperation, although the minority of evangelicals who launched the FCMS believed they could change that.

The first supporters of the FCMS were well-known people, involved elsewhere with benevolent activities which brought their names before the public. The Church of England was represented by Dr. Andrew Fernando Holmes, Capt. John Horatio Maitland, William Ogden, and Lt. Col. Edward Paston Wilgress; Methodists by the Hon. James Ferrier, William Lunn, the Rev. Robert L. Lusher, and John Matthewson; Congregationalists by the Rev. Henry Wilkes; and Presbyterians by the Revs. J. W. Perkins, William Taylor, and James Thompson, and businessmen James Court, William Lyman, and James Orr. The motion proposing the formation of the FCMS made specific mention of "assisting the present Swiss mission at Grande Ligne." Original plans seem to have called for an expansion of the Grande Ligne mission under local anglophone control, but Wilkes was rebuffed by the missionaries there. It was a disappointment to him that the Swiss work "was not upon the catholic basis that is felt to be so desirable in all foreign Missionary work, as this practically is." Wilkes' comment indicates the insensitive expression of anglophone superiority by FCMS leadership and supporters, called "bigotry" by detractors, which offended the franco-phones and which solidified Feller's determination to maintain control of the mission at Grande Ligne.[21]

The first blow to the society from an "ism" was the decision by Major W. Plenderleath Christie not to accept the proffered post as first president. Christie was the logical choice, a man of wealth and social standing who had advocated such a mission for a decade. He was, however, a member of the busy Special Council which governed the colony until the union with Upper Canada in 1841. His particular concern, too, was negotiations with Bishop George Jehoshaphat Mountain concerning churches of which he wished to be lay patron. Mountain was firmly opposed both to cooperation with non-Church of England groups, which he called "Sectarians", and to attempted "conversion" of a people he believed to be Christian already. Leadership of the FCMS would have jeopardized Christie's negotiating position with that prelate. Instead, Wilkes' friend Lt. Col. Wilgress was prevailed upon to serve as president of the FCMS, a post he held for many years.[22] A further cause of regret to the FCMS was that the local Protestant community was not forthcoming with much financial support -- circulars sent out that fall had netted only about one hundred pounds. Many Protestants clearly drew a line between cooperation in such ventures as distribution of literature and the disruptive work of proselytising. The widely-supported local Bible Society in fact did not wait long before instructing its agent, the Rev. James Thompson, to resign his membership on the committee of the FCMS. The implication was that the work of the two bodies could not be carried on with perfect harmony.[23]

By far the most severe blow to the hope of a sustained pan-Protestant mission to the French Canadians came with the 1839 Charge to his clergy by Bishop Mountain, in which he forbade any formal Church of England participation in the FCMS. The large Church of England community was "associated in the minds of men with the crown and empire of Britain" and this aloofness was interpreted by the evangelicals as a rejection of the FCMS by the respectable and the powerful. Mountain distrusted the evangelical motives and methods of the FCMS, but primarily he wished to protect exclusive Church of England claims to the Clergy Reserves. The bishop believed that Churchmen ought never to "adopt that language or lend ourselves to those proceedings in which the Church is regarded as a Sect among Sects." He agreed with the evangelicals that the greatest obstacle to Roman Catholic conversion was Protestant disunion, but his solution to disunion was that "sectarians" should return to the Church of England. Needless to say, Mountain won no friends for that cause. Such aloofness brought "sectarian" ire upon Church of England heads in Lower Canada as elsewhere, in what one Churchman described as "unholy alliances" of the smaller denominations promoting "violent excitements" against the Church of England.[24] For many Churchmen, at least, participation in the wider life of the state and British Empire by means of church establishment was a more attractive vision than the evangelical one of united Protestant cooperation.

In spite of these initial setbacks, the FCMS gamely went ahead with its plan to bring "spiritual religion" to the French Canadians. The FCMS committee delegated two of its number to make a fund-raising tour of Britain and the European continent, where aid and personnel were secured from many of the same evangelical friends in Glasgow, Edinburgh, London, and Geneva that Grande Ligne relied upon. In the meantime in Montreal, French colporteur Emile Lapelletrie of the Montreal Auxiliary Bible Society was engaged as an FCMS missionary, and Grande Ligne, "dans l'intérêt de l'oeuvre générale," loaned to the FCMS the services of an ailing man named Cellier, who soon died.[25] After a year of poor organization, the FCMS decided to concentrate its labours in Montreal and on the north side of the St. Lawrence River, and leave the south side and American border region to Grande Ligne. A great show was made of inviting the principal Swiss missionary, Louis Roussy, to help inaugurate the new FCMS station at Belle Rivière. A common Eucharist was planned, but the Grande Ligne contingent declined to participate; Feller and Roussy felt threatened because the FCMS had tapped into their overseas resources. They had reason to be cautious, for the FCMS began to make overtures to their American supporters soon after, when FCMS delegates to a Grande Ligne function took the opportunity to meet privately with representatives of the Foreign Evangelical Society of New York.[26]

The beginnings of the FCMS were small, but initial cooperation with the Grande Ligne mission made it seem that rivalry might be avoided. Rejection of the entire scheme by the Church of England was a disappointment but not without precedent. If Grande Ligne and the FCMS could at least work side by side, then it looked as though "Popery" would be eroded in Lower Canada. In this assessment the considerable strength of denominationalism and Roman Catholicism was seriously underestimated.

Ultramontanist Response and the Failure of Protestant Cooperation

The Roman Catholic bishop of Montreal, Ignace Bourget, was determined that he would lose none of his people to the Protestant drive. He
began a concentrated counter-attack against evangelical inroads as a
response both to the founding of the FCMS and to the announcement by
the British government of a plan to reunite Upper and Lower Canada in a
union designed to assimilate French-Canadian Roman Catholics. Bourget, a
convinced Ultramontanist, invited to Lower Canada the fiery French bishop
Charles-Auguste de Forbin-Janson, an Ultramontanist campaigner, to assist
in a Roman Catholic revival. The extravagant rhetoric and enormous
crowds which characterized Forbin-Janson's revival meetings were a rude
shock to evangelicals, exciting in them both indignation and fear. The
FCMS and Grande Ligne sent out colporteurs to the areas where the
Roman Catholic clergy were holding retreats -- an early end to the plan
of separate spheres of interest -- and the larger churches mobilized for
action.[27] Rather than join the nondenominational missions, however, the
Churches of England and Scotland aimed to protect their claims to
establishment by focusing their influence and expertise through their own
denominational missions. The weakness of anti-Roman Catholicism as a
unifying factor for Protestants was visibly demonstrated by these decisions
to found separate missions. The more subtle expression of Protestant unity
through the co-ordination of work was also jeopardized by the tendency of
the missions actively to compete with each other for personnel.

The man who might have begun the Church of England mission, and
who did begin the Church of Scotland mission, was an FCMS employee.
Emile Lapelletrie wanted to have a traditional congregational ministry. The
FCMS was unable to agree about the form his ministry was to take, and
Lapelletrie cast about for ordination elsewhere. He was engaged as
catechist and Scripture reader at Major Christie's new evangelical Church
of England parish, Trinity Church in Montreal, and solicited from Bishop
Mountain a licence to preach. Mountain was open to ordaining him to a
traditional ministry for his francophone congregation following the usual
year-long probation and further "conforming" study, but Lapelletrie was
enticed from the path with a better offer.[28] The Rev. Alexander Mathie-

son, a Church of Scotland minister out of sympathy with the strident evangelicalism of those Presbyterians who supported the FCMS, sought out Lapelletrie with the assurance that he could be ordained without further studies. Lapelletrie gave to the Quebec Presbytery testimonials he had solicited from Major Christie and Louis Roussy, and offered to bring into the Presbytery a ready-made congregation of seventy people. The Presbytery exempted Lapelletrie from the studies expected of probationers and hired him as a catechist. He was ordained a minister in the Church of Scotland in September 1841, given collections taken up in Kirk congregations for the new mission, and assigned to a church in Montreal. Following the Free Church separation from the Church of Scotland in Canada three years later, Lapelletrie remained loyal to Mathieson and kept his congregation within the Kirk.[29]

The entry of the Kirk into the field of French-Canadian missions gave impetus to similarly-minded Churchmen. In October 1841 Churchmen set up their own Church of England French-Canadian Missionary Society. Of the clergy and laity involved in forming the CEFCMS only some were evangelicals, such as William Anderson, William Dawes, and Mark Willoughby from the clergy, and Andrew Holmes and William Ogden of the laity. The mission was conceived to be broad-based enough to call on the support of all parties within the Church of England fold. There was no pretense of evangelical cooperation, however, nor was there any acknowledgement that any other French-Canadian missions existed. This mission was to be exclusively Church of England. News of the creation of the CFCMS was not well received by many Protestants. On the one hand, the FCMS, Grande Ligne, and Kirk missions perceived it to be a rival, and on the other Protestants opposed to any such missions were dismayed that the flames of religious discord were being fanned by the largest single Protestant church in the Canadas. Because so many British colonial officials were Churchmen, the reformist French-Canadian newspaper *L'Aurore des Canadas* warned ominously that the new mission should be immediately suppressed, "si . . . les autorités ne veulent pas se rendre solidairement complice à ses méfaits." This suppression, probably the work of Bishop Mountain, did in fact occur. Little record survives of this mission, and months later even the principal Church of England newspaper, *The Church*, heard of it only accidentally.[30] Determined anti-Roman Catholicism was by no means universal in the Protestant camp.

Non-Church of England observers eventually came to accuse the Church of England of "lack of concern" with the strength of Roman Catholicism, and to attribute this to the "pernicious" effect of Tractarianism, or the Oxford Movement, in undermining resistance to Romanism. If even the mighty Church of England could crumble at Rome's advance, the FCMS proclaimed, "their own union [in mission work] should be prized the more highly, and sought after the more earnestly."[31] At the 1842 FCMS annual meeting a sarcastic attack on Bishop Mountain's pro-Roman Catholic comments revealed something of the bitterness evangelicals felt in being denied even the appearance of united Protestant opposition to Roman Catholicism. Mountain believed that Roman Catholicism "if sincerely followed" had the power to bring its adherents to heaven. Evangelicals decidedly had no such belief, and did not fail to make a point of their difference "from this class of the community." Mountain's defenders responded to the evangelical critique in kind, deprecating French-Canadian evangelism as bigotry, harrassing the missionaries, and representing both the francophone missionaries and their anglophone supporters as mere religious agitators.[32] Relations between the Church of England and FCMS supporters were publicly very poor, and it was perhaps difficult for the public to remember that the president and several committee members of the FCMS were active Churchmen.

The FCMS tried in 1843 to build up an *esprit de corps* and to "dissipate the jealousies" amongst the various denominations and individuals supportive of French-Canadian evangelism by proposing that the FCMS, Grande Ligne, and Kirk missions hold their annual meeting on the same day and in the same place. This would have restored some public appearance of Protestant unity, for certainly prominent laity of every denomination would have attended and taken part. It was perhaps a sign of the fatal strains on nondenominational cooperation that nothing came of the proposal. Financial needs soon drove an enduring wedge between Grande Ligne and the FCMS. In 1843 staunch Grande Ligne supporter Major

Christie left Lower Canada for his health, and with his death in 1845 an important source of income and support was lost. By the mid-1840s, the Foreign Evangelical Society was seeking to expand and consolidate frontier and anti-Roman Catholic missions. In 1845 that society began to contribute to the FCMS as well as to Grande Ligne, and the illogicality of funding two similar missions caused the American body to insist on a stronger voice in the direction of the Grande Ligne mission. This would have meant some form of union with the FCMS and loss of control to the anglophone evangelicals. The American action precipitated a local crisis, the net result of which was the decision by the Grande Ligne staff to transfer control of the mission to the local Canada Baptist Missionary Society on terms allowing Henriette Feller and Henri Roussy continued control.[33]

For a decade, Feller and Roussy had steered a course clear of obligation to any denomination, but when given a choice between evangelical union with the anglophone FCMS or denominational liberty, the Swiss opted for liberty. After the move into the Baptist denomination was made, it was reported and long maintained in Grande Ligne materials that the shift was merely the public declaration of a long-held belief. Unquestionably the evidence points to an early sympathy of Feller and Roussy for believer's baptism, but Feller admitted later she had not expected the "violent rupture of ties" with longstanding non-Baptist supporters which resulted. There seems good reason to suspect that the change was precipitous and made from mixed motives. One Grande Ligne missionary even reported that not long before the change a colleague had been mercilessly hounded from the mission for advocating believer's baptism. The shock of the change was real to supporters, for those who had formerly been helpful actually shunned Feller on her next annual fundraising tour in the United States, and some even opposed her. Whether from theological difference or due to the sudden decline in funding, Grande Ligne lost at least two of its personnel at this time. Philippe Wolff severed his connection to Grande Ligne and was hired by the FCMS, and Daniel Gavin, who had become a tutor at the mission school after working for a time among the Sioux, left Grande Ligne and worked for the Presbyterians at Plattsburg, New York.[34]

The shift from nondenominational cooperation was harmful for Grande Ligne, for besides the loss of personnel and funds it was soon clear that the Canada Baptist Missionary Society was unable in 1846 and 1847 to meet the financial obligations it incurred in the transfer. The local Baptists in fact abandoned Grande Ligne altogether in 1848 to their more prosperous American equivalent. The American Baptist Home Missionary Society could not, however, by its constitution assume more than a third of the shortfall and so for years the Grande Ligne mission spent much of its time fundraising. Its schools had to accept cash-paying anglophone Protestant pupils as a means of bolstering income, and bilingual services were held to keep the mission before Baptist supporters. In addition, their new American friends seemed insensitive to the weakness of the Canadian mission. It took all the tact of the Swiss to prevent an agent of the American Baptist Home Missionary Society from using the appeal of their money to recruit personnel for work among French Canadians in the United States.[35]

Attempts at Renewed Evangelical Cooperation

The supporters who had been on the FCMS' first administrative committees were still involved in its affairs, and little real growth seemed apparent. Converts were shunned or persecuted by their Roman Catholic neighbours and many chose to emigrate to Upper Canada or the United States, where they were assimilated. The dream of a unified body of francophone Protestants looked as distant as ever. A small sign of hope for continued evangelical cooperation, however, was Methodist loyalty to the FCMS. Methodist circuit riders held public revival meetings, and caught some French Canadians in their evangelistic nets. These converts were directed to the FCMS, and Methodist churches invited the FCMS to hold its annual meetings in their facilities.[36] It did not seem enough, however. Debts were mounting and morale was poor.

Late in 1845 the new Presbyterian Church of Canada, the body created out of the Free Church movement away from the Church of Scotland, decided to throw its support behind the FCMS. The Presbyterians advocated evangelical cooperation and expressed particularly strong support for the FCMS. In December 1845 the Free Presbyterian paper, the *Ecclesiastical and Missionary Record*, devoted considerable space to an account of the FCMS in order to make the society "more generally known" and to encourage Presbyterians to give to it financially. Theological students at Knox College, the Presbyterian college in Toronto, heartily adopted the cause of French-Canadian evangelism in 1847 and one of their number, John Black, went to Montreal where he taught in the new FCMS educational institute and model farm at Pointe-aux-Trembles for several years. Black served also as a Collecting Agent and spoke on behalf of the FCMS before many different congregations, where he heard expressions of support. The Presbyterians consistently believed that "Home Missions, including Missions to the French Canadians, ought to be the first and principal enterprise of all the Evangelical Churches of Canada." Such forthright advocacy was a boon to the FCMS, as were the collections taken up in Free Church congregations for its support.[37] The new life given the FCMS by Free Church support encouraged the nondenominational American Tract Society to pay the salaries of three additional colporteurs in 1850, and talks were held early in 1851 with local Bible and Tract societies to coordinate colportage work.[38] The vision of evangelical unity in missions to the French Canadians was not dead.

With signs of hope for renewed evangelical cooperation within the FCMS, Church of England supporters now faced a dilemma. Their instinct was to cooperate but the reality was that their clerical leadership and probably a good portion of the laity were prejudiced against working with or contributing to the causes of those on the opposite side of the establishment issue. It is not surprising, then, that evangelical Churchmen wished to continue to work for a Church of England mission which would satisfy the scruples of their leadership and tap into untouched resources. The nucleus of what became the Church of England French-Canadian mission at Sabrevois, directly across the river from Grande Ligne, was the large family of local farmer Charles Roy. Roy had been given a Bible some time before by a passing soldier, and a French version of the Book of Common Prayer by a neighbour. He contacted the FCMS but decided in the end to join the Church of England; Bishop Mountain received him formally in July 1846. Amelia Bowman Christie, widow of the Major, secured the services of the peripatetic Swiss missionary Daniel Gavin at no cost to the diocese. In the Church of England diocese, Sabrevois was a part of Christieville parish, whose revenues came from Mrs. Christie's own Bleury seigniory and whose ministers were appointed by her through her late husband's trustees. Gavin worked as a catechist in the parish and went to Bishop's College at Lennoxville for his "conforming" studies, and was finally ordained deacon and priest by Mountain in 1848.[39]

The administrative committee of the FCMS hoped to co-ordinate the new missions's work with its own, and in 1847 invited two prominent Church of England priests, William Bennett Bond and Charles Bancroft, to join its membership. Neither priest then did so, indicating their caution with regard to Bishop Mountain, who had not yet given his support to a sustained mission. In fact, all Mountain ever did was to authorise an experimental bilingual parish on the Church of England model, and approve the terms of Gavin's licence restricting his activities to the approximate bounds of the seigniory of Sabrevois. Sabrevois was to be a welcome to inquirers, not a base for assault. It was a beginning the Evangelicals had no choice but to accept.[40]

The early 1850s saw efforts to expand all the missions and to secure an increase of support from all sources. This was due in large measure to the increasing influence of the Roman Catholic church in Canadian politics and the "Papal Aggression" crisis which erupted in 1850 when the Roman Catholic hierarchy was recreated in England. Protestants everywhere became "tremblingly and sensitively alive to the dangers of covered [sic] advances on the part of Rome."[41] The Church of Scotland sent Lapelletrie to Europe for funds and workers, but one of the two men who came soon left the work and the other, Louis Baridon, was hired away by the Presbytery of Champlain, New York. Lapelletrie returned to France with rumours flying of his having embezzled the funds he gathered, and at his death months later only a catechist, Thomas Charbonell, remained employed by the Kirk. The FCMS opened schools, including a "female school", expanded its colportage programme, and started a theological training class under Philippe Wolff, but the net result was a reduction in the number of active missionaries. Along with Wolff, the FCMS lost Jean-Frédéric Doudiet who was increasingly incapacited by blindness, and Jean Vernier who died at sea.[42]

The Church of England mission expanded in the only way open to it, the foundation of educational institutions. The burden of support was too great for a single individual to bear, and so evangelicals in the Church of England met to organize a Montreal Corresponding Committee of the strongly evangelical Colonial Church and School Society. After several years' battle Francis Fulford, bishop of the new diocese of Montreal, won control of the Committee over the threats of Amelia Christie to transfer the work to the Church of Scotland. The evangelicals' bid for independence was thus checked, and in order to preserve what influence they had with Fulford, they were obliged to keep their involvement in the FCMS circumspect.[43]

The End of Cooperation

In 1854 the divisive problem of the Clergy Reserves was finally settled, but it was too late to help the French-Canadian missions. They were now floundering in a sea of debt and had manifested few tangible results. In fact, the following year proved to be one of setbacks to the cause of French-Canadian evangelism and to evangelical cooperation. Free Church theological students who had undertaken FCMS summer placements gave up the work in discouragement. The FCMS model farm at Pointe-aux-Trembles had to close for lack of funds. Olympe Hoerner Tanner, mistress of the FCMS female school, died and it seemed impossible to find a replacement. Of the three remaining FCMS missionaries none were active in proselytism. Daniel Gavin died, putting the Sabrevois mission into turmoil; the Church of England mission entered into denominational isolation parallel to that of Grande Ligne. Henriette Feller was dangerously ill, and went to the United States for her health. A group of Grande Ligne and FCMS converts emigrated *en masse* with a former FCMS missionary to Grand Bend, on Lake Huron in Upper Canada.[44] By this time as well, it was clear on the political scene that the union of the provinces of Lower and Upper Canada had come to work in favour of the Roman

Catholics of Lower Canada, who were more numerous and apparently
stronger than ever before.

It is no wonder, then, that the Wesleyan Methodists of Lower Canada
began to be impatient for a "fresh start." An amalgamation in 1854 of
their work in Upper and Lower Canada "obviate[d] the scarcity of workers" in Lower Canada and infused new life into Methodist activities there.
A Methodist supporter of the FCMS, distressed at the forceful advocacy of
Calvinism by such FCMS mainstays as the *Montreal Witness*, brought
François Pépin to Quebec City late in 1854. Pépin, a French-Canadian
emigrant to Detroit, had been converted by the Methodist Episcopal church
there and worked as a colporteur for the American Bible Society. The
Christian Guardian brought Pépin to the attention of Wesleyans throughout
Canada, and the French Methodist mission was born. The Wesleyan
Methodist Missionary Society claimed it was not a rival to but a sincere
well-wisher of the other French-Canadian missions. Nevertheless, one of
its early acts was to entice Thomas Charbonell from the Kirk congregation
in Montreal, which then disbanded. The Society also engaged Amand Parent
(like Pépin a convert of the Methodists in the United States), who had
left work with Grande Ligne in 1845 when it became Baptist and took up a
trade.[45] The birth of the new mission meant that the FCMS gradually lost
most of its Methodist support and became for all intents and purposes a
Presbyterian body with some Congregationalist support. In practice,
nondenominational cooperation came to an end.

The FCMS vision of a united Protestant assault on the francophone
Roman Catholicism of Lower Canada was a tattered dream. Instead of
united Protestant support and a single French-Canadian Reformed Church,
which evangelical idealists had hoped for, there was a miscellaneous
collection of supporters and converts. Instead of a single strong mission
there were five struggling, isolated ones. The different denominational
visions propagated amongst the French Canadians did not, in the end,
translate into missions which complemented the FCMS, but into a fatal
weakening of the common enterprise. Anti-Roman Catholicism may have
been shared by a majority of Protestants in the province of Canada, but
that did not command a consensus nor prove to be the rock on which to

build united action. To paraphrase Major Christie's 1830 letter, Protestants could not, indeed, agree. The FCMS printed for wide circulation a brochure pleading for cooperative evangelical support, saying "if this work is to be done as all, it can best be done in connection with this Mission."[46] It was too late. An era of mutual isolation and competition had arrived.

Notes

1. *Church of England French Mission Record*, January 1861, 13.
2. Estimates of converts made by John Dougall in the *Montreal Witness*, 14 February 1857, 100, and 9 December 1857, 780. N. K. Clifford, "His Dominion: a Vision in Crisis," *Studies in Religion/Sciences Religieuses*, 2 (1973), 315-326, alluding to William T. Gunn, *His Dominion* (Toronto: Canadian Council of the Missionary Education Movement, 1917).
3. *Ecclesiastical and Missionary Record* [hereafter *E&MR*], February 1850, 60 *f*.
4. G. S. French, "The Evangelical Creed in Canada," in W. L. Morton, ed., *The Shield of Achilles: Aspects of Canada in the Victorian Age* (Toronto: McClelland and Stewart, 1968), 16, 17.
5. *E&MR*, November 1846, 216.
6. French Canadian converts who had lived in the United States noted their agreement with this conviction. *The Church*, 5 March 1842, 139; *Colonial Church Record*, February 1840, 142; A. Parent, *Life of the Rev. Amand Parent* (Toronto: Briggs, 1887), 39; W. N. Wyeth, *Henrietta Feller and the Grande Ligne Mission* (Philadelphia: Wyeth, 1898), 83.
7. John S. Moir, *The Church in the British Era* (Toronto: McGraw-Hill Ryerson, 1972), 44 *f*.; Reminiscences of Henry Wilkes, in *Montreal Witness*, 2 March 1846, 65; *cf.* 9 February 1846, 41; 7 February 1848, 42.
8. A. D. Stephenson, *One Hundred Years of Methodist Missions, 1824-1924* (Toronto: Missionary Society of the Methodist Church, 1925), 1:33 *f*.
9. *Montreal Witness*, 26 January 1846, 26.

10. John Campbell, "French Evangelization," in *Historic Sketches of the Pioneer Work and the Missionary, Educational, and Benevolent Agencies of the Presbyterian Church in Canada* (Toronto: Murray, 1903), 62; René Hardy, "La Rébellion de 1837/8 et l'Essor du Protestantisme canadien-français," *Revue d'Histoire de l'Amérique française,* 29 (1975), 166; Archives of the Anglican Diocese of Montreal, Christie Collection of Letters.

11. Ernest Hawkins, *Annals of the Diocese of Quebec* (London: SPCK, 1849), 240-4; J. M. Cramp, *Memoir of Madame Feller* (London: Elliot Stack, n.d.), 27.

12. A. Parent, *Life,* 20 *f.*; N. Cyr, *Memoir of the Rev. C. H. O. Côté, M.D.* (Philadelphia: American Baptist Publication Society, 1853), 18; *The Berean,* 31 December 1846, 22 April 1847; Wyeth, *Henrietta Feller,* 72, 83.

13. Cramp, *Madame Feller,* 63, 65; Public Archives of Canada [hereafter PAC], MG-8, F 99-9, 3:548, 562.

14. Reminiscences of the Hon. James Ferrier, in *Wesleyan Missionary Notices, Canada Conference,* February 1857, 158.

15. John Wood, *Memoir of Henry Wilkes, D.D., LL.D.* (Montreal: F. E. Grafton and Sons, 1887), 94.

16. Cyr, *Côté,* 107.

17. Cyr, *Côté,* 131.

18. Robert Campbell, *A History of the Scotch Presbyterian Church, St. Gabriel Street, Montreal* (Montreal: W. Drysdale, 1887), 450; Wood, *Wilkes,* 108.

19. Campbell, *Scotch Church,* 450.

20. Wood, *Wilkes,* 43, 51, 59; *Montreal Witness,* 18 June 1849, 146, rued that Protestants "are chiefly occupied with divisions amongst themselves; they are full of variances and distractions, and all are . . . more friendly with non professors than with professors of other denominations." 5

21. United Church of Canada Archives, FCMS Minute Book, 13 February 1839; Wood, *Wilkes,* 108.

22. R. M. Black, "Anglicans and French-Canadian Evangelism, 1839-1848," *Journal of the Canadian Church Historical Society*, 26 (1984), 20; Wood, *Wilkes*, 98; F. J. Audet, "Membres du Conseil Spécial," *Bulletin des Recherches historiques*, 7 (1901), 82-3.

23. FCMS Minute Book, 23 September 1839, 26 December 1839, 22 January 1841.

24. Hawkins, *Annals*, 155, 256 *f.*; *The Church*, 20 July 1839; A. Mountain, *Memoir of George Jehoshaphat Mountain, D.D., D.C.L., Late Bishop of Quebec* (Montreal: Lovell, 1866), 205.

25. Rieul Duclos, *Histoire du Protestantisme français au Canada et aux Etats-Unis* (Montreal: Librarie Evangélique, 1913), 1:142, 154; Glen Scorgie, "The Early Years of the French Canadian Missionary Society, 1839-50" (M.C.S. thesis, Regent College, 1982), 104-18.

26. Duclos, *Protestantisme français*, 1:142; FCMS Minute Book, 10 August 1840.

27. Léon Pouliot, *La Réaction catholique de Montréal* (Montreal: Imprimerie du Messager, 1942), *passim*; *Montreal Herald*, 27 September 1841, 8 November 1841; *Les Mélanges Religieux*, 8 octobre 1841; Cyr, *Côté*, 43.

28. FCMS Minute Book, 13 April 1841; *Annual Report of the Society for the Propagation of the Gospel*, 1841, cxvi-cxvii.

29. John Jenkins, *Life of the Rev. Alex. Mathieson, D.D.* (Montreal: Dawson, 1870), 127; McGill University Archives, St. Gabriel Street Church collection, Minute Book of the Presbytery of Quebec, 3 June 1841, 26 July 1841, 1-2 September 1841.

30. *The Church*, 25 December 1841, 98; *Montreal Herald*, quoted in *The Church*, 25 December 1841; *L'Aurore des Canadas*, 11 novembre 1841, 3.

31. *FCMS 4th Annual Report 1843*, f. 203, in FCMS Minute Book; *Fifth Annual Report 1844*, f. 265; FCMS *Missionary Record*, August 1843.

32. *FCMS 3rd Annual Report 1842*, f. 198, in Minute Book, quoting *The Church*, 20 July 1839; *FCMS 4th Annual Report 1843*.

33. *FCMS 3rd Annual Report 1842*, 7; Cyr, *Côté*, 131 *f.*, 137.

34. FCMS *Missionary Record*, August 1845, 297; A. Parent, *Life*, 60 *f.*, 70 *f.*; Cramp, *Madame Feller*, 153 *f.*; FCMS Minute Book, 5 August 1845; *Montreal Witness*, 22 February 1847, 57.

35. Cyr, *Côté*, 132 *f.*, 140; Cramp, *Madame Feller*, 181, 244; Duclos, *Protestantisme français*, 2:181, 218 *ff.*

36. FCMS Minute Book, 12 August 1844.

37. *E&MR*, December 1845, 140; May 1848, 95; August 1848, 145; September 1848, 78; August 1849, 195.

38. *E&MR*, February 1850, 60 *f.*; Montreal/Ottawa Conference Archives, United Church of Canada, McGill University, FCMS Minute Book, 11 February 1851.

39. Canon E. R. Roy, "Our Family's Debt to the Bible," in General Synod Archives, Anglican Church of Canada; Hawkins, *Annals*, 241 *f.*; G. J. Mountain, "Journal of a Summer Visitation ... 1846," *The Church in the Colonies*, 17 (London: SPCK, 1847), 46; PAC, MG-8, F 99-9, 7:11469.

40. FCMS Minute Book, 21 January 1847.

41. B. Andrews, "The Rise and Fall of the French Canadian Missionary Society, 1839-1880: A Study in Conflicting Aspirations" (Unpublished paper, 1977), 12.

42. *Montreal Witness*, 28 February 1855, 76, 23 August 1854, 300, 23 May 1855, 195, 25 July 1855, 271.

43. Archives of the Anglican Diocese of Montreal, correspondence of the Rt. Rev. Francis Fulford with the SPG, London, 10 November 1851, 195 *f.*

44. *Montreal Witness*, 8 November 1854, 395, 7 February 1855, 47, 29 March 1854, 113; *Canadian Messenger and Journal of Missions*, July 1855, 3; *The Echo*, 1 June 1855, 14 December 1855; Duclos, *Protestantisme français*, 1:218 *f.*

45. *True Witness & Catholic Chronicle*, 6 October 1854, 4; *Montreal Witness*, 20 September 1854, 335; *Christian Guardian*, 18 July 1855, 25 July 1855; Wesleyan Missionary Society, *Annual Reports*, 1856/7, x, 1857/8, xii, xlvii.

46. *A Brief Account of the French Canadian Missionary Society* (Montreal: n.p. 1860).

3

POVERTY AND PIETY: THE SAINT VINCENT

DE PAUL SOCIETY'S MISSION TO IRISH CATHOLICS

IN TORONTO, 1850-1890

Brian P. Clarke

After 1840, the Roman Catholic Church in Canada -- as in Ireland, France, and elsewhere -- experienced a religious revival which transformed Canadian Roman Catholicism. Known as the Ultramontane revival, this movement instituted a new type of piety and set a new standard for religious practice.[1] "The Catholic church," John Webster Grant has noted, "ceased to be a mere official presence and became a dynamic missionary force." One outstanding result of this missionary effort was the importation of a "plethora of voluntary associations, both local and national, that have become a familiar feature of Canadian church life."[2] The part played by these imported lay Catholic societies in furthering the Ultramontane revival, however, has often been overlooked. Once such association was the Saint Vincent de Paul Society, founded in Paris by Frederic Ozanam in 1833 for practicing Catholic men over the age of eighteen. Although the Saint Vincent de Paul Society is best known for its charitable relief, the primary goal of the Society was to convert non-practicing Catholics by disseminating the new Italian devotions which were integral to the Ultramontane revival. Material relief was but a means to an end.

The impact of the Saint Vincent de Paul Society in Victorian Toronto was directly related to the spiritual and material condition of the city's Roman Catholic population, the vast majority of whom were recently arrived Irish immigrants. Most Irish Catholic immigrants in Toronto were unfamiliar with the doctrines and piety of Ultramontane Catholicism. As a result their religious observances fell far below the minimum demanded by canonical Catholicism: attendance at Sunday Mass was rare, and the fulfillment of Easter duties and communion less frequent still. For the French Ultramontane Roman Catholic Bishop of Toronto, Armand de Charbonnel, who arrived in 1850, the Saint Vincent de Paul Society was a natural choice as an agency to reform the religious behaviour of the laity and to popularize the new style of religious practice. But if the spiritual needs of the Irish Catholic immigrants were pressing, their poverty was a still more immediate problem, and poor relief became the means of introducing them to Ultramontane piety.

The Poverty of Irish Immigrants

With the arrival of immigrants escaping the Irish famine of 1846-1849, the Irish Catholic population of Toronto increased from 3,678 in 1844 to 7,940 in 1850.[3] The Irish Catholic immigrants arrived in such a "destitute and weak" condition, observed John Elmsley, a leading Catholic layman, that they "made a very large demand" upon public charity.[4] Indeed, the sudden influx of the Irish taxed to the limit the charitable resources of the city.[5] The continuing strain that the famine-stricken Irish placed upon the city's charities was reflected in the dramatic increase of relief provided by the House of Industry, the largest nondenominational charity in Toronto. In 1845 there were 467 people receiving aid from the House of Industry, but by 1852 there were some 2,760 individuals, many of them Catholic, on the rolls.[6]

Leaderless after the death of Bishop Michael Power from typhus in 1847, without social institutions, and labouring under heavy debts, the Catholic Church was singularly unable to meet the material needs of the Irish poor.[7] Only a month after his arrival in October 1850, Bishop de Charbonnel founded the first Toronto conference of the Saint Vincent de Paul Society, a society which had been introduced into Canada by Dr. Joseph Painchaud of Quebec city in 1846. Bishop de Charbonnel had probably become familiar with the Saint Vincent de Paul Society in Lyons, France, where the first provincial branch of the Society was founded in

1836. He believed that the hierarchical structure of the Society, with its lay visitors organized in parish conferences under the direction of a local governing board, the Particular Council, was well suited to deliver essential relief to the poor in their homes efficiently and cheaply. The founding of such a parish organization circumvented the large investment required to establish an institution providing indoor care, an investment which the diocese could ill afford at the time. Because the Society in its early years primarily depended upon the donations of its members and timely contributions of provisions by merchants, it entailed no drain upon the diocesan treasury. Moreover, as the Society assigned each section of the city to a team of visitors, the Society's members could ensure personally that relief reached those who were in the most need.[8]

The founding of the Saint Vincent de Paul Society was a tacit recognition that poverty, far from being simply a short-term result of the Famine immigration, was likely to be a constant feature of the Irish Catholic existence in Toronto. While many Irish Catholics did arrive starved and diseased -- not surprising given their precipitous departure, the rigors of the transatlantic crossing, and the typhus fever raging in Ireland -- it would be misleading to view the entire mass of immigrants as one indistinguishable and pauperized lump.[9] Those who were best able to escape famine-stricken Ireland were precisely those who possessed ready capital: artisans, small tenant farmers, and the better-off cottiers who had cultivated cash crops on land rented in exchange for labour. Emigration during the Famine was largely a family phenomenon, and those who could afford the average family fare to Canada of £15 were by Irish standards moderately well off.[10] Yet, though these immigrants were not paupers when they left Ireland, little in their experience prepared them for the urban and rapidly industrializing society of Toronto.

The vast majority of Irish Catholic emigrants were rural residents in an underdeveloped country. Unlike other rural-born immigrants to Canadian cities, who in their home countries could gain experience and acquire skills by travelling the short distance to the nearest manufacturing town, Irish Catholics found few opportunities for work in Ireland's declining industrial sector and stagnant societies. Emigration abroad required Irish Catholics to

make the difficult transition from a rural, partly commercialized society to
an urban and industrial capitalist one. Irish Catholics in Toronto were thus
markedly over-represented in the least skilled occupations.[11]

In Canada lack of skills and low wages left many Catholics particularly vulnerable to the cyclical and seasonal fluctuations of the economy.
Labourers could earn about a dollar a day but would need to bring in
between four and four and a half dollars a week to support a wife and
two or three children. Irish Catholic labourers who enjoyed steady
employment could expect to work between 200 and 230 days of the year
and thus could provide for the families, but still the margin was very slim.
Most casual outdoor labourers were not so fortunate and on average could
only expect to work some 180 days in a year.[12] In these families the
earnings of older children, who could earn about two dollars a week, could
be absolutely necessary. For families of unskilled workers surviving on
what was at best a subsistence income, any interruption in employment
would bring with it extreme hardship. Although unskilled workers experienced severe deprivation during the depressions of 1857-1859 and 1873-
1879, even in good times they regularly faced unemployment caused by the
seasonal fluctuations of Toronto's economy. During the winter months not
only did outdoor work such as construction come to a standstill, but
factories were also closed to avoid the high cost of lighting and heating.
Because of the fierce competition in an over-supplied labour market, those
lucky enough to find work would accept deep cuts in their wages. When
food was already dearer and the cost of fuel -- almost a dollar and half a
week for a family -- would have strained a full wage packet, workers
found themselves without the means to meet the rigors of winter.[13]

One *Globe* reporter visiting the slums on Adelaide Street was shocked
to find "such a spectacle of misery and wretchedness." In one room he
found a family with only one piece of furniture -- a bed with icicles
hanging from it reaching to the floor. Without fuel or even clothes, many
a family huddled in bed to keep warm. Badly clothed, malnourished, and
living in cold, dank rooms, Irish Catholics readily succumbed to disease.
Not surprisingly, mortality rates among Irish Catholics were as much as
two times the norm for the rest of the population.[14] If the illness,

however brief, of a family's main wage earner forced them to rely upon the aid of kin or charity, the death of the husband was nothing short of disaster. The high incidence of mortality among Irish Catholic males, together with the proclivity of Irish Catholic men to abandon their families in their peripatetic search for work, meant that their wives and children were especially vulnerable to the depredations of extreme poverty.[15] Women's wages, even at the best of times, were insufficient to support a family. Charwomen and shirtmakers, for example, earned between thirty-five and fifty cents a day, and even the most experienced seamstresses could earn only between sixty-five and eight-five cents.[16] The division of labour according to gender condemned widows and their children to a life of indigence. For them, as with the chronically ill and the aged in reduced circumstances, poverty was endemic.

In keeping with the prevailing consensus that poverty was essentially a seasonal phenomenon, the Saint Vincent de Paul Society's charity was distributed only during the winter months and was limited to the barest necessities for those either unable to find work or incapable of working.[17] The Society's main form of relief was an allotment of oatmeal or barley, bread, and wood. Most families received between six and eight pounds of bread and two pounds of grain a week together with a quarter-cord of wood as needed.[18] Such relief provided the poor with the essentials, but even then it could not ensure the survival of the recipients. The Society's allotment of bread, while contributing a major staple to the diet of the poor, was no substitute for a balanced diet. Moreover, with cash grants sparingly distributed, most of the poor on the Society's rolls had to find other ways to procure food and to pay their rent.[19] Nonetheless, the Society's provision of clothing, bedding, and fuel did ensure that the poor won at least one battle against the vicissitudes of winter.

The Saint Vincent de Paul Society assisted only those who were without any other means of support.[20] While the Society did provide aid to families whose main wage earner, the husband, was unable to work, single women with children were the most likely to receive relief from the Society.[21] In 1850 four-fifths of the families who received relief were single-female parent families. The following year, in 1851, a little less than two-thirds of the families on the rolls were headed by women.[22] As late as 1886, slightly more than one half of the families receiving relief were women-headed families.[23] By 1888, however, single-female parent families made up one-third of the families aided by the Society.[24] This shift possibly reflected the relative decline of single-parent Irish Catholic families, but was more obviously a direct result of the Saint Vincent de Paul Society's improved finances and thus the wider range of those relieved.

As its financial resources grew, the Saint Vincent de Paul Society's impact on the Irish Catholic population increased: in the early 1850s between 2.5 and 3.5 per cent of the Irish Catholic residents of Toronto benefitted from the Society's charity; by the mid-1880s, the Society assisted from 4.5 to 6 per cent of the Irish Catholic population. These aggregate statistics, however, do not reflect the Society's impact accurately. Once these totals are analyzed by age and by sex, quite a different picture emerges. In the 1850s almost 6 per cent of adult Roman Catholic women received relief, and by the 1880s as much as 9 per cent of all Catholic women were under the Society's care. The proportion of children under twelve years of age on the Society's rolls increased from, 7 per cent in the 1850s to as high as 12 per cent in the 1880s.[25] If it is assumed that one half of the families from unskilled backgrounds lived in dire poverty, then about 25 per cent of the chronically poor women and children in the 1850s were aided by the Society. By the 1880s the proportion of these poor on relief rose to approximately 40 per cent.[26] The Saint Vincent de Paul Society reached a significant portion of the female and juvenile Catholic poor. Despite its improved finances, the Society still focussed its mission upon women and children.

Spiritual Poverty

For Bishop de Charbonnel, material poverty was a manifestation of a far more serious problem: the spiritual poverty of the Irish Catholic immigrants. Before 1850, the Catholic church in Ireland had been unable to create popular acceptance of the canonical requirements set down by the Council of Trent: attendance at Sunday Mass and the performance of the Easter duties of confession and communion. The eighteenth-century Irish penal legislation against the Catholic clergy together with the absence of effective episcopal control prevented the establishment of ecclesiastical discipline and the development of parochial piety.[27] By 1830, however, the bishops of Ireland, under the direction of Rome, had inaugurated an administrative reform of the church. A reformed church, having imposed new standards upon its clergy, could now initiate a concerted campaign to change the religious practices of the laity.

Galvanized by the piety and the reforming impetus of the Ultra-montane movement, the hierarchy and clergy of Ireland launched, to use Emmet Larkin's term, a devotional revolution.[28] This revolution marked a dramatic change in the character of popular religion: attendance at Mass increased and the range of devotions within the church was vastly expanded. The dissemination of this form of piety in pre-famine Ireland varied, however, according to the laity's social class. Only the middle class and prosperous farmers, who were receptive to outside influences and thus to new standards of propriety and respectability, enthusiastically adopted the piety of Ultramontane Catholics.[29] The vast majority of the laity simply ignored the clergy's new standards for religious practice. Because the church lacked priests and financial resources, most Irish Catholics rarely had the opportunity to approach the sacraments and their exposure to the doctrines of the church remained minimal. The church's inability to impose canonical religious practice resulted in the perpetuation among the peasantry of a popular religion which existed beside and exterior to the religious life of the church.[30]

Rooted in peasant culture, popular non-Christian religion was above all a communal and agricultural religion. Popular religious celebrations, such as the "patterns" (local festivities held in honour of a patron saint) and the annual feast days that marked the major turning points in the agricultural year, solidified communal bonds by expressing the community's dependence upon the apparently supernatural forces that guided the agricultural cycle.[31] Because of its essential link to agriculture, Irish popular religion was thus a vital part of day-to-day life. The precautions against the magical theft of dairy produce, the protective charms of the "fairy doctors" to protect cattle, and the propitiary bonfires to ensure fertility attest the extent to which the non-Christian supernatural impinged upon the daily lives of Irish peasants. Moreover, access to magical intervention necessarily lessened the laity's dependence upon the clergy and the church.[32] Canonical Catholicism, therefore, did not exhaust the religious possibilities open to the Irish laity who had ready recourse to the non-Christian supernatural.

With the exception of the wake, this localized and communal religion did not travel well.[33] Nevertheless, these popular beliefs and customs influenced the behaviour of Irish Catholic immigrants in Toronto. Many Irish Catholics continued to ignore most Catholic rituals, much as they had done in Ireland. Such indifference did not mean that these immigrants were irreligious, nor did it signify that they were not Catholic. For example, though the Irish felt that they could safely miss Sunday Mass, to die without receiving Extreme Unction was considered catastrophic. Irish Catholics believed Extreme Unction and the wake to be essential rites of passage and hence both were thought to be equally Catholic. Almost all Irish Catholic immigrants identified strongly with the Roman Catholic Church but also believed that being religious had little to do with obeying the precepts of official Catholicism.[34]

The immigrants' indifference to the norms of canonical Catholicism so shocked Bishop de Charbonnel that he was certain it was the nefarious product of irreligious Protestantism. After visiting a mission just outside of Toronto in 1852, Bishop de Charbonnel, wrote to Cardinal Fransoni, the Prefect of the Propaganda Fide, that he had "never found so much ignorance and rarely as much corruption." Many, he continued, "never go to confession . . . and communion, and if not positively Protestants are so in practice on account of their cold indifference."[35] Nor were matters much better in Toronto. "I have everywhere met," the bishop sadly admitted, "a great deal of ignorance and intemperance." Not only did Irish Catholics ignore canonical obligations of attendance at Sunday Mass and the performance of Easter duties, but many, de Charbonnel insisted, were completely unfamiliar with the most elementary Catholic devotions such as the Lord's Prayer or the Hail Mary.[36] Bishop de Charbonnel did not believe that the relationship between religious "ignorance" and poverty was coincidental: unless infused by the sacraments of the church, poverty resulted in idleness, and idleness inevitable led to intemperance, "familiar intercourses" between the sexes, and other vices.[37]

Although the bishop had mistaken the existence of pre-industrial work rhythms for idleness, he correctly perceived that the work patterns of the Irish immigrants were incompatible with the demands of canonical Catholicism. Pre-Famine popular religion was a product of traditional customs of work and leisure. In subsistence agriculture of modest commercial farming, work and social intercourse mingled: rather than methodical, disciplined labour, intense binges of work were followed by sprees of festivity. The communal festivals that punctuated the agricultural year were part of this pattern of work. Unlike pre-Famine popular religion canonical Catholicism was inimical to pre-industrial work rhythms. Rather, official Catholicism required the regular and methodical performance of religious duties at a precise time and place. Time-clock discipline and canonical Catholicism were thus mutually reinforcing, and the promotion of new forms of piety therefore depended upon the inculcation of the virtues of industry, self-discipline, and time-thrift.[38]

The influx of Irish immigrants to Toronto presented the Roman Catholic church with the immense challenge of transforming both their religious behaviour and their culture. While the material needs of the immigrants were no doubt pressing, Bishop de Charbonnel thought it more essential to redress their spiritual failings. Although this concern was reflected in the bishop's fear of "leakage" -- the "loss" of Irish Catholics, especially children, through the proselytism of Protestant charities -- much more was involved than simply plugging the leaks: it was necessary to convert nominal Catholics into practicing ones, and the measure of conversion was their participation in the new devotions of the church.[39] Only by participating in the full range of Roman Catholic piety could the laity be truly religious. Even among male, middle-class Catholics, those whose behaviour conformed to the canonical minimum fell well below this new standard. It was the middle-class laymen that Bishop de Charbonnel counted on to help disseminate the new devotionalism, and the bishop had no doubts that of all Irish Catholics, the poor stood most in need of spiritual rescue.[40] What Bishop de Charbonnel required was a voluntary association that could introduce both prosperous laymen and the poor to the new devotions of the church.

Through the Saint Vincent de Paul Society, Bishop de Charbonnel hoped to alleviate both the material and spiritual needs of the laity. As the only Roman Catholic benevolent institution until the founding of the House of Providence in 1859, the Society played a critical role in the formation of a Catholic network of social institutions. Even after 1859, when the House of Providence could have expanded its social program to include outdoor relief but did not, the Saint Vincent de Paul Society remained an important parochial institution. It maintained its role because, as part of the Ultramontane revival in France, the Society was intended to revitalize parochial piety. Bishop de Charbonnel, who himself shared the Ultramontane fervour and ideals of the Society, hardly could have been unaware of the Society's role in the French Ultramontane revival.[41] Moreover, the vertical structure of the Society, which linked the parish conferences to the General Council of Paris, the supreme governing board of the Society, insured that the aims and method of the Society would be transplanted with little or no modification. Through its dedication to inculcating Ultramontane piety in its male members, who were in turn expected to popularize these devotions among the poor, the Saint Vincent de Paul Society was a promising catalyst in effecting a devotional revolution.

Charity and Piety

The Saint Vincent de Paul Society had two related but distinct goals: the salvation of its members and the conversion of the poor. The "primary object" of the Society was in the words of the *Manual of the Saint Vincent de Paul Society*, "the salvation of souls, and in particular the souls of the members themselves." Acts of charity were the means by which the members of the Society gained their salvation. Thus, the visiting of the poor was not primarily a philanthropic exercise; visiting the poor was the "special object" of the Society because it was a form of active Christian virtue which required "but little time" and could be "easily practiced" by "men who live in the world."[42] Charity, then, enabled the members not only to atone for past deeds, but also to labour actively for their salvation and the salvation of others.[43] The physical wants of the poor, the *Manual* reminded members, are "the least of their misfortunes" for it is "the heart which is diseased." As a result, the highest form of charity, the "active love of our neighbour," was to labour for the salvation of others. Because the major function of the Society was to edify and supports its members in their quest for holiness, it was "not sufficient that religious improvement take place among the poor, it is necessary . . . that the conference should know that it has been effected."[44] The poor, by accepting their sufferings and by displaying the virtues of pious resignation and humility, were an inspiring model for the members of the Saint Vincent de Paul Society.[45] Relief was a way of gaining the confidence of the poor and effecting their spiritual improvement.[46]

As an active Christian virtue, however, charity became truly meritorious only as a result of the sanctifying grace communicated by the sacraments of the church. Without the aid of the sacraments, the members were warned, "our charity would be . . . but cold compassion -- a virtue completely human -- praiseworthy no doubt, but imperfect in the eyes of faith."[47] Through weekly meetings which included prayers and readings from the *Imitation of Christ*, the Society's *Manual*, and monthly *Bulletin*, the Saint Vincent de Paul Society sought to inculcate a life of piety which would "preserve the divine flame of charity."[48] The type of piety popularized by the Society, Roger Aubert has commented, constituted "the true triumph of Ultramontanism."[49] Under the sponsorship of the papacy a new style of devotionalism was introduced which transformed the nature of Catholic religiosity. Devotions such as the rosary and the stations of the cross which had languished during the eighteenth and the early part of the nineteenth centuries were resurrected in a Roman form and together with new Roman devotions such as frequent communion and the forty-hours devotion became part of the devotional repertoire of the church. This Roman piety was characterized by highly ritualized external observances accompanied by the frequent repetition of prayers.[50] This piety was designed to encourage the frequent reception of the sacraments

-- the means of sanctification and perseverance in a holy life -- and thus the personal quest for holiness became centered upon the parish church. At the same time, as a result of the necessarily regular performance of these devotions, day-to-day life was suffused with the sacraments.

The Saint Vincent de Paul Society encouraged its members to participate frequently in both private devotions such as the rosary and miniature stations of the cross and parish-focused devotions like the forty-hours' devotion, vespers, and the benediction of the Blessed Sacrament. By stressing the real presence of Christ, as in the case of the forty-hours devotion to the Blessed Sacrament, and the necessity of union with the suffering Christ, as in the stations of the cross, these devotions were calculated to encourage the reception of the sacraments. Consequently, members were expected to receive communion monthly, an unusually high frequency in mid-Victorian Toronto. Through the brotherly "union of prayer" and the sacraments of the church, the Saint Vincent de Paul Society attempted to cultivate the spiritual life necessary for "the practice of a Christian life."[51]

By providing a proper setting, the Society sought to nurture Ultramontane piety among "respectable" Irish Catholic men of all classes, especially young men.[52] W. J. Macdonell, president of the Particular Council, lamented that too many young men see joining the Saint Vincent de Paul Society as "one of the processes of 'making their souls,' to be undertaken only when white hairs begin to appear."[53] In fact, the Saint Vincent de Paul Society had difficulty recruiting men of any age. By 1865, the Society had gained only 207 members. Over the next two decades, the Irish Catholic population had almost doubled to over twenty thousand. Yet, by 1886 the Society had enrolled only 248 men, the largest figure ever.[54] The membership of the Society, then, never exceeded five per cent of the Roman Catholic adult male population.[55]

The most obvious reason for the Saint Vincent de Paul Society's failure to recruit members was its middle-class character. In a city where well over four-fifths of all Irish Catholic men held working-class occupations, between one half and three-quarters of the Society's members were from middle-class backgrounds.[56] This middle-class dominance put off many working-class men who were invited to join the Society. In general, it would seem that working men preferred to associate with their own class, as in the Irish Nationalist societies.[57] Although the middle-class character of the Society limited its appeal, the Society's religious cast had a much greater impact upon its ability to recruit members. The Saint Vincent de Paul Society's difficulty in attracting male members was also one shared by the parish confraternities or religious brotherhoods. While women and children joined the confraternities in large numbers, comparatively few men enrolled. Like the confraternities, the Saint Vincent de Paul Society demanded an intense commitment to and participation in the devotional life of the church. Yet, the ideals of Ultramontane piety ran counter to the mores of male working-class culture. Unlike women, when men joined a society such as the Saint Vincent de Paul Society, they had to give up old friendships and traditional recreational pursuits. Simply put, most Roman Catholic men did not choose to change their way of life and commit themselves to a life of piety.

It was precisely the religious character of the Society that made it such an attractive organization to the clergy. Because the members of the Society were dependent upon the sacraments of the church for the efficacy of their charity, the *Manual* affirmed "we should always remember that we are only laics" and should therefore "observe and follow with an absolute docility the directions which our ecclesiastical superiors may think to give to us." "It is the office of our pastor to expose our duties to us," the *Manual* concluded, "it is ours to discharge them."[58] As a result of this admission of clerical superiority, the parish clergy hoped that the members of the Saint Vincent de Paul Society would act as a leaven for the development of parochial piety. Whether forming the guard of honour in a religious procession or attending vespers and the forty-hours devotion, the members of the Saint Vincent de Paul Society together with other confraternities were essential to the emergence of parish-based devotions. The societies provided the original congregational nucleus for the novel parish devotions. By attending these devotions, the members of the Society were an example to others and acted as a magnet to attract the participation of the faithful. For example, when Bishop de Charbonnel introduced vespers in the early 1850s, it attracted few devotees outside the parish societies. By the 1880s, this service had gained a popular following. On a typical Sunday in early 1882, close to a quarter of the total Catholic population attended vespers, filling the churches almost to capacity. Far more important to the clergy, however, was the direct influence of the Society's members among the poor. The members of the Saint Vincent de Paul Society were to be the "servants" of the church and the "auxiliaries" of the clergy in bringing the consolations of religion to the poor.[59]

The members of the Saint Vincent de Paul Society visited the families on the Society's rolls weekly, intentionally avoiding visits at fixed times "so that the families may not be prepared, or 'got up' for their reception." The purpose of these visits was to determine whether the families were "worthy objects of their charity."[60] Although temperate habits among the poor were highly desirable, the visitors' most detailed questions were designed to elicit the nature of the families' religious practice. Did the family regularly attend church on Sunday? How frequently did members of the family receive the sacraments? Did the children attend Catholic separate schools where they would be educated in Catholic doctrine and piety? Had the children received baptism, confirmation, and first communion? Did they know how to recite the Lord's Prayer? These were the questions that concerned the visitors of the Saint Vincent de Paul Society.[61] As these questions illustrate, the Society's visitors sought to introduce the poor to the devotional life of the parish and they were particularly concerned with the piety of children. As Father Laurent of Saint Patrick's parish put it, "on the youth of to-day will mainly depend the progress of the Catholic church of the future."[62] The Society, therefore, took charge of the supervision that should belong to the parents, but "which through carelessness or want of time, they sometimes acquit themselves badly" in order to initiate Catholic children into the sacramental life of the church.[63] The first task of the Society was to enroll the children in the Roman Catholic schools or the catechetical classes conducted by the Society where they could be inculcated with the values and ideals of Ultramontane Catholicism. During their visits to the family home and in the schools, the members sought to oversee the

children's educational and spiritual progress and ensure that they attended
the separate schools regularly. At the same time, the visitors applied moral
suasion to make sure that the children were confirmed and made their
first communion -- the initiations into the full sacramental life of the
church -- as well as ensuring that they said their daily prayers and
attended Sunday Mass.[64] If the parents proved recalcitrant, the Society
frequently would threaten to remove the children and place them with a
pious family where the children would be nurtured in the piety of official
Catholicism.[65]

In order to have any impact upon the children's religiosity, the
Society of necessity had to recast the religious practice of their parents.
Adults too were encouraged by the visitors to attend church regularly and
fulfill their Easter duties, but the visitors were not satisfied with this
minimal canonical observance. They distributed rosaries, crucifixes, prayer
books, and religious literature as well.[66] These devotional aids were a
means of popularizing new, Roman forms of piety: the cults of the Virgin
Mary, the devotions to the Sacred Heart of Jesus, and the pilgrimage of
the stations of the cross. As a discipline of piety, these highly ritualistic
and external observances were the means of consolidating sacramental
conversion. If the sacraments were essential for a life of holiness, these
devotions in turn, by preparing their practitioners for the reception of the
sacraments, fostered the perseverance in a sacramental way of life.[67]

Religious literature in particular played a critical role in the dissemination of piety by the Society's visitors. Because visitors "may be embar-
rassed in the choice of words" in instructing the poor, observed W. J.
Macdonell, President of the Particular Council such books could be an
indispensible aid in explaining devotions and "so fortify the faith of our
poor." After having read the tracts aloud, the visitors could then question
the poor in order to determine the effects of the Society's efforts to
reform popular religious beliefs.[68]

The discipline of piety popularized by the Saint Vincent de Paul
Society entailed not only assiduous praying but also right living. For the
poor, this meant embracing a life of "holy poverty." The poor were God's
children: by resigning themselves to their condition they could, in effect,

make a virtue of necessity; by accepting their lot, they could gain
sanctification. Poverty, instead of being an obstacle to salvation, could
become the means by which salvation could be gained.[69] The other side of
this sanctification of poverty, however, was a rigorous moralism: parties,
dancing, drinking, easy familiarity with members of the opposite sex, even
between children, were all condemned, and the members of the Society did
not hesitate to use their weekly visits to enforce this strict moral code.[70]
Self-discipline and sobriety were thus indispensible virtues in the sanctification of poverty. In short, the recasting of Irish Catholic religious
practice depended upon the reform of a whole range of behaviour; as in
work and recreation, religious observances were to be discharged punctu-
ally and with propriety.

The Saint Vincent de Paul Society's contact with the poor was
limited to two specific groups. Although comparatively few men were on
the Society's relief rolls, the Society did reach a significant proportion,
perhaps as much as two-fifths, of the female and juvenile Irish Catholic
poor. How, then, did the Roman Catholic poor respond to the Saint
Vincent de Paul Society's mission to reform their religious and social
behaviour? The Society rarely made relief directly dependent upon the
conversion of the poor. Yet, the complete dependence of the Irish Catholic
poor upon the resources of the Society undoubtedly persuaded many to
cooperate. Such external compliance, however, would have been as
ephemeral as it was artificial. The ability of the Saint Vincent de Paul
Society to influence the poor depended upon the immigrants' inherent
loyalty to their church. Catholicism had become by 1830 an inextricable
part of Irish national consciousness. Although if judged by the norms of
official Catholicism many of these immigrants were not practicing Catholics, they themselves had no doubt that they were Catholic and thoroughly
identified with the Catholic church. Further, the notoriety of "souperism",
the use of hot meals by Protestant charities to proselytize Irish Catholics,
led the Catholic poor to turn to the Saint Vincent de Paul Society for
help. Most Irish Catholics therefore welcomed the visitors of the Saint
Vincent de Paul Society.[71]

Especially during the 1850s, these visits would have been the first time that they were exposed to the doctrines and devotions of the Roman Catholic church. The response of the poor to this message was largely divided by sex and age. Many of the poor women and children on relief, it would seem, adopted the piety promoted by the Society. In the 1850s, less than half the Catholic population frequented church, but by 1882 over 70 per cent attended Sunday Mass.[72] During the late 1860s and after, contemporary observers were especially struck by the large number of poor women and children at church on Sundays.[73] These poor, whose spiritual fate particularly worried Bishop de Charbonnel, had become church goers. Besides discharging this canonical minimum there is also evidence that poor women and children practiced Ultramontane devotions. By the 1880s, the Society's visitors could rely upon children to read religious tracts to their parents and to answer their parents' questions that arose during these readings. This literacy would indicate that poor children had attended separate schools long enough to gain a basic knowledge of Catholic dogma and practice.[74] The separate schools and the Saint Vincent de Paul Society together encouraged children to join confraternities, and the vast majority did in fact enroll. Parish confraternities also had many poor women members. In fact, from the mid-1860s on, poor women were among the most likely to become members of a confraternity.[75] because the purpose of the confraternities was to foster Ultramontane piety, the extensive involvement of poor women and children in these parish societies indicates that they did engage in a wide variety of devotions.

The intense religiosity of Irish Catholic poor women and children was in stark contrast to that of Irish Catholic men from all social backgrounds. Few men took up the new devotions and a significant minority only entered the church for the major rites marking birth, marriage, and death.[76] Poor men certainly had much less contact with the Saint Vincent de Paul Society than women and children. As a result of the Society's efforts, however, some men did become practising Catholics, though it is impossible to be sure just how many.[77] If the Society did not always influence them directly, perhaps the example of their wives and children did. Like most men, only a small number of poor men incorporated

Ultramontane devotionalism into their daily lives, but by the 1880s it is likely that a majority, if only a bare majority, of them fulfilled their canonical duties. Compared to pre-Famine Ireland, when no more than 40 per cent of the population attended Sunday Mass, this was nonetheless a substantial change.[78]

A Devotional Revolution

The founding of the Saint Vincent de Paul Society in Toronto was an important step in the formation of a network of Catholic social institutions parallel to those of the Protestant majority. As a microcosm of the Ultramontane movement, the Society's main goal was to transform the religious behaviour of the laity. The Society's attempt to recruit male Catholics, particularly young men, was a notable failure. Yet by forming a devotional middle-class elite, the Society was then able to set out and integrate into the religious life of the parish an important segment of the Catholic population -- the impoverished women and children of the city -- who would have otherwise remained uninfluenced by the church.

Through its promotion of Ultramontane piety, the Saint Vincent de Paul Society played a key role in effecting a devotional revolution among Toronto's Irish Catholics. In this devotional revolution not only did the observance of canonical obligations become more widespread among the laity as a whole, but the range of devotions practised by women and children in particular was also vastly increased. In turn, this change in popular religious practice entailed the reform of immigrant culture and the inculcation of such values as self-discipline and sobriety. Like work in industrial society, Ultramontane Catholicism required the punctual and methodical discharge of duties. Through its outreach program, then, the Saint Vincent de Paul Society facilitated the transition of many Irish Catholic immigrants to an urban and industrial environment. In so doing, the Saint Vincent de Paul Society consolidated Irish Catholic identification with the church, and -- along with temperance societies, confraternities, and clubs for young men -- contributed to the creation of a religious subculture in Toronto that revolved around the parish. Lay initiative played an essential role in the making of Toronto's devotional revolution among Irish Catholics.

Notes

I would like to thank Professors Jerald C. Brauer, N. Keith Clifford, and Emmet Larkin, and Ms Edith Killey for their helpful comments and suggestions on earlier versions of this paper.

1. Roger Aubert, *The Church in the Age of Liberalism*, 7, *History of the Church*, ed. Herbert Jedin (New York: Crossroad, 1981), 23-7; Emmet Larkin, "The Devotional Revolution in Ireland, 1850-75," *American Historical Review*, 77 (1972), 625-52; and Nive Voisine, "Jubilés, missions paroissiales et prédication au xixe siècle," *Recherches sociographiques*, 13 (1982), 125-37.

2. John Webster Grant, *The Church in the Canadian Era* (Toronto: McGraw-Hill Ryerson, 1972), 13, 57.

3. *The Churchman's Almanac for the Year of Our Lord, 1846* (Toronto, 1845), and *Census of Canada, 1851* (Quebec, 1853), 1:30-1, 66-7.

4. Archives of the Roman Catholic Archdiocese of Toronto [hereafter AAT], Charbonnel Papers [hereafter CP], John Elmsley to John Carroll, 18 August 1849.

5. Gilbert Tucker, "The Famine Immigration to Canada, 1847," *American Historical Review*, 36 (1930), 540, and G. J. Parr, "The Welcome and the Wake: Attitudes in Canada West toward the Irish Famine Migration," *Ontario History*, 66 (1974), 108-10, 113.

6. *Report of the Trustees of the House of Industry* (Toronto, 1853). Unfortunately the House of Industry reports did not provide religious statistics. As the total city population had increased by approximately seventy per cent between 1845 and 1852, while the number on relief had increased almost six times, it is not unreasonable to conclude that this increase was in part, at least, caused by the growing number of Irish Catholic poor.

7. J. R. Teefy, *Jubilee Volume: The Archdiocese of Toronto and Archbishop Walsh* (Toronto: George Dixon, 1892), 151-4; AAT, John Elmsley Papers, "The Total Cost of Erecting St. Michael's Cathedral up to

21st March 1850," AAT CP, Bishop de Charbonnel to the central council of the Society for the Propagation of the Faith, 12 May 1852, and Pastoral, 19 October 1850.

8. Jean-Baptiste Duroselle, *Les Débuts du Catholicisme Social en France* (Paris: Presses Universitaires de France, 1951), 178; "Summary Statement from 10 November '50 to 1 May 1851," in *A Documentary Contribution to the History of Saint Vincent de Paul Society in Toronto 1850-1975*, James S. McGivern, ed. (Toronto, n.p., 1975) [hereafter *Documentary History*], 60; "Families Relieved," 1850-1853; *Rules of the Society of St. Vincent de Paul* (Toronto, 1861), 56-7, 61; *Conference of Our Lady*, Minutes [hereafter *OL*], 7 August 1853, 12 May 1857.

9. Helen I. Cowan, *British Emigration to British North America: The First Hundred Years* (Toronto: University of Toronto Press, 1961), 177-8, 193, 216-18; William F. Adams, *Ireland and Irish Emigration to the New World from 1815 to the Famine* (New Haven: Yale University Press, 1932), 392-2; Frances Morehouse, "Canadian Migration in the Forties," *Canadian Historical Review*, 9 (1932), 319-20; and Tucker, "Famine Immigration," 537, 539. For an important analysis of the social background of the Irish see Donald H. Akenson, "Ontario: Whatever Happened to the Irish?" *Canadian Papers in Rural History*, D. H. Akenson, ed. (Gananoque: Langdale Press, 1982), 228-31.

10. S. H. Cousens, "The Regional Variation in Emigration from Ireland between 1821 and 1841," *Institute of British Geographers Transactions*, 37 (December 1965), 26-8; S. H. Cousens, "Emigration and Demographic Change in Ireland, 1851-1868," *Economic History Review*, 14 (1961), 284-6; S. H. Cousens, "The Regional Pattern of Emigration during the Great Irish Famine, 1846-51," *Institute of British Geographers, Transactions*, 218 (1960), 122-3, 126, 128; M. R. Beames, "Cottiers and Conacre in Pre-Famine Ireland," *Journal of Peasant Studies*, 2 (1975), 352-4; James S. Donnelly, Jr., *The Land and the People of Nineteenth-Century Cork: The Rural Question and the Land Question* (London: Routledge and Kegan Paul, 1975), 127.

11. Joel Mokyr, *Why Ireland Starved: A Quantitative and Analytical History of the Irish Economy* (London: George Allen and Unwin, 1983), 176-8, 191-4; Lynn Lees and John Modell, "The Irish Country-man Urbanized: A Comparative Perspective on the Famine Migration," *Journal of Urban History*, 3 (1977), 395-400, 404-6.

12. C. J. Houston and W. J. Smyth, "The Irish Abroad: Better Questions through a Better Source, the Canadian Census," *Irish Geographer*, 13 (1980), 10. Unfortunately, reliable employment statistics apparently start only in the 1880s, when the Toronto daily press became interested in the "Labour Question." In the case of casual outdoor labourers, it is probable that there was little change in employment and underemployment between the early 1850s and the 1880s. Aside from cyclical fluctuations, the major constraint on employment was the seasonal nature of outdoor work. *Globe*, 19 June 1855, 17 May 1856, 26 July 1870, 12 October 1876, 2 April 1881, 30 April 1881, 3 February 1883, 22 September 1883, 27 October 1883.

13. *Globe*, 8 December 1882, 3 February 1883; Bettina Bradbury, "Family Economy and Work in an Industrializing City: Montreal in the 1870s," Canadian Historical Association, *Historical Papers* (1979), 78-82, 86; Gregory S. Kealey, *Toronto Workers Respond to Industrial Capitalism, 1867-1892* (Toronto: University of Toronto Press, 1980), 58; Bryan D. Palmer, *Working-Class Experience: The Rise and Reconstitution of Canadian Labour, 1800-1980* (Toronto: Butterworth, 1983), 64-6; Judith Fingard, "The Winter's Tale: The Seasonal Contours of Pre-Industrial Poverty in British North America, 1815-1860," Canadian Historical Association, *Historical Papers* (1974), 66-72; Ian Davey, "The Rhythm of Work and the Rhythm of School," in Neil McDonald and Alf Chaiton, eds, *Egerton Ryerson and His Times* (Toronto: Macmillan 1978), 237-8.

14. *Globe*, 10 February 1855, 1 January 1858, 11 February 1866.

15. *OL*, 27 April 1856, 26 January 1868, 30 January 1876, 10 December 1876, 23 December 1877; *Conference of St. Patrick*, Minutes [hereafter *StP*], 31 January 1874, 28 February 1875, 3 January 1876, 2 March 1884, 1 December 1889.

16. *Globe*, 8 December 1882.
17. Fingard, "Winter's Tale," 65-94. For a detailed examination of Catholic charitable efforts in Toronto see Murray W. Nicolson, "The Irish Catholics and Social Action in Toronto, 1850-1900," *Studies in History and Politics*, 1 (1980), 30-54. As Nicolson seems to define Catholic social action as social reform his description of Catholic charity as social action is puzzling.
18. "Minutes of the First Meeting of the St. Vincent de Paul Society in Toronto," 10 November 1850, *Documentary History*, 32; *OL*, 11 December 1853, 14 January 1855, 1 February 1857, 9 February 1868, 4 January 1872, and 6 December 1874.
19. *OL*, 28 January 1854, 28 October 1866, 19 March 1871, 9 December 1872, 3 October 1879; *StP*, 5 March 1876, 17 December 1876, 10 February 1878, 21 January 1883.
20. Families that had children capable of working were thus not considered for relief. *OL*, 18 April 1857, 1 December 1867, 16 February 1868, 5 April 1868.
21. AAT, St. Vincent de Paul Society, "Families Relieved," 1850-3.
22. AAT, St. Vincent de Paul Society, "Families Relieved," 1850-3; "Summary Statement," in *Documentary History*, 36.
23. *Société St. Vincent de Paul -- Rapport du Conseil Superieur de Quèbec pour l'année 1886* (Quebec, 1886).
24. *Report of the Superior Council for the year 1888* (Quebec, 1889).
25. "Summary Statement," in *Document History*, 36; *Conseil Superieur 1886*, and *Superior Council 1888*. My calculations are based on the assumption that the distribution of the Irish Catholic population by age and by sex resembled that of the population as a whole. See *Census of Canada, 1851* (Quebec, 1853), 1:288-90 and *Census of Canada, 1881* (Ottawa, 1882), 1:288 and 2:100-1.
26. As Houston and Smyth have shown, about 65 per cent of all Irish Catholic workers in St. David's Ward in 1861 had unskilled occupations. Father Jamot's census of Catholic ratepayers indicates, however, that St. David's Ward had an unusually large number of unskilled Irish Catholics. In any case it is doubtful that an occupation

profile of all workers which includes domestics, boarders and the like, reveals the occupational standing of families. A survey of household heads provides a better measure of occupational background for families. In his study of Hamilton during the 1850s, Michael Katz finds that between 57 and 58 per cent of Irish Catholic household heads had unskilled occupations. In these calculations I have therefore assumed that 55 per cent of the Irish Catholic families were from unskilled backgrounds. Given that 45 per cent of those who either owned or could afford to rent a house were from unskilled occupations, the estimate that one half of these families were chronically poor is a conservative one. Houston and Smyth, "Irish Abroad," 10; Michael B. Katz, *The People of Hamilton, Canada West: Family and Class in a Mid-Nineteenth Century City* (Cambridge, Mass.: Harvard University Press, 1975), 57; AAT, Father Jamot's census of City Wards, circa early 1860s.

27.   John Brady and Patrick J. Corish, *The Church under the Penal Code*, 14, *A History of Irish Catholicism* (Dublin: Gill and Macmillan, 1971), 6-8, 21-2, 27-33, 41, 49-50; S. J. Connolly, *Priests and People in Pre-Famine Ireland 1780-1845* (Dublin: Gill and Macmillan, 1982), 60-1.

28.   Emmet Larkin, "Devotional Revolution in Ireland," 625-52, and Connolly, *Priests and People*, 98-9, 268, and 272-8.

29.   Eugene Hynes, "The Great Hunger and Irish Catholicism, *Societas*, 8 (1978), 242, 143; Emmet Larkin, "Church, State, and Nation in Modern Ireland," *American Historical Review*, 80 (1975), 1254.

30.   Larkin, "Devotional Revolution in Ireland," 627, 638-9; David Miller, "Irish Catholicism and the Great Famine," *Journal of Social History*, 9 (1975), 83-7 and 89-91.

31.   Connolly, *Priests and People*, 105-6, 135-8; Miller, "Irish Catholicism, 90-1, and Séan O. Súilleabháin, *Irish Folk Custom and Belief* (Cork: Mercier Press, n.d.), 66-8.

32.   Connolly, *Priests and People*, 101-4, 106, 109-10, 115, 119-20; Miller, "Irish Catholicism," 89-90.

33.   "Summary Statement 1850," *Documentary History*, 37; *OL*, 30 October

1853, 4 May 1856, 22 September 1867, 15 December 1872, 24 December 1876.

34. *Mirror*, 19 March 1852, 16 April 1852, 16 July 1852, 23 March 1853, 17 June 1853, 29 September 1854, 14 March 1856; Connolly, *Priests and People*, 75, 88-9, 91, and 110-13.

35. AAT, CP, Bishop de Charbonnel to Cardinal Fransoni, 30 May 1852.

36. AAT, CP, Bishop de Charbonnel to de Mérode, 12 July 1852. AAT, CP, Circular, 28 December 1852, Bishop de Charbonnel to Cardinal Fransoni, 30 May 1853, Bishop de Charbonnel to John Wardy, 1 December 1854, and Bishop de Charbonnel to Father Rooney, 25 July 1858.

37. AAT, CP, "Address of His Lordship to the Irish Catholics of Toronto, 1856," "Regulations for the Retreat Preceding St. Patrick's Feast," 1859, and Pastoral, 10 February 1859.

38. Connolly, *Priests and People*, 171-4. For an incisive analysis of pre-industrial patterns of work and recreations see E. P. Thompson, "Time, Work-Discipline, and Industrial Capitalism," *Past and Present*, 38 (December 1967), 56-97.

39. AAT, CP, Bishop de Charbonnel to Cardinal Fransoni, 30 May 1852, and Circular, 20 December 1852.

40. "Minutes of the First Meeting," *Documentary History*, 31-2, 34; "Summary Statement," *Documentary History*, 35; AAT, CP, John Elmsley and S. G. Lynn to Bishop de Charbonnel, 18 October 1850.

41. Duroselle, *Catholicisme Social*, 175, 179, 186-7; R. P. C. Causse, *Evêque d'or, Crosse de Bois: Vie de Monseigneur de Charbonnel, Evêque de Toronto* (Parish: S. F. D'Anine, n.d.), 34, 40-8.

42. *Manual of the Society of St. Vincent de Paul* (London: n.p., 1867), 30-3 [hereafter *Manual*].

43. "Twenty-Fifth General Meeting," *Documentary History*, 57.

44. *Manual*, 9, 20-1, 31, 57, 112, 273, 413; *Bulletin of the Society of St. Vincent de Paul* [hereafter *Bulletin*], June 1887, 166, August 1889, 228.

45. *Bulletin*, June 1878, 80, June 1879, 173, October 1888, 348, February 1889, 40.

46. *Rules of the Society of St. Vincent de Paul,* 29; *Manual,* 60; *Irish Canadian,* 15 December 1880; *OL,* 27 April 1856, 17 December 1871, 9 December 1877, 2 March 1879, 25 April 1880; *StP,* 10 January 1875, 3 January 1876, 24 February 1878, 25 November 1883, 22 June 1890.

47. *Manual,* 20, 422.

48. *OL,* 8 February, 18 June, and 8 October 1854.

49. Roger Aubert, *Le Pontificat de Pie IX* (Paris: Bloud and Gay, 1963), 465.

50. Roger Aubert, *The Church in a Secularized Society* (New York: Paulist Press, 1978), 119-225; Kenneth Scott Latourette, *The Nineteenth Century in Europe,* 1, *Christianity in a Revolutionary Age* (New York: Harper and Row, 1958), 356-65.

51. *OL,* 16 September 1853, 1 June 1854, 4 December 1854, 16 November 1865; *Bulletin,* September 1872, 295-9, May 1873, 152, June 1875, 161, February 1889, 45, September 1889, 257; *Manual,* 20, 31.

52. *Manual,* 6, 20, 24, 26, 30-1, 87.

53. "Toronto Particular Council Report," *Bulletin,* March 1882, 90.

54. "Twenty-Fifth General Meeting," *Documentary History,* 65; *Conseil Superieur 1886.*

55. This figure has been calculated on the assumption that only one quarter of the total Catholic population would have been eligible for membership. See *Census of Canada, 1861* (Quebec, 1863), 1:511-2, 518; *Census of Canada, 1881,* 1:188, 2:100-1.

56. Because the Society's *General Register* listed all who were nominated for membership, but who did not necessarily join, the occupational profile of the Society's membership is based upon the minute books of the Our Lady and St. Patrick's conferences.

57. Compared to middle-class men, workers were far more likely to refuse membership in the Society, especially after having attended one or two meetings. *OL,* 13 November 1853, 8 June 1854, 14 October 1866, 20 December 1868, 12 March 1871; *StP,* 22 August 1875, 10 March 1878, 3 December 1882, 18 November 1883, 18 March 1884, 29 November 1885, 16 January 1887; *Irish Canadian,* 18 March 1863, 23 March 1864.

58. *Manual*, 26, 223.

59. *OL*, 19 September 1875, 10 June 1877, 19 June 1881; *StP* 18 June 1875, 17 June 1877; *Canadian Freeman*, 22 June 1865, 22 June 1871; *Irish Canadian*, 21 September 1875, 29 April 1889; *Globe*, 7 February 1882; *Manual*, 6, 26.

60. "Twenty-Fifth General Meeting," *Documentary History*, 59, 63.

61. "Visitors' Report," J. J. Murphy, *Scrapbook of Newspaper Clippings*, 4, 5.

62. *Irish Canadian*, 16 November 1870.

63. *Manual*, 477.

64. *OL*, 9 October 1853, 27 November 1853, 19 March 1854, 2 September 1855, 27 January 1856, 13 April 1879, 27 April 1880; *StP*, 23 December 1877, 28 October 1878, 2 March 1879, 28 January 1883, 30 November 1885, 9 November 1886; "Presidential Address -- 8 December 1878," *Bulletin*, February 1879, 61; "Toronto Particular Council Report 1887-1888," *Bulletin*, November 1890, 346; "Summary Statement," *Documentary History*, 37; "Visitors' Report," Murphy, *Scrapbook*, 4, 5.

65. *OL*, 3 September 1854, 10 December 1854, 24 February 1874; *StP*, 10 February 1889; "Saint Vincent de Paul Society, Toronto," *Bulletin*, November 1879, 339.

66. "Visitors' Report," Murphy, *Scrapbook*, 4, 5; "Saint Vincent de Paul Society, Toronto," *Bulletin*, November 1879, 329; March 1882, 93-9, January 1884, 20; *Hospital Board Minutes*.

67. *Bulletin*, April 1871, 125-6, September 1872, 298-300, May 1873, 152, June 1875, 161-3, June 1879, 172-81, April 1882, 100, and March 1888, 70; "Toronto Particular Council Report," *Bulletin*, March 1882, 92; *Superior Council of Canada Report for the Year* (Quebec, 1883) 20; *StP*, 30 December 1883.

68. "Toronto Particular Council Report," *Bulletin*, March 1882, 92-3.

69. *Manual*, 225, 234-5; *Bulletin*, May 1877, 165, June 1879, 173; *Canadian Freeman*, 21 September 1871; *Irish Canadian*, 9 February 1879.

70. *Manual*, 29, 60, 263, 272, 330, 480; *OL*, 4 June 1854, 19 September 1854, 23 February 1855, 26 January 1868, 15 March 1868, 17 December 1871, 21 January 1872, 14 June 1876, 9 December 1877, 3 August 1879,

24 October 1880; *StP*, 10 January 1875, 14 February 1875, 27 February 1876.

71. *Globe*, 22 January 1853, 28 Mary 1855, 25 September 1856; Connolly, *Priests and People*, 75-6 and 109-10.

72. Attendance for the 1850s is based upon the capacity of the parish churches and the number of Masses offered as well as Bishop de Charbonnel's comments to Cardinal Fransoni, 26 May 1851, AAT, CP; *Globe*, 7 February 1882.

73. John Ross Robertson, *Landmarks of Toronto* (Toronto: Toronto Telegram, 1914), 4:307; *Globe*, 16 April 1881; *Irish Canadian*, 16 October 1869, 14 March 1877.

74. "Toronto Particular Council Report," *Bulletin*, March 1882,

75. AAT, Lynch Papers, "St. Mary's Report," 15 August 1881; *Bulletin*, August 1887, 228; *Irish Canadian*, 20 June 1877, 7 June 1883; *Register of the St. Joseph's Bona Mors Society*, 1863-1873.

76. *Mirror*, 23 February 1852, 7 October 1853, 9 June 1854, 22 February 1855; *Canadian Freeman*, 6 October 1870; *Irish Canadian*, 16 October 1869, 14 March 1877.

77. *Bulletin*, January 1878, 179-80; "Particular Council Report," *Bulletin*, November 1888, 382-4.

78. *Globe*, 23 February 1882, 26 March 1883, 21 April 1885; Miller, "Irish Catholicism," 84-7.

4

THE ROAD TO WINSOME WOMANHOOD:

THE CANADIAN PRESBYTERIAN MISSION AMONG

EAST INDIAN WOMEN AND GIRLS

IN TRINIDAD, 1868-1939

Geoffrey Johnston

The Canadian Presbyterian mission among East Indians in Trinidad was one of the most significant of the overseas missions of the Presbyterian Church in Canada. Although small compared to the work in China or India, Canadian Mission to the Indians (CMI) was of crucial importance in helping the East Indians make their adjustment to life in the Caribbean. Within the context of the adjustment of an immigrant community to their new environment, the work among East Indian women and girls served as an alternative form of training for wives and mothers, something to replace the patterns which had developed in India. This study will describe the development of work among East Indian women and girls in Trinidad from its origins in 1868 to the beginning of the nationalist period in 1939.

The East Indians in Trinidad and the Beginnings of the Mission

The East Indians first came to Trinidad as labour for the sugar industry. When slavery ended in the West Indies in 1838 Trinidad was one of the few sugar frontiers left in the Caribbean. Much of the colony was still in forest, lacking only the labour to clear it and transform the island after the pattern of the rest of the Caribbean. Given the previous association of sugar and slavery, however, the recently emancipated blacks avoided work in the sugar fields except as a last resort. After all, they now had alternatives, such as squatting, petty trade, or subsistence farming. The sugar barons, accustomed to a reliable labour force, had to look elsewhere for workers and after a couple of false starts settled on indentured, or contract, labour from India. The first boatload arrived in 1845, and the system continued until 1917 when it was abolished by act of the British government. A labour contract normally bound a labourer for five years. After two contracts labourers were entitled to a free, or later, an assisted return passage. After 1869 the colonial government began the practice of offering cheap land as a substitute for a return passage. It was a popular offer and became one of the keys to the development of a settled East Indian peasantry in Trinidad.[1]

By law, the recruiting agents had to include women among the contract labourers. Between 1845 and 1870, 28,030 adult East Indians came to Trinidad, of whom something under a third, 9,280, were women.[2] In due course, as the East Indian population became established in Trinidad, the numbers of men and women became more even. The systems which the East Indians had developed in India for the training of girls for adult life did not take root in the new world. The one which seems to have been most common was one in which young girls were betrothed by their parents and sent to live in their husband's home at about age twelve. It fell to the mother-in-law to train the new arrival in the arts of house-wifery.[3] While the system itself did not weather the passage from India, the fundamental assumption, that a woman's place was in the home, lost none of its native vigour.

If a woman's place was in the home, and that home was her husband's, or more precisely that of her husband's family, a girl's parents were reluctant to invest much in her since any benefits would accrue, not to them, but to the in-laws. There was little point, for example, in keeping the girl in school for very long, as a sophisticated education was not a prerequisite for household management or child bearing. This reluctance to keep girls in school posed a serious problem for the Canadian mission, for it had begun from early days to use the schools as primary means of reaching the Indian community.[4]

The Canadian mission began in 1868, the same year in which Governor Gordon instituted the land-in-exchange-for-passage policy which changed the face of the Trinidad countryside. The pioneer missionary was John Morton, a young man from Pictou County, Nova Scotia, who had been a minister in Lunenburg, Nova Scotia. A chance voyage to the West Indies brought the spiritual state of the "coolies," the East Indians, to his attention. He pressed the American Presbyterians, the Scottish Presbyterians, and his own church, the Presbyterian Church in the Lower Provinces of British North America, to start a mission among the East Indians, but nothing happened until he volunteered to go himself. In January 1868 he arrived in Port of Spain with his wife Sarah and their daughter Agnes to begin what was the second of the overseas missions of the Presbyterian churches in Canada.[5]

Morton was not the first Presbyterian on the island. The United Presbyterian Church of Scotland had a small work among Europeans and blacks, and their ministers had formed a Presbytery in 1845. It was to that Presbytery that Morton presented his certificates. They sent him to Iere, a village in the southern part of the island, not far from San Fernando, where they already had a small outstation.[6]

In due course Morton was joined by other Nova Scotian ministers, and a strategy developed based on Canadians settled in key centres -- San Fernando and Princestown in the south, Couva in the west, and Tunapuna, near Port of Spain, in the north. Each of these men supervised a corps of East Indian teachers and catechists, and a few ordained ministers, rather in the fashion of a second century bishop. In addition to a good deal of time spent on the primary school system, the mission also worked hard at what might be called routine evangelization, including street corner disputations, a kind of theological Hyde Park which, besides being reasonably effective, was enjoyed by all and sundry. As time went by, they added a secondary school, a teacher training college, and a theological school to their list of institutions. For a small mission their work is impressive, but it was a strategy best suited to reach men and boys, not women and girls.[7]

Work among Women

A strategy for women was slow in developing. At first there were no women on the mission staff, and when they began to be appointed after 1876 they were located in the school system. The missionary wives were young women, busy having children themselves. Nevertheless from the beginning Sarah Morton went with her husband on his visits to the barracks, the living accomodation provided for the East Indians by the sugar estates. While John Morton spoke to the men, Sarah took the women aside, later organizing them into small meetings. There was never any doubt about what the work among women was intended to do. The mission intended to develop Christian wives and mothers. At first the work was hard going:

> They have great freedom of intercourse and much evil example around them. Sad to say they often show themselves as degraded as they are ignorant. On the other hand, many are beautiful and lovable, faithful to their husbands and devoted to their children.[8]

The first recorded reference to work among women, dating from 1874, clearly shows its domestic bias: "Mrs Grant taught her girls needlework and was almost daily engaged in sewing up garments."[9] Mrs. Grant was the wife of George Grant, missionary in San Fernando, the principal town in southern Trinidad. One of the earliest of the single missionaries, Adella Archibald, who was appointed in 1889, regarded her work to be finished when the girls were married into Christian families.[10] Although the scope of their work among women changed over the years, it never entirely lost this domestic bias. Until 1889 the work among the women was something of a sideline to the mission, an activity the women in the mission staff took up when they had time left over from their families or the schools.[11]

In 1889 the programme was put on a more permanent footing. During their furlough that year the Mortons decided to start a home for young women, and while in Nova Scotia collected enough money to get the project under way. The Mission Council, the assembly of missionaries which controlled the mission's day-to-day affairs, thought the scheme was premature but nonetheless allowed the Mortons to spend the money they had collected on a new building. Once the school moved to its new quarters the space under the manse became vacant, and the Mortons promptly filled it with a home for girls.[12]

Sarah Morton's objectives for the home were quite clear and straightforward. She wanted to train wives for the catechists and teachers of the mission staff. These men were socially and geographically mobile, and in addition traditional East Indian patterns for the training of wives did not appear to be suitable. Thus, the girls' home was an effort to provide not so much an alternative as a replacement system. In effect, Sarah Morton set herself up as a surrogate mother-in-law.[13]

Many in the Indian community appreciated the home, and by 1902 sixty girls had gone through it. Nevertheless, only sixteen, or less than a third, had married teachers or catechists. In 1892, Mrs. Morton gave a sketch of the twenty-two girls who had been, or still were under her care at that time. Of these, only two had married teachers. Four of the twenty-two had come from within the mission's school system, while most of the remaining girls could be described as coming from the flotsam and jetsam of a society based on contract labour.[14]

As one might expect in a missionary home intended to produce wives and mothers, the training combined religion, drawing heavily on the Hindi Bible, and the housewifely arts of laundry, sewing, cooking, and gardening. Indian cuisine was the norm, but when Agnes Morton came home from her domestic science course in Edinburgh, they varied the diet to include Scottish dishes. Normally the girls graduated by getting married. Mrs. Morton took an active part in screening male suitors, and once she was satisfied that a man was a suitable husband, a girl was free to say yes or no. Occasionally Mrs. Morton had to go out and find a husband:

I have been greatly engaged in husband hunting; two notices were put up yesterday. The prettiest young lady is always the hardest to settle, her love affairs being ruinous; therefore the "belle" is not settled yet. Four wanted her, two seem to have

drawn back; the others are not altogether desirable. I am
looking for Providence to open my way with regard to the girls.
I have for some time made it a subject for prayer.[15]

Mrs. Morton arranged the wedding feast in the school building nearby,
attended by friends of the Mortons. She prepared the Morton buggy to
take the couple to the train, and gave them the standard Morton present,
a hoe and a broom. The last of the girls graduated in 1909 with a triple
wedding, and Mrs. Morton closed down the home. It is not clear why she
decided to set the work aside, but her advancing years is the most likely
explanation. By 1909 she had served forty-one years in Trinidad.[16]

Adella Archibald carried on a similar work, however. Miss Archibald,
who had come as a teacher in 1889, had opened in 1905 a home for girls
in Iere in the southern part of the island, not far from San Fernando. The
Mission Council minute authorizing the school spoke of it as operating
"along the same lines, and to meet the same class of people, as present
effort," that is, as the home under the Morton's house.[17]

Adella Archibald was not a carbon copy of Sarah Morton, nor was
Trinidad the same place in 1905 as it had been in 1889. Miss Archibald
would have no waifs and strays, but only promising orphans, girls from
Christian homes and, if any space were left, girls whose families could pay
the full cost.[18] Nor was the training exactly the same. While there was
the same emphasis on religion and housewifery, the girls could attend the
nearby Canadian mission school for the kind of primary education which
the state supported mission schools offered all over Trinidad. Nor was
marriage the normal form of graduation. Between 1905 and 1917, 142 girls
went through the home, but by 1918, only fifty were married.[19] While
these observations indicate a shift in method, the fundamental objective of
the school was the same as Sarah Morton's -- to develop Christian
mothers. The Bible was not just to be learned, it was to be applied:

Only thus may self-control be learned and Christian character
formed. If thereby the roll of Christian mothers in this land

should be increased, then the existence of the Iere Home will have been more than justified.[20]

When the Iere Home burned down in 1928, the mission resumed the same kind of programme in Tunapuna near Port of Spain, not far from the site of the Morton's original home for girls. Known as the Archibald Institute, half the work was in academic subjects, English, Hindi, household and personal accounting, religious and general knowledge with special attention to current events and geography. The other half of the course dealt with the skills of competent housekeeping, sewing, budget analysis, design and pattern making, and cooking. The cooking classes went beyond the art of preparation to deal as well with the elements of a balanced diet.[21] It was clearly a more sophisticated approach, but still very much in the tradition of the school for wives and mothers that Sarah Morton had begun over forty years before.

This increasing sophistication of the programme for wives and mothers reflects developments within the Indian community. By the time the British government abolished indenture in 1917, East Indians had been living in Trinidad for seventy years, and had been able to buy land on the island for almost fifty years. The East Indians, no longer a people in transit, had become a settled part of Trinidad. Several generations had been to the primary schools and many boys had attended a secondary school begun in San Fernando in 1900. At the same time, a trickle of qualified East Indian students went to Britain for an advanced education, and it was this group of young men that in a way precipitated the formation of a high school for girls.[22]

In January 1912 the mission paper, the *Trinidad Presbyterian*, announced the opening of a high school for girls at Naparima under the supervision of Dr. F. J. Coffin, the senior educational missionary, with a Miss Doyle, a local woman, as teacher. The mission sources make this new venture sound like a routine Canadian initiative, but there is more to it than meets the eye. The stimulus apparently came from the Indian National Congress, a communal organization of Trinidadian East Indians, one of whose leading figures was C. D. Lalla, then a catechist in Couva, the headquarters of one of the mission districts. The Congress was concerned that the young East Indian men going abroad for study would come back with foreign wives if there were no properly educated East Indian girls available. The Congress went to Coffin, persuaded him to take the project under his wing and offered a grant towards the salary of the first teacher.[23]

The Naparima Girls' High School later became part of the mission's educational system, and over the years between the two world wars grew to rival the older high school for boys. When Grace Beattie arrived to take charge of the school in 1916 she found eighteen girls, six doing teacher training and the rest in the ordinary high school course.[24] Naparima Girls' High School was not simply a high school; in 1917 it acquired a primary department. The statistical returns sent home to the Women's Missionary Society in Canada do not always make clear how many girls were in the primary department and how many in the high school. But the institution's growth was impressive. By 1922 the enrolment had become eighty-five, and by 1936 it was 265. In April 1937 Mission council granted approval for an extension of the buildings, the second such expansion since the start of the Depression.[25]

An institution of that size was beyond the financial resources of the mission. Grace Beattie had not been long on the job before she opened conversations with the government about a grant. In 1921 the government recognized the school as an intermediate high school, and in 1924 as a full secondary school.[26] With government financing came the government-approved curriculum, and a willingness to admit other than East Indian girls. The mission accepted these conditions although they were not entirely consistent with their usual strategy. As part of the case for full status as a secondary school, the mission argued that the girls' high school was the only one in San Fernando, and that there was a need and a desire in the community for facilities that would allow girls to proceed to the Cambridge examinations, the normal conclusion to a secondary education.[27]

The acceptance of the Cambridge examinations as the last hurdle in a secondary education set up a tension between an academic education and one intended as preparation for marriage. This tension the mission never entirely resolved. The annual reports in the late twenties and thirties to the United Church of Canada which now supervised the mission, tended to speak less about homemaking and more about success at the Cambridge examination. On the other hand, as Marion Outhit, one of the early teachers at the girls' high school, put it:

> The progress towards the attainment of missionary ends must necessarily be slow until the Indian women are trained in the fundamental principles of home making and taught to keep themselves and their children clean by the observance of laws and rules to which they are strangers.[28]

In the same article she made the same point in somewhat more picturesque language: "there is a species of mental and physical discipline of far more importance to these people than that which is to be derived from grubbing through a tangle of Latin roots." The mission never lost track of this emphasis, even at the high school, and indeed, neither did the East Indians. While there was clearly a demand for secondary education for girls, most students looked forward to marriage as their career. Agnes Rampersad, a graduate of the school and a member of the staff from the late twenties, said that most girls went through to Form Four and then took up teaching as a way of keeping bread on the table until they married. She and Stella Abidh, who became a doctor, were the only graduates of the school she could think of who did not marry.[29] The level of sophistication within the educational programme for girls might change, but the basic objective did not.

The District Work

Institutions like Naparima Girls' High School or the Archibald Institute could influence only the relatively small number of people who attend them. The Trinidadian countryside was full of women who never entered a girls' school. Work with women in their homes began with the origins of the mission, when Sarah Morton took the women aside while her husband spoke with the men. As long as people lived mainly in sugar estates, in relatively dense and relatively accessible communities, this procedure was possible. Mrs. Morton, when she had time left over from her own family, worked extensively among the women on the sugar estates. Some of those she met she took in for further training, and with their assistance was able to cover more ground than she could by herself. Deborah Talaram and Fanny Subaran are examples of these protegées of Sarah Morton, early examples of what later became known as the Bible Women, a kind of female version, though with less training, of the catechists.[30]

The sugar crisis of the late nineteenth century, however, had far reaching consequences both for Trinidad and the mission. As European beet sugar, often subsidized by public funds, came on the market in the late nineteenth century, the profits of the Trinidadian sugar barons declined. The barons shut down their estates or reduced their staffs. The East Indian labour force moved out, some to relatively adjacent empty land, but others farther afield, into the hill country to grow cocoa. Many of those who moved out were families with whom the mission had some contact. Male catechists carried on regular church activities, such as Sunday worship, but there was no parallel development among the women. In 1903 the number of Bible Women peaked at fourteen, while there were forty-five male catechists. In 1916 there were only seven Bible Women, but fifty-seven catechists.[31] The essential difficulty was that in a society where virtually every woman had domestic responsibilities, it was extremely difficult to develop trained, full-time women staff. Apart from the occasional widow, female leadership came, in the first instance at least, from women who were willing and able to take time off from their family duties. The Mission Council discussed establishing a programme for such women but nothing happened until 1920 when Adella Archibald was detached from the school system to take the programme in hand.[32]

Miss Archibald started with the girls she had known at Iere, many of whom had married and settled "in conditions not helpful to Christian living." The key to the programme was the meeting, the small gatherings of Christian women and their friends, where they could be encouraged to read, to teach others to read, to deepen their spiritual life, and in general to develop homes that could be centres of "light and good influence."[33] Initially the missionaries provided the leadership, Miss Archibald full-time and other single women in the institutions in their spare time. In due course a class of Bible Women, the successors of Deborah Talaram and Fanny Subaran, began to appear.[34]

In 1928 the *Missionary Monthly*, an organ of the United Church of Canada, published an account of a probably not untypical example of meeting for women:

> After a beautiful drive through the sugar cane fields we drive up before our meeting place. No, it is not a church, or a public hall, or even a school house -- it is a karat roofed mud hut. It holds perhaps fifty people.

The meeting was conducted by a Trinidadian woman, Marion Alibaksh, a widow and an adult convert. She began with Bible study and then went on to discuss the control of flies and mosquitoes. The gathering was well attended and the message, apparently, well received.[35] Unlike most East Indian women, Marion Alibaksh was well versed in the Hindi sacred texts before becoming a Christian. After her conversion she married a catechist, and on his death served with distinction as a Bible Woman until she married again in 1934 and was available only for part time work. She stands out among the new class of Bible Women that grew up under Miss Archibald's care. There were very few such women when she began district work in 1920, but by 1930 there were seventeen, most of whom worked only in the afternoons. They had been trained in a kind of extension programme which stressed bible study, Hindi missions, devotional subjects and, always, hygiene.[36] In a society where diseases like hookworm were endemic, the stress on hygiene was eminently sensible.

While the basis of the district work was the meeting for women, often held in humble circumstances and led by women of humble attainments, it was not surprising that a mission in the twentieth century would develop the superstructure they had known at home. the Trinidad Women's Missionary Society appeared in 1928, an island-wide organization with a president, two vice-presidents, a secretary and a treasurer. In 1934 the annual meeting heard speeches on social obligation, child raising, and the place of women in the church. The last was provided by J. C. MacDonald, one of the senior ordained missionaries. One afternoon's worship was led by the members of the Fyzabad Trinidad Girls in Training.[37] The Trinidad Girls in Training was an import pure and simple, modelled on the Canadian Girls in Training, a classic instance of the transfer of a Canadian programme with minimal adjustment into the Trinidadian scene. They even had an annual camp:

> There are the physical 'jerks', morning dip and flag salute; jolly meal hours with songs and stunts, morning watch and solemn worship periods, Bible Study and World Friendship classes, handwork, swimming, hikes, treasure hunts, even the Camp Fire. . . .[38]

The camp fire, as the author conceded, was not the same thing on a tropical island as in Canada. Fires in a warm climate do not carry the same symbolism as in the north. But the salient point about the programme for women in this mission is that so much was transferable.

The Patterns of the Work

In their initial stages the various programmes undertaken by the mission worked because both missionaries and East Indians agreed that the place of women was in the home. The problem for the mission was to provide a Christian replacement for the domestic apprenticeship that had been the responsibility of the mother-in-law in India. Contemporary reaction to the programme is a study in the choice of words. Harold Sitahal, a leading minister in the Presbyterian Church of Trinidad, was sharply critical:

> To complete the creation of a small but significant elite group among East Indians, the mission groomed East Indian girls to be suitable wives for the young men. This was also a direct thrust

against the East Indian attitude toward women and East Indian marriage customs.[39]

On the other hand R. G. Neehal, another leading minister from the same church, sees in the mission's work among girls "a general emancipation of women from the inferior position they occupied in the thinking of East Indian men." He continued, "Perhaps most importantly of all was the development in the minds of women of a consciousness of their own worth and a realization of the important place they filled in the progress of the race."[40] Both men are right. The girls' schools were a direct attack on Indian marriage customs, for, as Bernard Cohn and others have pointed out, Indian society is incorrigibly hierarchical, the older over the younger, the men over the women.[41] Anything that led to the emancipation of women from this hierarchical system was an attack on the marriage patterns of Indian immigrants. One may infer from Neehal's comment that he agrees that East Indian marriage patterns were under attack, but that he regards the attack to be a good thing, leading to emancipation.

Whatever assessment one may make of the ethical validity of East Indian marriage patterns, those patterns were disintegrating in Trinidad. On the one hand there was, at the outset at least, an acute shortage of women, something which gave them considerable bargaining power, and on the other, the structure which had provided for the training of brides in the mother-in-law's house did not survive the passage from India. By setting themselves up as surrogate mothers-in-law the ladies of the mission were providing a substitute. The missionaries, however, understood their task differently. They saw themselves as training Christian mothers, and therefore laying the foundation for Christian homes. Everybody agreed that properly trained wives were desirable, and therefore the girls' schools found a wide measure of acceptance in the Indian community. The missionary reasons and the East Indian reasons, while they overlapped, were not exactly the same. Because the missionaries saw their work as part of their Christian mission, it was natural for them to extend the programme for women beyond the simple training of wives and mothers into more specifically Christian activities, following the patterns with which they were most familiar, the ones they had known in Canada.

They were able to proceed as far along this route as they did, including the transfer of such Canadian institutions as the Women's Missionary Society and the Canadian Girls in Training, because the East Indian community did not suggest indigenous alternative patterns. Why was there an absence of such alternatives and why did the the Canadian Presbyterian Mission to girls succeed as it did? The basic answer lies deep in the nature of the colonial experience in Trinidad. Trinidad was, according to M. G. Smith a "plural society" in a "colony of immigration."[42] For the purposes of this discussion one may speak of three kinds of colonies in the modern world -- colonies of conquest, of settlement, and of immigration. A colony of conquest is one in which the host culture, although overcome by force of arms, remains substantially intact. There may be important changes in the society as a consequence of the imperial experience, but a a whole people do not lose touch with their roots. India and Africa are examples of colonies of this type. A colony of settlement is one in which the immigrants come predominantly from the same society as the colonizing power, as in Canada or Australia. In this case immigration on a large scale takes place, and in the new environment changes do occur, but they are variations on the imperial theme, as it were. In a colony of immigration the newcomers are from a different cultural tradition from the imperial power. In the West Indies the immigrants came either as slaves or as contract labour, and the transition to the new land was a difficult one indeed.

In the Trinidadian case the situation is further complicated by the existence in Trinidad of two major and a number of minor cultural entities. The vast majority of Trinidadians are either East Indian or black, but there are also the Chinese and the Europeans. Trinidad is a plural society, a political or territorial jurisdiction comprised of differing communities, but held together by the dominance of one section, in this case the British. The British controlled the state and the economy, and British cultural patterns dominated the island as the standards of "civilized" people. In this situation it is easy to understand why the East

Indians accepted as many Canadian patterns as they did, not just for the women, but in church life as a whole. Both as a result of their immigration and of their becoming Christian, the East Indian Christians were, in a sense, rootless people in a society where British, and by association Canadian, patterns were the norm. Naturally they accepted them, because they had no real alternatives.

This study ends in 1939, during the "Butler days," those disturbances in the sugar industry which mark the beginning of the nationalist period in Trinidad. Trinidad became independent in 1961, and with the departure of the British governor has gone a good deal of the lustre of the British standards. Since independence a significant number of West Indian intellectuals have actively pursued a new Caribbean identity, a sense of identity which does justice to those aspects of West Indian life derived from Africa or India, or indigenous to the Caribbean itself. Within the church, people have decided that they had accepted more of the missionary patterns than they should.[43] Between 1869 and 1939, however, the times and patterns were different. The road to marriage and motherhood served both Canadian Presbyterians and Trinidad East Indian girls simultaneously.

Notes

1. The literature on the East Indians in Trinidad is extensive. See, for example, Morton Klass, *East Indians in Trinidad* (New York, London: Columbia University Press, 1961); John La Guerre, ed., *Calcutta to Caroni: the East Indians of Trinidad* (N.p.: Longman Caribbean, 1974); and Keith Laurence, *Immigration into the West Indies in the Nineteenth Century* (Kingston: Caribbean University Press, 1971).
2. Donald Wood, *Trinidad in Transition* (Oxford: Oxford University Press, 1968), 154.
3. Bernard S. Cohn, *India: The Social Anthropology of a Civilization,* (Englewood Cliffs, N.J.: Prentice-Hall, 1971), 117-20.
4. Geoffrey Johnston, "The Canadian Mission in Trinidad, 1868-1939: Studies in a Colonial Church" (Th.D. thesis, Knox College, Toronto, 1976), 6, 174.

5.   Sarah Morton, *John Morton of Trinidad* (Toronto: Westminster, 1916),
      7-10, 17.
6.   Morton, 21, 40.
7.   Morton, chapters 4-6.
8.   Morton, 185.
9.   Presbyterian Church Archives [hereafter PCA], Morton Papers, Box 6,
      Sarah Morton, "Address to a Conference of Workers at Susamachar,
      1915."
10.   United Church of Canada Archives [hereafter UCA], Adella Archibald,
      Diary, I:22, 23, 54.
11.   Morton, 236.
12.   Morton, 346-7.
13.   Morton, 343-4, 350 *ff*.
14.   *The Record*, March 1903.
15.   PCA, Morton Papers, Box 6, Sarah Morton to A. S. Morton, 21 March
      1909.
16.   Morton, 433-4.
17.   UCA, *Minutes of the Trinidad Mission Council*, 29 December 1904.
18.   *The Message*, April 1912. *The Message* was the publication of the
      Women's Missionary Society, Eastern Division, of the Presbyterian
      Church in Canada.
19.   *The Message*, April 1912.
20.   *The Message*, April 1912.
21.   *The Trinidad Presbyterian*, September 1932.
22.   Conversation with Agnes Ramporsad, 12 March 1976; Grace Beattie in
      The Trinidad Presbyterian March 1938.
23.   Notes on a conversation between the author and Agnes Rampersad, 12
      March 1976, and Grace Beattie in the *Trinidad Presbyterian* March
      1938.
24.   Grace Beattie, in *The Message*, June 1917.
25.   Johnston, 90.
26.   *Minutes of the Trinidad Mission Council*, 19 September 1924, and 13
      January 1925.

27. *Minutes of the Trinidad Mission Council,* 17 September 1924, 13 January 1925.
28. *The Theologue,* May 1913. *The Theologue* was published at Pine Hill Theological College, Halifax, Nova Scotia.
29. Notes on a conversation of the author with Agnes Rampersad, 13 March 1976.
30. Morton, 35-9, 340, 353 *f.*
31. Johnston, 199.
32. Johnston, 201.
33. *Acts and Proceeding of the General Assembly of the Presbyterian Church in Canada,* 1921, Report of the Board of Foreign Missions, 10.
34. Morton, 434.
35. *The Missionary Monthly,* January 1928.
36. Johnston, 205.
37. *The Trinidad Presbyterian,* April 1934.
38. Mission Council of Trinidad, *East Meets West* (Toronto: Committee on Young People's Missionary Education, United Church of Canada, 1934), 74.
39. Harold Sitahal, *The Mission of the Church in Trinidad* (S.T.M. thesis, McGill University, 1967), 64.
40. R. G. Neehal, *Presbyterianism in Trinidad: A Study of the Impact of Presbyterianism on the Island of Trinidad in the Nineteenth Century* (S.T.M. thesis, Union Theological Seminary, New York, 1958), 63.
41. Cohn, *India,* 12.
42. M. G. Smith, "West Indian Cultures," *Caribbean Quarterly,* 1:3 (1961-2), 112-18.
43. For examples of the nationalist critique of the colonial, including the missionary experience, see the work of the late Dr. Idris Hamid, a minister of the Presbyterian Church of Trinidad, *In Search of New Perspectives* (Bridgetown, Barbados: CADEC, n.d.); and a volume of essays edited by him, *The Troubling of the Waters* (San Fernando, Trinidad: Publisher, 1973).

5

FAR INDEED FROM THE MEEKEST OF WOMEN:

MARION FAIRWEATHER AND

THE CANADIAN PRESBYTERIAN MISSION IN

CENTRAL INDIA, 1873-1880

Ruth Compton Brouwer

During the last third of the nineteenth century in Protestant North America the foreign missionary movement came to be regarded as an appropriate outlet for the spiritual and intellectual energies of the much discussed "new woman."[1] A contributor to *The Knox College Monthly* of Toronto was thus expressing a widely shared sentiment when in 1888, following the designation of a trained nurse for the Canadian Presbyterian Church's mission field in North China, he wrote:

> This appointment . . . illustrates the prominence that must be given to woman's work in the evangelization of the world. Here is a sphere less injurious to true womanhood than many into which women are clamoring for admission, more in harmony with her better nature and with God's evident designs, in which her own long pent-up energies and powers may find full scope to her own advantage and the immeasurable blessing of humanity.[2]

A few years later, however, an ordained Canadian missionary, writing from India, used the phrase "ecclesiastical Amazons" to describe a group of women colleagues who had sought an equal role on the mission council.[3] Once again, the sentiment, if not the phrase was representative.

As these two perspectives suggest, women's participation in the foreign missionary enterprise was characterized by a complex interweaving of opportunity and constraint: women workers in foreign fields could look forward to career opportunities that were virtually unavailable in Canada, and to the full approbation of the church and community from which they had come, so long as they remembered that even the peculiar needs of a mission station would not be allowed to blur unduly long-standing notions of appropriate female behaviour. This combination of opportunity and constraint may be seen as a particularly striking example of a broad and persistent pattern in the Judaeo-Christian heritage, a pattern which one scholar has labelled "the central paradox of women's religious history."[4]

The present study illustrates this paradoxical tendency by focussing on the experience of Marion Fairweather, an Ontario woman who played a key role in founding the Canadian Presbyterian mission in Central India in the 1870s. As an unordained missionary worker, Fairweather demonstrated a high level of initiative, ambition, and intelligence, as even her sharpest critic was prepared to acknowledge. But when these qualities were combined with an "unwomanly" assertiveness and a certain want of discretion and exercised in a mission where the lines of authority had not yet been elaborated, they aroused resentment and disapproval among her co-workers of both sexes and ultimately proved fatal to her missionary career. Recalled in 1879 after the all-male Foreign Missions Committee had received reports of improprieties in her relationship with an ordained male colleague, Fairweather endeavoured to respond to the allegations and persuade the Committee to retain her on its staff. Her efforts were unsuccessful, and her service as a missionary for the Presbyterian Church was formally terminated in October, 1880.

The Founding of the Mission

When Marion Fairweather volunteered for foreign missionary service in 1872, the overseas outposts of Canadian Presbyterianism were feeble and far-flung. The union of Presbyterian churches in 1875 that would alter this situation had not yet taken place, and the formation of a woman's foreign missionary society to finance and publicize women's work was still four years distant. But like their brethren in other evangelical denominations, Canadian Presbyterian leaders had come to believe that full participation in the foreign missionary enterprise was essential to the life and health of their church.[5] They were most familiar with the missionary activities of their Scottish and American fellow Calvinists and aware of the fact that even these conservative churchmen had come to regard the participation of single women workers as a necessary aspect of foreign missionary outreach. Such workers, they believed, could gain access to secluded Oriental women and, through the educational and medical services they provided, attract a clientele that would not normally be drawn by the Christian message itself. As social service became an increasingly important part of overseas evangelism, female workers came to predominate on the staffs of many mission boards.[6]

Given these circumstances, the Foreign Missions Committee (FMC) of the Canada Presbyterian Church was prepared to respond positively to Fairweather's request in 1872 that it find a field of labour for her and her friend Margaret Rodger.[7] It arranged to have the two women attend the Ottawa Ladies' College for a brief period of preparatory study and wrote to Presbyterian foreign missionary committees in Scotland and the United States about a possible field of labour for them.[8] By October 1873 it had been decided that the two would join an American Presbyterian mission in North India until such time as the Canadian church could stake out its own spiritual territory in the sub-continent.[9] On Christmas Eve of that year Fairweather and Rodger arrived in the city of Allahabad.[10] A sense of vocation, alloyed, in all likelihood, by more worldly motives, had launched their missionary careers.[11]

On the surface, the church's two pioneer women missionaries appeared to have a good deal in common. Both were in their mid-twenties, Canadian born, of Scottish background. Both had obtained elementary- and model-school-teaching diplomas from the McGill Normal School, where Fairweather had also received an honourable mention for elocution. While living in Montreal they had attended Erskine Church, which was, even then, strongly missions-oriented.[12] Both came from modest but respectable backgrounds: Fairweather's father had been a shopkeeper in Bowmanville, Ontario, while Rodger was from a large farm family near Lachute, Quebec.[13] Beyond these surface similarities, however, the women seem to have had strongly contrasting personalities, and while FMC members may not have had an opportunity to meet the two before they left Canada, the correspondence exchanged in preparation for the trip should have given them some indication that Marion Fairweather might prove to be an assertive, even troublesome, worker, while Margaret Rodger would function largely in the role of silent labourer.[14] In September 1873, for instance, Fairweather had written the Committee a strongly-worded letter to express her frustration at its failure to inform her and Rodger about specific plans for their deployment. She had passed up a good teaching job on the assumption that their departure was imminent, she maintained, and was inconvenienced as well as grieved by the uncertainty. "If the Committee do not think it worth while to treat us with common politeness," she had warned, "I fancy the sooner we dissolve the partnership the better."[15]

Notwithstanding these somewhat strained preliminaries, the Committee evidently sent the two women off with its full confidence and approval. Writing in December 1873 to inform them that no ordained candidates had yet come forward to offer themselves for India, Secretary Thomas Lowry indicated what was expected of them under the circumstances. "As you are our pioneers," he explained, "we must be guided very much in our future plans by the information which we may get from you and from other sources respecting the state of affairs in the place to which you have gone."[16]

The task of advising the FMC about its future course of action in India was one that Marion Fairweather took up with alacrity. Early in 1874 she urged the American missionaries with whom she and Rodger were associated to inform the Committee about an appropriate location for a Canadian Presbyterian mission. Subsequently, she endorsed their suggestion that her church should begin operations in the princely state of Indore, Central India, and exhorted Committee members to act promptly on the Americans' advice. "Would it not be well," she wrote, "to advance this idea at the [next] General Assembly."[17] In the two years that followed, in letters describing the educational, orphanage, and evangelistic work that she and Rodger were doing in the several American mission stations to which they had been posted, Fairweather would continue to press the Canadian church about opening its own mission station in India.

While she was clearly happy with her new life, and grateful to the FMC for making it possible[18] Fairweather did not hesitate on occasion to write sharp letters to its Executive, expressing her displeasure at its administrative failures and conveying her views about the most appropriate course of action for those contemplating service in India. Thus, in November 1874, in a somewhat peremptory letter to the FMC Convenor William McLaren, she deplored the arrears in her own and Rodger's salaries and urged that the problem be dealt with immediately.[19] The following year she was equally forthright when she heard that the Reverend J. Fraser Campbell was coming to India not to begin work in Indore but to join an existing English-language mission in Madras. Disappointed with Campbell's apparent reluctance to undertake language study and do pioneering work in the interior, she told McLaren that if Campbell were not prepared to learn a new language, he should "change his mind and remain at home," since speaking the vernacular and trans-lating were essential skills in any mission. She was not pressing the claims of Indore for any personal reason, she insisted -- perhaps somewhat disingenuously. Indeed, she and Rodger were quite happy working with the Americans. But millions of souls were waiting in that benighted part of India with "*not one* Missionary to tell the glad tidings." Then, skilfully appealing to her fellow Presbyterians' sense of denominational pride, she held out the possibility that some other missionary group might occupy the field and thus prevent the Canadian church from establishing "the last clasp in the chain of our Presbyterian frontier."[20]

Reaching a consensus about a new mission field and finding an ordained worker to superintend it were undoubtedly more difficult matters for the newly united Presbyterian Church in Canada than Fairweather seemed to realize,[21] but in the summer of 1876 she at last received word that the church had agreed to begin a mission in Indore and that a

Princeton-trained minister, the Reverend James M. Douglas of Cobourg,
Ontario, would probably come out to India as its founding missionary.[22]
Her response was enthusiastic and characteristically voluble. In the months
that followed she wrote a series of letters -- to Douglas, to the FMC, and
to the newly formed Woman's Foreign Missionary Society (WFMS)[23] --
about the nature of the institutions the church should establish in its
India mission and her own efforts to prepare the ground.

Fairweather took it for granted that the mission should operate its
own printing press and with that goal in view proposed to arrange a
marriage between one of her most promising orphanage girls and a young
man with mission printing experience and bring the two to Indore as
mission employees.[24] Similar steps were taken to recruit a team of native
evangelists.[25] On the subject of educational work she had strong and
positive views. In response to a WFMS enquiry about the relative merits of
teaching school and visiting the high-caste Hindu women secluded in
zenanas, she urged the desirability of supporting both forms of missionary
activity. She explained, however, that the former was more valuable, since
children were generally more open to the gospel than the high-caste
women in zenanas who accepted the visits of a missionary only as a
diversion from the seclusion and boredom of their daily lives. Children,
moreover, could themselves serve as missionary agents by disseminating a
knowledge of Christian teaching in their homes.[26] To McLaren she stressed
the desirability of starting a high school at an early date as a vehicle for
attracting older boys.[27] The missionary agency about which Fairweather
was most enthusiastic, however, was women's medical work. In a letter to
McLaren in 1874 she had confided, "I always at home had a kind of horror
of a lady physician but since I came to India I have not ceased to regret
my ignorance of this subject."[28] In the course of working with the
American Presbyterians Fairweather had come to know their pioneer
woman medical missionary, Dr. Sara Seward, niece of the late American
Secretary of State. She was greatly impressed with Seward's accomplishments and with the opportunities that medical work offered for
gaining access to high-caste Hindu families and winning the tolerance and
support of native princes.[29]

By the time she and Margaret Rodger had joined James Douglas in Indore in the early months of 1877, Fairweather had made recommendations or preliminary arrangements for establishing virtually the full range of contemporary missionary agencies in her church's new field. Her advice reflected her experience in three American stations and her commitment to the school of missionary thought which emphasized a multi-faceted approach to conversion efforts. By the last quarter of the nineteenth century such an approach had largely superseded an exclusive reliance on direct evangelization,[30] so that while some of the measures she advocated may have been premature ones for a new mission, they were not unconventional. Similarly, when she turned to the subject of the training and deployment of those who were soon to be her colleagues, her advice appeared to reflect sound experience and shrewd common sense. Yet the outspoken language in which it was occasionally delivered could offend as well as inform. Fairweather's belief in the importance of sending out only fully-trained medical workers, for instance, made her critical of two missionary candidates still in Canada. One of the two, Mary McGregor, who would later contribute directly to Fairweather's recall, had particular reason to be resentful, for in May of 1877, in a letter to McLaren, Fairweather had scornfully dismissed her plan to acquire some basic nurse's training: "You will pardon me . . . if I say I believe Miss McGregor is wasting time. What earthly use nursing is to be to her I cannot well make out." Without taking care to explain clearly why nursing skills would be of minimal value in a new mission in India, she urged that McGregor acquire the training of full-fledged medical missionary or else learn to teach fancy needlework and Bible object lessons as preparation for zenana visiting and school work. There was no place in a new mission, she warned, for "half-way people." In the same letter, Fairweather described some evangelistic work that she proposed to turn over to Mrs. Jane Douglas when the latter joined her husband in Indore. Sounding more like a supervisor than a future colleague, she added, "I fear some times my plans may be more than she will be able to overtake."[31]

By writing in this fashion, Fairweather may have sown seeds of discord with her future co-workers, for while her own experience un-

doubtedly seemed to her sufficient justification for instructing those still
at home, there were no formal guidelines giving her the pre-eminent role
she seemed to be assuming and no acceptable precedents for her sometimes
imperious tone. McLaren himself showed occasional irritation with his
missionary's forthright style.[32] On the other hand, after three years'
service in American stations, Fairweather and Rodger had won praise from
their ordained colleagues for the effective way they had taken up language
study and the several branches of mission work.[33] Fairweather's letters to
the home church were thus written from the self-confident perspective of
a successful, knowledgeable missionary.

Difficulties Begin

By the end of its first year, the Canadian mission in Central India
had six staff members occupying two stations. During the summer, J.
Fraser Campbell had decided to leave Madras and settle in Mhow, a small
British cantonment town some fourteen miles from the city of Indore. In
Indore, Fairweather, Rodger, and Douglas shared the only accomodation
they had been able to obtain. The two new missionaries, Mary Forrester
and Mary McGregor, had arrived from Canada in December, accompanied
by Jane Douglas and three of her children. In view of the Indore housing
problem, it was decided that Rodger and Fairweather should join Campbell
in Mhow.[34] About a year later, Forrester married Campbell and in so doing
surrendered her official status as a missionary.[35] No further changes would
take place in the mission staff until the autumn of 1879 when Marion
Fairweather would be recalled to Canada.

In the three years leading up to her recall, Fairweather played a
prominent role in developing the work of the mission and appeared to
enjoy the full confidence of the church at home.[36] In addition to being
involved in missionary education work and providing private tuition to a
young princess, she visited a large number of zenana women during her
first year in Indore and made evangelistic trips to villages outside the
city. In the evenings, she and Margaret Rodger joined Douglas in receiving
enquirers in their bungalow.[37] By the early months of 1878 she was
participating with Douglas and an ordained Indian missionary in the

struggles that resulted from their efforts to baptize their first converts, two young Brahmins.[38] That summer she was also given responsibility for a new endeavour, the Christian Girls' Industrial School and Orphanage. Located in the bazaar across from Douglas's office, this institution now became both her home and the school, workplace and residence where a small number of girls and women were given domestic training and taught to perform simple tasks for the mission press.[39]

Converting Indian gentlemen was generally regarded as outside the sphere of the "lady missionary."[40] Yet in a non-British state like Indore the conversion and friendship of this group was seen to be particularly crucial.[41] To Fairweather, considerations of gender came to seem less important in the task than the ability to present an intelligent case for the merits of Christianity.[42] By 1878, therefore, her letters contained frequent references to even this form of evangelism. Men as well as women were approached in the bazaar and welcomed to her home. Copies of missionary literature were then presented and their contents explained.[43] Some of these efforts were particularly ambitious -- and perhaps naive. In one letter, for instance, Fairweather described a chance encounter in a railroad station with a gorgeously attired maharajah: observing that, despite his evident curiosity about the leaflets she was distributing, he appeared reluctant to approach an "English lady," she initiated a conversation and invited him to pay her a visit.[44] Such initiatives did not mean that Fairweather had abandoned "woman's work" or relegated it to second place. Nevertheless, by the end of 1878 it was clear that she had developed a very expansive view of her missionary role, a role whose only constraints appeared to be those inherent in being an unordained worker.

As late as the autumn of 1879 Marion Fairweather was still sending confident, detailed accounts of her work to correspondents in Canada,[45] apparently unaware of the fact that her missionary career was in jeopardy. Yet by the summer of that year the FMC had begun to receive reports of dissension and scandal in Central India in which Fairweather's name figured prominently. The reports appear to have been as unexpected as they were disturbing, for while there had been hints of differences between James Douglas and J. Fraser Campbell, the two ordained missionaries, from the first year of the mission's existence,[46] the Foreign Missions Committee could not have anticipated that such differences would come to involve the entire mission staff and threaten the very future of the church's India endeavour. The first word of unusual difficulties seems to have reached the Convenor of the FMC in a brief note from an Indian catechist formerly employed by the mission. The badly flawed English in which it was written made the burden of his message doubly difficult to grasp: the behaviour of Fairweather and Douglas had been causing gossip in the Indian community, he maintained, and when he, McGregor, and Rodger had reported the problem to Campbell, Douglas had retaliated by dismissing him from the mission and placing the two women under suspension.[47] Some weeks later, the FMC received a second, equally confusing, communication: acting in what she called "the interests of truth and justice," Mary McGregor had forwarded a note which she had reportedly received from Douglas' wife. The key passages in Jane Douglas's note constituted a denial of the rumours involving her husband, but they were no less sensational for all that, particularly with their reference to "things done *sufficient* to cause remarks by those who did not understand English people."[48]

In the wake of this troubling correspondence, the FMC wrote to Campbell, McGregor, and Rodger for further information about the allegations involving Fairweather and Douglas. All three denied any knowledge of immoral behaviour by their colleagues, but all spoke of disturbing rumours reported by mission workers, or of imprudent conduct likely to fuel such rumours.[49] The FMC also heard from ordained workers at other Presbyterian missions in India.[50] Writing from Bombay, two Scottish missionaries declared that the rumours were unfounded and that Campbell, Rodger, and McGregor had ill-served the mission by circulating them.[51] The Reverend J. S. Beaumont of Poona, senior missionary of the Free Church of Scotland in India, attempted to put the mission's problems in historical perspective. The Indore difficulties were not unusual, he maintained. Rather, jealousies and troubles were the norm in a new mission. "As a matter of fact patent to all," he continued, "Miss Rodger and Miss McGregor are very jealous of Miss Fairweather, and Miss

Fairweather, I am sorry to say, is far indeed from the meekest of women." Another source of difficulty was the converts themselves: "To play off one missionary . . . against another is not a game begun . . . in your Canadian mission."[52] Like his colleagues in Bombay, Beaumont depicted Douglas as the unjustly maligned founder of a promising mission. It was a picture that contrasted sharply with that painted by Campbell, McGregor, and Rodger, who portrayed him as a high-handed and arbitrary director, interfering with their work and salaries on the one hand and demonstrating favouritism towards Fairweather on the other.[53]

Faced with bizarre and conflicting information from sources thousands of miles away, the FMC decided in October 1879 that some action was necessary even if no firm conclusions could be reached: Douglas was to remain in the field, though he was to be replaced as mission treasurer by a newly appointed missionary from Canada, the Reverend John Wilkie.[54] As for Marion Fairweather, though the FMC had not previously contacted her in connection with the case, it now instructed her to return to Canada at once. At the end of December, just six years after her arrival in India, Fairweather wrote from the mission station at Poona to say that she would comply with the instructions as soon as she could safely travel.[55]

Fairweather's Removal

Fairweather's prompt note of compliance left the FMC unprepared for the vigorous campaign which she subsequently mounted to salvage her name and position. In the months before leaving India she forwarded to the FMC a formal statement describing the complex circumstances that had led to the rumours about her and Douglas. She stressed particularly the absence of adequate housing in Indore, a situation which had made it necessary for her and Rodger to share quarters with Douglas, and her role as his mentor during a period in which he had lacked both language skills and a knowledge of mission routines. She and Douglas had worked as a team, especially on the mission press, and they were, therefore, necessarily, in frequent contact. These circumstances, she maintained, had given rise to gossip with the Indian community, made Jane Douglas and her sister missionaries jealous of her role, and Campbell resentful of what he called her "influence." Now, by recalling her, and her alone, the FMC was contributing, however unintentionally, to the destruction of her reputation, and its use of the word "furlough" did not alter that fact.[56]

Fairweather's letters were well written and well argued, and in the early months of 1880 they were supported by strong testimonials from both ordained and lay Europeans working in India. The correspondents paid uniform tribute to her ability and missionary zeal. One spoke of her as "the mainstay, the righthand [sic] of Mr. Douglas" and, like Beaumont, suggested that she had been a victim of jealousy.[57] Another, a former Church of England chaplain in Indore, wrote: "I never met a person who impressed me more as a vigorous worker and competent administrator than yourself." Unfortunately for her cause, the chaplain's subsequent comments may well have fuelled doubts in the FMC's mind about Fairweather's discretion, for he went on to observe that her efforts to proselytize Indian gentlemen, however commendable, were scarcely orthodox for a "lady missionary."[58]

The testimonials were probably of limited value in any case, for the FMC had evidently made up its mind that Marion Fairweather's removal was necessary for the good of the cause. Convenor McLaren clearly expected that Fairweather would accept her recall quietly and was therefore dismayed when on her return to Canada she endeavoured to enlist supporters and persisted in efforts to salvage her position.[59] Following a meeting with her in June 1880, held at her request, the FMC formally decided that her employment as a missionary would officially end in October.[60]

Even after this meeting, however, Fairweather did not obligingly fade into obscurity. From her home in Bowmanville, she sent the FMC a spirited critique of the way it had handled her case and insisted that it acknowledge the double standard it had applied.[61] She dismissed the FMC's claim that it disbelieved the scandal and had recalled her from India only to end friction within the mission. If that were so, she wrote, then only an official statement "so clearly and precisely worded as to be tantamount to a censure on both the originators and disseminators of the scandal" would be sufficient to remove the impression created by her recall. The

FMC's contention that if it had believed the rumours it would not have removed her alone, was not convincing, she continued, since to have removed her alleged partner in the scandal would have involved the church in a costly and embarrassing investigation, a course it obviously wanted to avoid.[62] The existing state of affairs was particularly unfair to a woman, she pointed out: "You will pardon my reminding you that it is by no means necessary that the guilt of *both the parties . . . be believed* to seriously injure if not ruin a woman's character." Referring to the Committee's complaint that she had spread knowledge of the affair throughout other India missions and in Canada, she pointed out that such news spread all too quickly on its own and then asked rhetorically what else she could have done: "You surely could not expect me to sit calmly by and submit without a struggle to being robbed of that which among the things of time is a woman's *all in all. . . .* Fatherless and brotherless, to whom was I to turn. . . . Where else could I turn but to friends in other missions[?]" She concluded by appealing to the FMC to return her to Central India or else give her the kind of strong recommendation that would enable her to obtain a similar position on another foreign mission staff.

The theatrical language in Fairweather's letter reflected her intense frustration at the injustice of her situation. She had not been formally accused of any wrongdoing; yet she had implicitly been found guilty. If the evidence before FMC members had led them to believe her guilty of sexual misconduct, they were logically compelled to believe the same of James Douglas; yet only she had been recalled. Even if they had reached no such conclusion but rather had acted on strictly pragmatic grounds. She correctly recognized that she had been sacrificed in a hard-headed calculation that the end justified the means.

McLaren and other members of the FMC may have had some misgivings about the way they had handled Fairweather's case, especially in view of the issues raised in her August letter,[63] yet there is nothing to suggest that they reconsidered returning her to Central India or helping her to find a new position. Any thought of such a course of action would have been discouraged by the letters they had begun to receive in early 1880 from their newest missionary in India, John Wilkie. Though he had evidently never met Marion Fairweather, having arrived in Indore after her departure, the young Knox College graduate soon undertook a campaign to discredit all aspects of her missionary career.[64] Acknowledging that his chief sources of information were Mrs. Douglas, Margaret Rodger, and Mary McGregor, Wilkie wrote at various times to say that Fairweather had never acquired a proper use of native languages, had exaggerated her missionary accomplishments, and was extravagant in her use of mission funds.[65] She had undoubtedly been ambitious and clever, he conceded, but she had lacked "staying power" and was "*too clever* for a mission agent."[66] Though he was careful not to accuse her directly of sexual immorality, he insisted that Fairweather's indiscreet behaviour towards Douglas and his wife, and her practice of receiving Indian gentlemen, had made her the deserving target of gossip, and he more than once alluded to other, discreditable rumours, as yet unknown to the Committee.[67] The hostility of British government officials towards the mission, continuing friction among mission staff members, and Douglas's weaknesses as a missionary adminis-trator were also, he maintained, largely a result of her lingering, baneful influence.[68]

Wilkie's attacks on Fairweather, however intemperate, were consistent with his opposition to "lady workers" who could not be "kept in their place"[69] and clearly designed to prevent her return.[70] They were also part of a complex strategy to engineer Douglas's recall and establish his own authority at Indore.[71] It was to become a familiar pattern: before his own controversial recall in 1902 Wilkie would quarrel with virtually all of his ordained colleagues and write a seemingly endless stream of letters to the FMC, describing their shortcomings.[72] Unlike Fairweather, however, the male missionaries would be aware of the paper wars being waged against them, and as ordained workers they could, if necessary, take action to protect themselves through the courts of the church.

Given Wilkie's campaign to discredit her and the FMC's anxiety to safeguard its overseas ventures, Fairweather could look for no further opportunities in her church's missionary institutions. A letter to McLaren in the autumn of 1880 vaguely hinting at legal action was probably no more than a dramatic final gesture, for in the absence of family and financial resources, she had no real chance of seeking legal redress.[73] A single line in *The Presbyterian Record* in 1881 announced her "retirement."[74] After that, the church virtually ceased to mention its once prominent missionary.[75]

In the years that followed, however, Fairweather was able to demonstrate that she was by no means a passive victim of hostile colleagues and arbitrary ecclesiastical officials. With characteristic energy and determination she undertook a course of action that would facilitate her return to India. Between 1880 and 1884 she contributed three series of articles on India to a privately owned journal, *The Canada Presbyterian*.[76] Collectively, the articles served as the literary testament of a woman who had been broadened and enriched by her missionary experience, exposed to the aspirations of educated Indians and led to a new and more enlightened view of the missionary task in India. At a more fundamental level, they perhaps helped to refurbish her tarnished image and provided a small source of income to aid in financing the medical studies she had decided to undertake.

Fairweather had begun training as a nurse in the autumn of 1880 at Charity Hospital, New York. After obtaining a diploma there, she had moved to the Woman's Medical College, Chicago, and begun studying to become a doctor, working as a nurse between sessions to pay her way. Following her graduation in 1885, Dr. Fairweather practised briefly in Chicago to obtain money for medical supplies before sailing for India at the end of 1886. With the help of ordained Scottish and Indian missionaries, she had obtained a position as superintendent of the Native Woman's Medical College and the General Hospital for Women at Agra.[77] Her previous difficulties, she now concluded, had been part of God's plan for her life. His finger had led her through "the crimson of anguish" to the path of a new form of service.[78]

An Unconventional Woman

Marion Fairweather's assertive nature and the initial absence of male missionaries allowed her to play a leading role in establishing the Canadian Presbyterian mission in Central India. Even after the arrival of ordained

Canadian workers, however, she rejected the conventional role of "lady missionary." In doing so, and particularly in attempting to work as a close and equal colleague of a married male missionary, she created jealousy and offended the sensibilities of her Indian and Canadian fellow workers. The evidence does not support any supposition of sexual wrongdoing in her choice of this course of action, but it does suggest that she was guilty of imprudence and naivety. The combination proved fatal to her missionary career.

How representative was Fairweather's experience in the foreign missionary movement? Clearly, Marion Fairweather was a rather exceptional figure even within a movement that attracted unconventional women, and the particular set of circumstances that led to her recall was probably unique. Yet the foreign missionary careers of other women who served the church in the years before the First World War suggest that, in a broad sense, her experience was part of an ongoing pattern within a movement that both encouraged and circumscribed the ambitions of Victorian women.

By 1914 the Presbyterian Church in Canada had sent more than one hundred single women to overseas mission fields.[79] There they had opportunities to run schools, orphanages, and hospitals, and to engage in various forms of direct evangelism. In the Indian context, such work could take them, quite literally, from the palace of a maharajah to the homes of the poor and untouchable. Both as part of their service and on furloughs, they had opportunities to travel that were not otherwise available to women of the backgrounds from which most of them came. In addition, many of the medical missionaries and some of those who had prepared for other forms of service had some or all of their training financed by the church. Overseas missionaries could have all of this, and at the same time bask in the admiration of missions enthusiasts at home, for they had become participants in an enterprise invested with romance and glory. But if, in the course of their service, the women undertook initiatives or behaved in ways that constituted too great a challenge to prevailing views of the sexes' proper roles, they risked being perceived as unbiblical and unwomanly -- and even as "ecclesiastical Amazons." They risked being factionalized by the rivalries of their ordained male colleagues and, ultimately, they risked being rebuked or recalled by mission authorities in Canada.

Few women in the church's overseas missions in fact shared with Marion Fairweather the humiliation of being recalled.[80] Disputes involving women's place in the mission did not disappear after 1880; indeed, those touching on questions of mission government and administration often dominated mission politics. But as the FMC gained experience in supervising overseas fields, it generally showed a greater readiness to let missionaries sort out their own differences and was correspondingly less inclined to act precipitately than it had been in Fairweather's case. Moreover, with the formulation of written regulations defining the responsibilities of male and female workers there was less room for ambiguity and experiment in regard to women's roles.[81] At various times before 1897 these regulations were updated to defuse discontent and give women a greater voice in mission politics.[82] Finally, and perhaps most important, as the FMC adopted procedures for weeding out applicants who might prove "troublesome" or "unsound," and especially as it involved the Woman's Foreign Missionary Society in the details of this process,[83] it became increasingly less likely that a woman of Marion Fairweather's expansive views and ambitions would be sent to a mission field. In these circumstances, the overseas service of the church's women missionaries was more apt to be terminated by old age, ill health or personal choice than by the arbitrary decision of a church committee whose commitment to a double standard was no less evident for being denied.

Notes

An earlier version of this paper was presented to the 63rd Annual Meeting of the Canadian Historical Association, Guelph, Ontario, June 1984.

1.   See, for example, several articles in B. F. Austin, ed., *Woman: Her Character, Culture and Calling* (Brantford: The Book and Bible House, 1890).

2.   James A. Macdonald [J.A.M.], "A Trained Nurse for Honan," *The Knox College Monthly and Presbyterian Magazine*, 7 (July-August, 1888), 179.

3.   United Church of Canada Archives [hereafter UCA], Presbyterian
      Church in Canada, Foreign Missions Committee, Western Section,
      Central India Mission, General Correspondence [hereafter Corres-
      pondence], Box 5, File 58, W. A. Wilson to R. P. MacKay, 25 March
      1897. The phrase had been used by a Scottish missionary and was
      approvingly quoted by Wilson.

4.   See Janet Wilson James' Introduction to the special "Woman and
      Religion" edition of *American Quarterly*, 30 (Winter 1978), 581. This
      theme has been an important one in the impressive body of literature
      on the history of women and religion which has appeared in the
      United States since the late 1960s. Influential works include Nancy F.
      Cott, *The Bonds of Womanhood: "Woman's Sphere" in New England,
      1780-1835* (New Haven: Yale University Press, 1977); Ann Douglas,
      The Feminization of American Culture (New York: Knopf, 1977);
      Amanda Porterfield, *Feminine Spirituality in America: From Sarah
      Edwards to Martha Graham* (Philadelphia: Temple University Press,
      1980); Barbara Welter, "The Feminization of American Religion, 1800-
      1860," in Mary S. Hartman and Lois Banner, eds., *Clio's Consciousness
      Raised: New Perspectives on the History of Women* (New York: Harper
      and Row, 1974). Recent writings which illustrate the theme while
      focussing on denominational patterns in women's religious involvement
      include Lois A. Boyd and R. Douglas Brackenridge, *Presbyterian
      Women in America: Two Centuries of a Quest for Status* (Westport:
      Greenwood Press, 1983); and Hilah F. Thomas and Rosemary Skinner
      Keller, eds., *Women in New Worlds: Historical Perspectives on the
      Wesleyan Tradition* (Nashville: Abingdon, 1981). All of the above touch
      at some point on women's involvement in the missionary movement,
      but book-length monographs on the subject are both recent and rare;
      see Jane Hunter, *The Gospel of Gentility: American Women Mission-
      aries in Turn-of-the-Century China* (New Haven: Yale University
      Press, 1984); and Patricia R. Hill, *The World Their Household: The
      American Woman's Foreign Mission Movement and Cultural Transfor-
      mation, 1870-1920* (Ann Arbor: University of Michigan Press, 1985).
      The most comprehensive overview of the subject remains R. Pierce

Beaver's *American Protestant Women in World Mission: A History of the First Feminist Movement* (Grand Rapids: William B. Eerdmans, 1980; orig. ed. 1968, but see also Barbara Welter's widely cited article "She Hath Done What She Could: Protestant Women's Missionary Careers in Nineteenth Century America," *American Quarterly*, 30 (Winter 1978), 624-38. In English Canada, the history of women's role in religion is till largely unwritten. Two articles that deal with women's home-base involvement in missions are Christopher Headon, "Women and Organized Religion in Mid and Late Nineteenth Century Canada," *Journal of the Canadian Church Historical Society*, 20 (March-June 1978), 3-18; and Wendy Mitchinson, "Canadian Women and Church Missionary Societies in the Nineteenth Century: A Step Towards Independence," *Atlantis*, 2:2 (Spring 1977), 57-75.

5.   John S. Moir, *Enduring Witness: A History of the Presbyterian Church in Canada* (Toronto: Presbyterian Publications, n.d. [1974]), 145 and chapter 8; *Enkindled by the Word: Essays on Presbyterianism in Canada* (Toronto: Centennial Committee of the Presbyterian Church in Canada, 1966), especially "Our Overseas Adventures."

6.   In 1880, 57 per cent of the personnel of six major American mission boards were women; figure cited in Beaver, 111.

7.   UCA, Presbyterian Church in Canada, Minutes of the Foreign Mission Committee, Western Section [hereafter Minutes], 1:5 March 1872, 128, and 3 July 1872, 132. The Canada Presbyterian Church was by far the largest of the four bodies that united in 1875 to form the Presbyterian Church in Canada.

8.   Minutes, 1:15 July 1873, 153-4.

9.   Minutes, 1:1 October 1873, 156.

10. Correspondence, Box 1, File 5, Marion Fairweather to Rev. Thomas Lowry, 26 December 1873.

11. There are no formal statements of motivation available for Fairweather and Rodger, as there are for many of the church's later missionary candidates. This sentence is based on their later correspondence and behaviour and on other, more general evidence of missionary motivation.

12. UCA, United Church of Canada, *One Hundred Years of Erskine Church Montreal* (n.p., 1933), 31.

13. Biographical data on Fairweather and Rodger come from a variety of sources: Canada Census; McGill University Archives, Record Group 30; *The Presbyterian Record*, 20 (April 1895), 94. Helpful information on Margaret Rodger's background was provided by the Reverend Howard Doig and by Miss Elizabeth Black and Miss Jean McOuat.

14. Rodger was evidently a very reluctant correspondent; see Correspondence, Box 1, File 7, Rev. Thomas Lowry to Rodger, 1 July 1875. At that point Lowry had received no letters from Rodger in India, and only one written prior to her departure. In 1887 her colleague Dr. Marion Oliver would praise Rodger's labours as an example of "work without words;" see Correspondence, Box 2, File 29, letter from Dr. Oliver, 14 March 1887.

15. Correspondence, Box 1, File 5, Fairweather to "Lowrie" [*sic*], 13 September 1873.

16. Correspondence, Box 1, File 5, Lowry to "My dear Friends," 13 December 1873.

17. Correspondence, Box 1, File 6, Fairweather to Lowry, 20 March 1874; see also Rev. A. Broadhead to Lowry, 18 March 1874, and Rev. Joseph Warren to Lowry, 24 March 1874, for the American missionaries' advice about Indore.

18. For example, Correspondence, Box 1, File 8, Fairweather to Lowry, 7 August 1876.

19. Correspondence, Box 1, File 6 Fairweather to McLaren, 5 November 1874.

20. Correspondence, Box 1, File 7, Fairweather to McLaren, 16 August 1875. American Presbyterians were active to the north and northeast, in the Punjab and the United Provinces, while Scottish missionaries were a strong presence in Rajputana and the Bombay Presidency. Irish Presbyterians were also at work in the latter region.

21. See, for example, Correspondence, Box 1, File 6, Rev. John Morton to Lowry, 31 October 1874; File 5, Lowry to Rev. J. Fraser Campbell, 12 April 1875, and Campbell to Lowry, 21 April 1875. Morton had started

a mission in Trinidad in 1868 and regarded the proposal to begin work in distant India as an impractical and "romantic" one. Campbell was being pressed by the FMC to undertake the task of mission founder, but some Committee members wanted him to go out as a married missionary and he was not prepared to oblige.

22. Correspondence, Box 1, File 8, Fairweather to Lowry, 7 August 1876. Unlike missionary wives, single women workers were regarded as full-fledged missionaries. Nevertheless, the church took the position that only an ordained missionary could establish a new mission.

23. The Woman's Foreign Missionary Society was organized in Toronto in 1876 as an auxiliary to the FMC, Western Division, with Convenor McLaren's wife as its first president. A similar society was begun in Halifax in the same year. See *The Story of Our Missions* (Toronto: The Women's Missionary Society of the Presbyterian Church in Canada, 1915).

24. Correspondence, Box 1, File 8, Fairweather to Lowry, 7 August 1876. It was common practice for missionaries who ran orphanages to arrange marriages for girls in their care.

25. Correspondence, Box 1, File 8, Fairweather to McLaren, 12 August 1876.

26. Fairweather to WFMS Secretary, as printed in *Record*, 2 (June 1877), 155-6. Fairweather's relative lack of enthusiasm for zenana visiting reflected her impatience with its slow pace and the need to use needlework as a "decoy"; see Fairweather to WFMS Secretary, as printed in *The Canada Presbyterian*, 1 (26 July 1878), 611-2.

27. Correspondence, Box 1, File 8, Fairweather to McLaren, 12 August 1876.

28. Correspondence, Box 1, File 6, Fairweather to McLaren, 5 November 1984.

29. Correspondence, Box 1, File 8, Fairweather to Lowry, 7 August 1876, and Fairweather to McLaren, 12 August 1876; Fairweather to WFMS Secretary, as printed in *Record*, 2 (January 1877), 15-6.

30. See, for example, Stephen Neill, *A History of Christian Missions* (Hammondsworth: Penguin Books, 1964), 254-5; L. S. S. O'Malley, ed.,

Modern India and the West (London: Oxford University Press, 1941), 325-6; Julius Richter, *A History of Missions in India* (Edinburgh and London: Oliphant, Anderson & Ferrier, 1908), chapter 3, especially 230.

31. Correspondence, Box 1, File 9, Fairweather to McLaren, 14 May 1877; see also File 8, Fairweather to Lowry, 7 August 1876 for more such advice.

32. For example, Correspondence, Box 1, File 6, Fairweather to McLaren, 5 November 1874.

33. Correspondence, Box 1, File 6, Warren to Lowry, 24 March 1874; File 7, Broadhead to Lowry, 23 January 1875; File 8, J. C. Lowrie to Lowry, 1 July 1876.

34. *Acts and Proceedings of the Fourth General Assembly of the Presbyterian Church in Canada* [hereafter *A and P*, with year], 1878, Report of the Foreign Missions Committee, Western Section 1877-8, Appendix lxxiv-lxxvii.

35. Correspondence, Box 1, File 11, Campbell to McLaren, 5 February 1879.

36. The letters in which Fairweather described her work for WFMS auxiliaries and other church groups were passed on for publication in Presbyterian periodicals, where they generally outnumbered those from her sister missionaries.

37. *A and P*, 1877, Appendix, lxix-lxx, and 1878, lxxv; Fairweather to Mrs. Harvie, as printed in *Record*, 2 (October 1877), 269-70, and 3 (April 1878), 103-4; also Fairweather to Mrs. Harvie, as printed in *Presbyterian*, 1 (26 July 1878), 611-2.

38. Fairweather to Hamilton WFMS, as printed in *Record*, 3 (June 1878).

39. Fairweather to Secretary, Juvenile Mission Scheme, as printed in *Record*, 4 (June 1879), 155-6; also, letter of James Douglas, as printed in *Presbyterian*, 2 (8 November 1878), *Presbyterian*, 2 (16 May 1879), 452.

40. The woman missionary's particular province was seen to be work among women and children (though efforts to convert male servants seem also to have been acceptable). When the Western Division WFMS

was formed in Canada in 1876, it described its mandate in terms of the promotion of such work; see UCA, Woman's Foreign Missionary Society of the Presbyterian Church in Canada, *First Annual Report*, 1877, 7.

41. For the perceived importance of winning the support of the elite, see, for example, Correspondence, Box 1, File 8, Fairweather to Lowry, 7 August 1876, and letter of James Douglas as printed in *Presbyterian*, 2 (8 November 1878), 21.

42. Correspondence, Box 1, File 9, Fairweather to McLaren, 14 May 1877; Fairweather to WFMS Secretary, as printed in *Presbyterian*, 3 (5 March 1880), 277-8.

43. For example, Fairweather to WFMS Secretary, as printed in *Presbyterian*, 1 (8 November 1878), 21; also, letter of Fairweather's as printed in *Record*, 4 (October 1879), 271.

44. As printed in *Presbyterian*, 1 (9 August 1878), 644-5. The question of how initiatives such as this one -- and indeed the very presence of single women missionaries -- were regarded in host societies is a complex one. In 1907, Arthur Judson Brown, an eminent and much travelled missionary bureaucrat, downplayed the charge that "[s]ingle women missionaries often create scandal by ignoring native ideas as to propriety." Focussing chiefly on China, he first belittled the claim that they created offence by travelling alone, or residing or travelling with single males, but later in the same work he wrote: "In many lands, a single man is often misunderstood; a single woman is nearly always misunderstood." See his *The Foreign Missionary: An Incarnation of a World Movement* (New York: Fleming H. Revell, 1907), chapters 16, 342-3, and 17, 366. Indian missions historian Julius Richter maintained that Hindus easily became reconciled to the sight of women missionaries travelling alone and that the latter were perfectly safe in doing so, since Hindus were generally so "harmless." See Richter, *Missions*, 345.

45. See letter of 23 September 1879, as printed in *Record*, 5 (February 1880), 47-8, and undated letter in *Presbyterian*, 3 (5 March 1880), 277-8.

46. Correspondence, Box 1, File 9, Douglas to McLaren, 26 October 1877.
47. Correspondence, Box 1, File 12, Madhi Hoosein [sp.?] to McLaren, 4 May 1879; Minutes, 2, 17 June 1879, 93-4.
48. Correspondence, Box 1, File 12, McGregor to McLaren, 12 June 1879, enclosing Mrs. J. Douglas to McGregor, undated. In the final paragraph of her note Mrs. Douglas had asked Mary McGregor to destroy it and "think no more about it." A year later she wrote to McLaren to deny that she had ever written letters accusing Fairweather of improper behaviour with her husband and to affirm that she stood beside him despite all the gossip; see Correspondence, Box 1, File 15, letter of 6 March 1880.
49. Correspondence, Box 1, File 13, Campbell to McLaren, 7 August 1879; McGregor to McLaren, 12 August 1879; Rodger to McLaren, 20 August 1879; Campbell to McLaren, 21 August 1879. Rodger's letter was guarded and obscure: "Regarding the truth of the Munshi's [Catechist's] complaint," she wrote, "I know nothing, except in one or two instances, which came under my observation." McGregor was also somewhat obscure. Fairweather's greatest fault, she seemed to suggest, was in criticizing Mrs. Douglas, while James Douglas himself "never manifested any firmness in resisting Miss Fairweather's encroachments or checking her ill-advised remarks concerning his wife or any missionary in the field." She went on to speak of the relations between Fairweather and James Douglas as "no more than imprudence but yet calculated to injure the cause in the eyes of native people." The strongest indication that there might be some basis for the rumours came in Campbell's August 21 letter: when the Indian catechist, in the presence of Douglas and Campbell, alleged that improper behaviour had taken place between Fairweather and Douglas, the latter "positively denied all the more serious [statements]. . . . he also spoke of avoiding for the future what, while done in the simplicity of his heart, without thought of harm might be misinterpreted." Campbell went on to report that under his cross-examination, Douglas had confessed to behaviour that was astonishingly imprudent for a missionary living in a foreign culture:

working until late in the evening in the same building that contained Fairweather's bedroom, for example, and having sleeping arrangements on an evangelistic outing that were open to misinterpretation by the Indian workers accompanying them. Yet Campbell had ended his August 7 letter by reporting that two Scottish missionaries investigating the case had concluded that "Mr. Douglas came out without a stain on his character" and that he "concurred in that expression." Clearly, Committee members had reason to be confused by the correspondence they received on the subject.

50. Minutes, 2, 21 October 1879, 100-1, 105.
51. Correspondence, Box 1, File 13, D. McPherson and R. Jeffrey to McLaren, 12 September 1879.
52. Correspondence, Box 1, File 13, Beaumont to Douglas, 6 August 1879, co-signed by John D. Morrison, Chaplain, Church of Scotland, Mhow, and -- [illeg.], and forwarded to the FMC; see also Beaumont to McLaren, 14 August 1879. Beaumont and Morrison were the two missionaries who had joined Campbell in investigating the case.
53. Correspondence, Box 1, File 11, Campbell to McLaren, 5 February 1879; File 12, Rodger to McLaren, 25 June 1879; File 13, McGregor to McLaren, 12 August 1879, and Campbell to McLaren, 28 August 1879.
54. Minutes, 2, 23 October 1879, 106-8.
55. Minutes, 2, 23 October 1879, 106-8, and Correspondence, Box, Box 1, File 14, Fairweather to McLaren, 31 December 1879; see also File 15, Fairweather to McLaren, 20 February 1880.
56. Correspondence, Box 1, File 15, Fairweather to McLaren, March 1880.
57. Correspondence, Box 1, File 15, James Larey [sp.?] to Fairweather, 9 January 1880; see also Rev. John Morrison to Fairweather, 6 January 1880, Rev. J. S. Beaumont to Fairweather, 4 March 1880, and Rev. A. L. Mitchell to Fairweather, 30 January 1880.
58. "I should have been proud if a sister of mine had had your zeal and ambition," he wrote, "but I should not have let her try to convert native gentlemen." Correspondence, Box 1, File 15, Rev. Oscar D. Watkins to Fairweather, 22 February 1880.
59. Correspondence, Box 1, File 16, McLaren to Lowry, 27 May 1880.

60. Correspondence, Box 1, File 16, Fairweather to McLaren, 29 May 1880; Minutes, 2, 9 June 1880, 119, and 10 June 1880, 122.

61. Correspondence, Box 1, File 17, Fairweather to McLaren, 14 August 1880.

62. Fairweather's use of the term *fama* demonstrated her familiarity with the church's formal provisions for investigating a minister charged in a scandal. These were set out in Presbyterian Church in Canada, *The Constitution and Proceeding of the Presbyterian Church in Canada* (Toronto: Hart and Rawlinson, 1879). Provision number 248 (page 48) stated that no rumour was to be considered for investigation unless it "specifies some particular sin or sins, is widely spread, generally believed and has strong presumption of truth."

63. Correspondence, Box 1, File 18, Fairweather to McLaren, 27 October 1880.

64. See, especially, Wilkie's letters to McLaren in Correspondence, Box 1, File 15-20. His criticisms of Fairweather were most frequent in 1880, but as late as 1885 he was still maintaining that the internal problems in Central India were partly a result of her influence; see Correspondence, Box 2, File 26, Wilkie to Wardrope, 24 August 1885.

65. See, for example, Correspondence, Box 1, File 16, Wilkie to McLaren, private, 27 May 1880, and Box 2, File 19 Wilkie to McLaren, 15 January 1881.

66. Correspondence, Box 1, File 16, Wilkie to McLaren, 27 May 1880. In depicting Fairweather's cleverness as a liability rather than an asset to the mission, Wilkie claimed to be reporting local views.

67. See, for example, Correspondence, Box 1, File 16, Wilkie to McLaren, private, 3 June 1880.

68. British authorities in Indore had in fact been opposed to the Canadian mission from the outset. See, for example, Correspondence, Box 1, File 10, Douglas to McLaren, 28 August 1878, and Box 2, File 20, Lieut-Col. Thomason to McLaren, 25 September 1881. For Wilkie's references to British hostility see Correspondence, Box 1, File 16, Wilkie to McLaren, private, 3 June 1880. For Fairweather's allegedly negative influence on the mission staff and on Douglas in particular,

see Correspondence, Box 1, File 16, Wilkie to McLaren, private, 16 April 1880, and Box 2, File 19, Wilkie to McLaren, 4 May 1881 and 23 July 1881. Wilkie's opposition to Fairweather may have been influenced to some degree by denominational politics. He was very critical of the Free Church of Scotland missionaries at Bombay and Poona who had championed her cause. See especially Correspondence, Box 1, File 16, Wilkie to McLaren, private, 16 April 1880 and 27 Mary 1880.

69. Correspondence, Box 2, File 20, Wilkie to McLaren, private, 22 November 1881. Ironically, in later years when he had quarrelled with a majority of his ordained colleagues, Wilkie took pains to cultivate the support of the women missionaries and advocated an equal voice for them on the mission's council.

70. Wilkie was very much concerned about this possibility, and on several occasions, in response to rumours, he wrote to the FMC to ask that action be taken to prevent it. See Correspondence, Box 2, File 19, Wilkie to McLaren, 4 May 1881, and File 23, Wilkie to McLaren, 14 May 1883. Though the second letter bore Campbell's name as well as Wilkie's, it was clearly the product of the latter's pen.

71. Correspondence, Box 1, File 16, Wilkie to McLaren, 6 April 1880 and 16 April 1880, and Box 2, File 20, Wilkie to McLaren, private, 23 July 1881. Douglas was recalled in 1882 and subsequently became a missionary in Manitoba, a Member of Parliament and a Senator; see *A and P*, 1883, Appendix, ci, and James Henry Morgan, ed., *The Canadian Men and Women of the Time* (Toronto: William Briggs, 1912), 340.

72. Regarding Wilkie's recall, see *A and P*, 1902, Appendix, 104. For one review of the difficulties between him and his brethren, see Correspondence, Box 5, File 81, "Statement of the Situation in India Before the Foreign Mission Committee," undated, by Rev. Murdoch MacKenzie.

73. Correspondence, Box 1, File 18, Fairweather to McLaren, 27 October 1880.

74. *Record*, 6 (March 1881), 63. See also *A and P*, 1880 Appendix, lxxxiv-v.

75. Subsequent accounts of the church's missions typically passed quickly over the troubled beginnings in Central India and made only brief or indirect reference to Fairweather and Rodger. An exception was William MacLaren [sic], "Central India, *Knox College Monthly*, 14 (September 1891), 262-77. McLaren compared the early staff difficulties in Indore to those which had afflicted the Apostolic Church and in a striking act of clerical revisionism claimed that following the troubles of 1879 "Miss Fairweather *was permitted to return to Canada on furlough* and ultimately *allowed to retire* from the service of the church." (266, italics added).

76. *Presbyterian*, 3 (20 August - 10 December 1880); 9 (17 June - 21 October 1881); and 12 (27 February - 16 April 1884).

77. For an account of these years see "Miss Fairweather, M.D.," *Presbyterian*, 16 (5 January 1887), 21. Though the article did not say so, Fairweather's new medical work was under the auspices of the Countess of Dufferin Fund, a non-missionary agency for providing Indian women with medical services and training. See *Canadian Statesman*, Bowmanville, 16 January 1889, for Fairweather's account of her involvement with this work both before and after her marriage to Dr. Charles Stirling in Agra in 1888.

78. *Presbyterian*, 16 (5 January 1887), 21.

79. See *A and P*, 1914, Appendix, 148-54, for a list of the church's active and retired or deceased foreign missionaries.

80. Ironically, the next woman to be recalled was Mary McGregor, in 1888. See Minutes, 3, 17 May 1888, 182-5.

81. Regulations drafted by the FMC were sent to India in the spring of 1879, about the time that news of the scandal was reaching Canada. See Minutes, 2, 4 April 1879, 81-86.

82. In 1897 women missionaries in India were given a separate but subordinate council after a brief attempt to give them a full voice on a common mission council had aroused strong opposition among most of their male colleagues. See *Minutes*, 10, 29 June 1897, 7-8, 21-4.

83. From 1891 the WFMS was given responsibility for investigating and reporting on the background of missionary applicants, though the

FMC retained final responsibility for all appointments; see UCA, Woman's Foreign Missionary Society, Western Division, Board of Management Minutes, 8, 16 June 1891. The "vetting" of would-be missionaries was a central function of the Ewart Missionary Training Home, founded in 1897; see UCA, "The Ewart Missionary Training Home," undated pamphlet (probably 1907 or 1908), 4.

6

EVANGELICALS, CIVIC MISSION, AND

PRISONERS' AID IN TORONTO, 1874-1896

Ronald G. Sawatsky

In the fall of 1896, the Hon. Samuel Hume Blake, well-known lawyer and former Chancellor of Ontario, addressed the Prisoner's Aid Association in the Metropolitan Church in Toronto with these words:

> Now, take the daily farce going on at our Police Court. The constant sending down of law-breakers to a place which is not infrequently called the Criminal Club, where the culprits are reasonably well fed, well housed, and which is made the rendez-vous where the criminal class is glad to meet and discuss all matters of general interest to their profession.

> How this process of contamination hardens! Take the daily illustration of the first offence. A culprit sentenced to prison, often a mere child, miserable, wretched, in tears, ashamed, sits down, apart by himself. He gets wearied of this, gradually draws near, and soon becomes a companion of others, and thus enters, placed there by the State, a first-class school of vice.[1]

Blake, a Church of England evangelical, was speaking before an interdenominational and evangelical group of friends and associates who had founded the Prisoners' Aid Association (PAA) in 1874. For the members of the PAA the creation of major changes in the penal system in late Victorian Toronto and Ontario was an important goal to be achieved.

Blake and the PAA were committed to addressing the problem of prison reform more directly than had been done by either the governments or the churches of the day. They were determined to be faithful to the biblical injunction "to feed the hungry, clothe the naked, and visit those in prison." For them the fulfillment of this social concern was realized in what they called "civic mission."

The people who participated in the meetings and work of the PAA were, in fact, part of a larger evangelical movement active during the last quarter of the nineteenth and the early part of the twentieth centuries. During this period evangelicals inaugurated a number of theologically conservative enterprises such as Bible and prophecy conferences, denominational and faith missions, Bible schools, a publishing company and a variety of philanthropic, social service ventures for the urban poor of Toronto.[2] In reality, these people were proto-fundamentalists -- forefathers of the conservative, evangelical Protestants who became known as Fundamentalists in the 1920s.[3]

The term "evangelical" as used here refers to the proto-fundamentalist movement as described above. Its religious roots lie deep in the main tradition of orthodox Protestantism of the nineteenth century. Some of the main beliefs springing out of this included the revivalist emphasis on a personal religious conversion and devotional piety, a belief in the finality of the Christian religion and attendant desire to tell the world about it, an affirmation of the uniqueness of Jesus, and an emphasis on the special nature of the Bible as divine revelation. Out of this conservative theology came, amongst other things, a strong, new interest in foreign and home missions as well as the desire to establish various humanitarian organizations which would assist in reclaiming the fallen of their society.

It is particularly important, at the outset, to note that the evangelicals appear to have evinced a strong social conscience throughout the life of their movement. Generally, it has not been known, or perhaps sufficiently acknowledged, that nineteenth century evangelicals made significant contributions in this area. Historians have traditionally separated those who emphasized individual salvation from those who were concerned with the Social Gospel. In retrospect, this separation appears to have been artificial, a direct result of attitudes and opinions generated during the fundamentalist controversy of the 1920s, and scholars have begun to revise this earlier inaccurate assumption. For example, Ferenc Morton Szasz in *The Divided Mind of Protestant America, 1880-1930* devotes a full chapter to a description of the social conscience and activities of the evangelical conservatives during the period 1901-1917.[4]

Two of the major actors in the Canadian evangelical movement were William H. Howland and Samuel H. Blake. It was Howland, mayor of Toronto for two years (1886-1888), who was the first major political figure in Toronto to demonstrate concrete concern for the plight of the urban poor.[5] On the other hand, Blake, a well-known lawyer and tireless labourer for numerous good causes, worked more quietly in the background and made his contribution through other means.[6] The two men, however, worked very closely together in the whole process and in fact drew in many other middle and upper class Torontonians to help.[7]

Toronto in the late nineteenth century was a rapidly growing city. The increasing urbanization of Canada's population was bringing with it the usual problems associated with too rapid urban growth. Before 1880 there was no provision for public utilities such as garbage and sewage disposal. Rampant alcoholism and prostitution were only the overt signs of the hard facts of poverty. Everywhere there were conditions which needed changing -- housing, nutrition, education, abandoned children, battered wives, unemployed men, and crime and prisons, all attracted the attention of the evangelicals.

The evangelicals' main response to the moral challenges of the city was to create social programmes which would assist in helping those adversely affected by this rapid urbanization. The main focus for these programmes was the Toronto Mission Union, an organization that served as both a formal and informal clearing house for most of the evangelicals' activities. Before examining one of the important programmes connected with the Mission Union, the Prisoners' Aid Association and its work with male and female inmates, a brief summary of the broad scope of the Mission Union activities provides some context for our analysis, although the PAA actually predated the Toronto Mission Union by about a decade.[8]

The Toronto Mission Union

For approximately ten years before 1884, Howland, together with Blake and several others, had been in the forefront of efforts to establish a residence for old people, to set up a "Help and Aid Society," and to engage in other charitable activities for the residents of St. John's Ward, the poorest part of Toronto's downtown.[9] In April 1884 Howland proposed a scheme which would bring about the unification of a number of the existing programmes for the urban poor and place them under one management. This new institution was to be known as the Toronto Mission Union and its objective was "to extend the knowledge of the Gospel of our Lord Jesus Christ among the inhabitants of Toronto and its vicinity, and especially among the poor and neglected classes, without reference to denominational distinctions or the peculiarities of Church Government."[10]

From a small beginning in April 1884 the Toronto Mission Union grew quickly to include various components. A report in 1887 indicated that the following agencies were operating under the auspices of the Toronto Mission Union: a corps of district visitors, Home for the Aged, day nursery, savings bank and provident fund, lodging house work, Young Men's Mission Band, clothing sales, Sunday afternoon Bible class, Sunday School teachers' training Bible class, morning Sunday School, children's church, day school and Band of Hope. A Ragged School set up and funded personally by Howland had an attendance of one hundred vagrant children.[11]. In 1886 a newspaper report indicated that an Aged Women's Home had been added recently and that the Sewing Society had given away 350 garments and ten pairs of boots.[12] In addition to all of the above, the Mission Union also maintained several Gospel Halls or Mission Halls in the east and west parts of the city.[13]

There were two places where most of the activities were concentrated -- the area around the Central Mission Hall on the corner of College and Emma streets (Emma was actually renamed Mission Street for a time) and at the Sackville Hall. The Central Hall was the main locus where the general meetings and planning for the Mission's activities occurred. In several adjacent buildings there were a Home for the Aged, a

Day Nursery, a Deaconess House, a Coffee Palace, a Bible Women's Home and the Nursing-at-Home and Free Dispensary House. In 1896, for example, the twelfth annual report of the Toronto Mission Union noted that over four thousand children were being cared for in the day nurseries. This meant that, for a sum of ten cents, the children would be fed, washed and cared for while their mothers were away at their daily work.[14]

The Nursing-at-Home and Dispensary Branch was one of the most important aspects of the work of the Mission Union with the urban poor. At a time when there were no universal medical plans, the services provided were free of charge to those not able to secure a nurse in times of sickness. The trained nurses were all volunteers with a two-month probation and a practical training course of two years. Training lectures were provided by some of the city's doctors.[15] There were usually five nurses on staff plus a female superintendent. All cases brought to their attention were visited, with emergencies getting first priority. Two hundred and sixty-one patients were attended in 1897. The dispensary was open every day between 2:30 and 3:30 and, for those who could afford it, a charge of fifty cents was made for all medicines handed out. Most of the money for the nursing and medicines came from donations and the whole enterprise was able to operate at a break-even level.

The superintendent's report of 1897 dealt with one of the most common questions which was asked about the Mission, "Why not send the sick poor to the hospitals?" The response was fourfold:

1. The Health Office had a rule that a person admitted as a city patient could only be admitted once in a year.
2. Hospitals did not generally admit chronic or advanced malignancy patients.
3. Many calls come from patients too ill to be moved or from situations where a sick parent in the hospital would mean the breakup of a home because of lack of care for the children.
4. The Mission was also committed to the care of consumptives (lung tuberculosis) who could not generally receive care in the hospitals.[16]

The second major locus of effort was the Sackville Street Hall which had its beginning in an attic on Patterson Street in 1885 with a committee which included Rosalind and Jonathan Goforth.[17] In 1887 a new Hall was opened at 205 Sackville Street in order that the evangelization of the east end of the city might receive more impetus. Aside from the usual Bible and Sunday School classes which were conducted at the Hall, there were also a day nursery and a band of hospital visitors who "daily visit the sick and suffering, and endeavour to brighten the weary hour of inmates with comfort, counsel and reading . . . ."[18] In March 1889 a Hospital Home was opened at the rear of the Sackville Mission Hall. The new enterprise was described as follows:

> The home is intended as a temporary resting place for men who are discharged from the hospital as cured, but who have no homes in which the later work of convalescence can be satisfactorily accomplished.[19]

According to the report, the Hospital Home consisted of sitting rooms and a dormitory for thirteen men. The Home also had "all modern conveniences in their proper places" and was under the care of a matron and superintendent "who are mother and father to the temporary occupants who are getting ready for another bout in the tussle of daily life."[20]

The Toronto Mission Union presents an excellent window on the evangelical movement as a whole. Here was a concrete demonstration of how concerned friends came together to bring about joint action against the various social and moral evils of their society. The *Evangelical Churchman*, a Church of England periodical which was virtually the official organ for the social aims of the movement, provided a strong endorsement of Christians as the agents of social reform. It approved of many of the ideas of a Chicago-based, liberal journalist, W. T. Stead, who visited Toronto in 1893 and spoke to large crowds. The *Evangelical Churchman* reported his visit as follows:

The gist of his words was: Organize for concerted attack upon the physical and moral evils of your town or city; make use of "applied Christianity." His speech was a most powerful plea for an imitation of Christ in His going about doing good to *all*, even the lowest and most degraded. And what fruit of the Christian life is comparable to this? Only let it not be forgotten that the source of all strength for such work and the fountain of cleansing for all moral uncleanness is in the divine person of Christ, Son of God and Son of Man.[21]

Almost a year later the same theme was still being reiterated. Christians were duty-bound to raise their voices against social wrongs. "In this nineteenth century, it is treason to Christ to hold back."[22] The editor of the *Evangelical Churchman* was speaking for the evangelicals when he urged Christians to combine their efforts as a "civic church" to combat the moral evils of the community:

The spiritual regeneration of the individual lies at the root of all true reforms; but to effect that, to make possible the preaching of the Gospel and to remove countless unnecessary sources of temptation, some social, municipal, and political reforms should be concurrently attempted by the church. True, the highest attitude of the soul to its Maker is that of worship; yet divine worship is an inspiration for an incentive to human service. If Christ were to come to our city, or town, or village, what would He think of us and our lives? How do we show our belief in Him by helping the least of these, His brethren?[23]

The Prisoners' Aid Association

For these evangelical activists one very practical way of living their faith was to be found in giving aid to prison inmates. It has already been noted that Howland and Blake and some of their friends created the Prisoners' Aid Association in 1874 in order to provide active engagement with this often forgotten segment of society. Both Howland and Blake had conducted Sunday School classes and religious services in the Central Prison for many years. Quite soon, however, both men felt that there was a serious need for major reforms and that the way to ensure support for this was to found an organization which addressed the problem of prison reform more directly.

During its first years the work of the PAA was based upon a single principle:

> that the chief point aimed at in the punishment of the criminal,
> is not, as is too often thought, chiefly or exclusively the
> protection of society or the vindication of the law, but the
> reformation of the criminal and the prevention of crime.[24]

The Prisoners' Aid Association advocated several different means to achieve the reformation of the convicted person and to prevent further crime. First, the Association lobbied to change public opinion in order to apply pressure for positive change in the penal system in Ontario. In a major series of articles which filled most of one issue of *The Evangelical Churchman*, the problem of how to deal with prison reform on a theoretical basis was fully addressed.[25] The group's public programme for prison reform had two main components: prevention and cure.

One article defined prevention as "the diminution of the criminal class" through "the care taken of the children [of] vicious or criminal parents."[26] The author noted that the recently formed Children's Aid movement (1893) was a key factor in this part of the programme. No longer would orphaned, abandoned, or vagrant children be placed in orphanages or other institutions where "the herding together of large numbers" was producing a negative effect. Rather, placing children in good Christian foster homes would, no doubt, yield beneficial effects and lead to orphanages and asylums for dependent children becoming a thing of the past.[27] The Association was attacking the disease at what it felt was the root cause -- the "aim to preserve the sanctity of the home, by insisting upon parents properly looking after their children."

The second main element of the programme of prison reform was the cure. This was contingent on the adoption of five components: the probation system, the cellular system, indeterminate sentences, the employment of prisoners inside and outside of prison, and religious influences. The probation system was based on the principle that first time offenders would be saved from a life of crime if their sentence were suspended and they were forced to report regularly to parole officers whose job it would be to help them find work and give them social and moral support to keep them from getting back into bad company. .

The PAA was deeply troubled by the fact that the prisons themselves were so often the schools of crime. Persons who had committed comparatively small crimes were usually forced to mingle with others convicted of greater crimes and in the process were subjected to the corrupting influence of hardened criminals. As its second recommendation, the Association called for proper classification and segregation of prisoners. No longer should prisoners be kept in large common rooms but they would be locked in individual cells. The Association made it very clear that this "separate system" of having inmates in cells was quite different from the "solitary system" where the individual has no contact with anyone. The cellular system was more expensive to build but more effective in producing reform. The prisoner would receive daily visits from relatives, the chaplain, the jailer or his assistants, or the magistrate. The proposal continued:

> He has work, he has exercise in the open air, he has instruction from his teacher, he has books, and he can earn various privileges by good conduct. It is found that this system facilitates reflection and religious counsel and it promotes reformation . . . . Since the adoption of the separate system in Great Britain in 1877, there had been a large diminution in the volume of crime in the United Kingdom.[28]

The third recommendation in the reform programme dealt with the need for "indeterminate sentences." The Association recommended that all sentences passed on juveniles going to reformatories or industrial schools and for young men going to reformatories have no time limit. Parole and release would be conditional on good behaviour and thorough reformation. Furthermore, sentences for repeating offenders should be progressive or cumulative. The prisoner should know that the penalty would increase in severity as convictions increase in number.

The employment of prisoners was the fourth plank in the PAA reform platform. The Association accepted the notion that it is good for prisoners to do useful work while in prison. The problem, however, was that the work being done, under the auspices of the government, provided unequal competition for any entrepreneur on the outside who was trying to make a living. The Association suggested two adjustments which it thought would preserve the principle of "convict labour." First, the government should adopt a policy that prison labour be used only for providing supplies for the various departments of government so as not to compete with the private sector. Second, since the spouses and families of prisoners are usually placed in financial hardship because of their loss of support, it was recommended that a portion of a prisoner's earnings be applied to the family's support or that some of a prisoner's earnings be set aside as a fund so that he or she would have some financial means upon being released.

The religious influences, the fifth but not the least component, was the area in which the Prisoners' Aid Society was able to do the most work. The Association believed that reformation must also include a religious transformation:

> The soul of the prisoner must be the great stronghold to be attacked and won for the Lord Jesus before any permanent amendment can be looked for. It is the supreme object of religion to seek the salvation of the soul; it does not matter to the servant of Christ whether his work be among the respectable and law-abiding members of a Christian congregation, or among the inmates of gaol or reformatory. The object is the

same: to reach the heart and secure its allegiance to the Divine
Master.[29]

The association in fact gave solid support for a series of religious efforts
in the Toronto prisons. There were Sunday Schools in the Mercer Reformatory, the Central Prison, and the Toronto Jail. There was a Sunday
School mission in the women's reformatory and a Bible woman and an
agent were employed for the prisoner' welfare. At the same time the
Association also maintained a night school for secular education in the
Central Prison.[30] The religious emphasis was certainly in the forefront but
secular education was not neglected.

The Prisoners' Aid Association was deeply concerned that the prison
system was not doing what it should to reform the criminals of their
society. Blake spoke for all the members when he criticized the general
organization of Toronto's and Ontario's prisons: "In the common [as
opposed to cellular] gaols, this Satanic work of inoculating the young with
vice and crime, this work of manufacturing criminals, this work of
discouraging morality and virtue, all this is done under the aegis of law,
with the co-operation of judges, sheriffs, and other legal functionaries,
and with the implied sanction and approval of society at large."[31]

The Prisoners' Aid Association was, however, not only concerned with
the theoretical considerations regarding prison reform. It also advocated a
practical programme particularly for those who were coming out of prison.
The Association would take the inmate who had just been released and
attempt to assist his re-entry into society through the re-establishment of
self-support, through employment, and also through the restoration of
confidence on the part of the rest of society. The Association opened up
workshops where employment was given to just-released convicts until
more permanent employment could be found.

Furthermore, it was thought that the answer to the problem of
vagrancy was to be found in creating industrial schools where young
derelicts could learn useful trades and skills in a reform-oriented environment. By the end of the nineteenth century two industrial schools had
been established in Ontario, both founded by Howland. The Victoria

Industrial School in Mimico near Toronto had its beginning in the 1880s with its main building being completed in 1887. It was on fifty acres of farmland and over the years a large number of other buildings were added, including a gymnasium named Howland Memorial Hall. In 1897 there were 250 boys living there. The other institution was the Alexandra Industrial School for Girls in East Toronto (four miles east of Toronto on Kingston Road). It was under the same management as the Victoria School, but in 1897 had only seventeen girls between the ages of seven and fourteen.[32]

The Prison Gate Mission

While the evangelicals were concerned about male criminals and delinquent boys and girls, they also made a commitment to help female prisoners. Parallel with the PAA the Toronto Prison Gate Mission was organized in January 1878 by the Gaol Committee of the Women's Christian Association and by "other benevolent ladies and gentlemen." The main task of this Mission was "to provide a temporary refuge for discharged female prisoners, with the view of preventing, if possible, their return to the haunts of vice."[33] The temporary refuge was a lodging house called the Haven, located at 186 Berkeley Street in central Toronto. A matron was placed in charge of this plainly furnished residence.

The system that was used to the find the women who were being released was quite simple.

> The Mission undertakes to meet every female, who may be discharged from the Toronto Jail, *at the Gate* . . . . The hour of discharge . . . has been fixed at nine o'clock in the morning; and *all* discharged, are forthwith invited to breakfast at the Haven; where Christian women meet them, and endeavour by loving words, kindly counsel, and all persuasive arguments, . . . to induce them to renounce their evil lives . . . . but the difficulties that surround the mission to this depraved class, can be well understood, for this is no new saying, painful as it is, "that when women are bad they are bad indeed.[34]

The response of the women was apparently gratifying. During the first two years of its existence, the Mission admitted over seven hundred female prisoners. A small number of these were admitted more than once; the Mission workers were always willing to try again. The policy was,

> None refused, no matter how wretched, how sinful, how utterly depraved they may be. No promises extorted -- it is simply "Come with us and we will do thee good.[35]

The evangelical programme of the Prison Gate Mission was quite aggressive. Bible Readings were held by the ladies in the City Jail every Thursday afternoon, in the Mercer Reformatory every Thursday evening, and in the Haven every Thursday afternoon and on Sunday afternoon and evening. In addition, there was regular visitation to the Maternity Hospital, the "Locked Ward" in the General Hospital, and even the houses of ill-fame. The administration reported regularly on its progress in reclaiming women. There were "hard cases" who were reformed and even a few, it was believed, were truly converted. One former street walker was reported to have held one job for the past thirteen months -- a sign of true progress.[36]

Although the Haven apparently did not have a direct administrative tie with the programme of the Toronto Mission Union, there is enough evidence to indicate that the two organizations worked very closely together. Many of the people who supported the Mission Union financially also did the same for the Prison Gate Mission. In March 1883, as was often done in the late nineteenth century, a partial list of subscribers was published. Among those who gave two hundred dollars (a substantial sum in that day) were Blake and Howland.[37]

Like most other projects supported and initiated by the evangelicals, the work of the Haven and Mission grew significantly. In 1883 a new wing was added to the "haven" and at its official opening Blake and several other evangelicals were the speakers.[38] In 1888 another fundraising drive was launched for an enlarged building.[39] In 1893 the Haven inaugurated a letter campaign in which there was a request for funds to assist in erecting a wing to contain forty new beds. The Mission was then in its fifteenth year of operation[40] and it continued to operate until at least the turn of the century.[41]

The Prison Gate Mission and a number of the missions operated in connection with the Toronto Mission Union were important not only because they assisted the poor of the Toronto slums but also because they provided openings for some of the middle and upper class women to participate in practical Christian work. Many of the women who supervised the sewing clubs, taught cooking, read to the convalescents, nursed the sick and counselled the female prisoners were the wives or daughters of the men of the evangelical movement. For example, Howland's daughter was a prominent member of the committee of women (and a few men) who actually operated the Prison Gate Mission and Haven.[42]

Against Capital Punishment

Finally, it is interesting to note that the evangelicals exhibited progressive thinking with regard to the question of capital punishment. The issue was raised only on rare occasions but then it was spoken to clearly. The problem was presented in the form of a question: Is the execution of murderers by the State a justifiable homicide? The *Evangelical Churchman* in reporting on an execution of four men in New York State gave a negative answer. The argument ran along the following lines: Weak states may need executions for protection. For example, in Mosaic Israel the infant State was allowed to protect itself from criminals by killing them. The periodical commented,

> But surely in civilized and Christian lands, after eighteen centuries of Christian teaching, something more Christlike should be done with a criminal than to kill him. Surely it is not necessary for self-preservation that the State should inflict the death penalty; . . . . The very obloquy visited on the executioner is a virtual admission by the State that something more Christian should be attempted with prisoners. The problem is, indeed, a most difficult one, but is worth the serious considera-

tion of all philanthropists -- of all, indeed who wish to see Christ's Kingdom more widely and completely established upon earth before the Lord comes.[43]

Blake struck a somewhat similar note when ending his speech to the PAA in the Metropolitan Church in 1896: "In conclusion, I would solemnly ask that each one here consider what criminals we ourselves are; how much we have been forgiven; and, in this same spirit of love and forgiveness, proceed to do our best for other criminals in our land."[44]

Prison Work as Civic Mission

The fact that evangelicals became interested in the mission to the "criminal elements of Society" probably has as much to do with their Christian, humanitarian concern as the fact that a number of them were lawyers by profession. In any case, it is clear that many evangelicals placed prison reform high on the list of priority changes to be effected in late nineteenth century Ontario society. By the end of the period under examination here, the interest in prison reform had spread beyond their smaller group to the larger society. Indeed, there is little doubt that under the direction of Blake, its long-time president, the continual lobbying of the PAA had to a considerable degree helped mould public opinion, and had motivated the provincial government to create the Ontario Prison Reform Commission in 1890.

The over-riding impression that one receives of the evangelicals was that they were all deeply concerned and active on behalf of the urban poor. Blake, Howland, and others were all equally concerned about social and spiritual reform. It was this concern which was the major reason for their willingness to participate actively in the Toronto Mission Union and the work of the PAA.

The case of the work among prisoners and for prison reform makes it clear that the evangelical movement in Toronto clearly affirmed and supported a strong social ministry. In fact, the evangelicals were in the vanguard of the social reform movements of late nineteenth century Toronto. In light of this it is possible to understand why, for instance,

Howland is still remembered as the first reform mayor of Toronto, the one who made Toronto "good."

At the same time, however, it must be noted that the group also set certain limits in their programme for reform. In 1894, the *Evangelical Churchman* raised the social reform issue again in an editorial. This time the question was whether the church should enter the arena of social politics and take part in the industrial and economic conflicts of the day. The people calling for this approach were those who were saying that the preaching of doctrines (such as Christ and His salvation) was of little use. They wanted something practical and "up to the times." The editor responded to them without equivocation:

> It is not the duty of the Christian minister to preach politics or social science, or to hold forth, as some do, each recurring fad, each new and untried economic theory, as the panaceas and heal-all for the ills of society; but it is his duty and privilege to preach Christ, His atoning death, His abiding fulness, His truth, with all the eternal principles of right thinking and right living. Other foundation can no man lay that that which is laid, which is Christ Jesus.[45]

The pattern is clear. The true Christian is required to work not only at the task of saving society from corruption but also at saving the individual from eternal damnation. While the two tasks move forward in parallel, they are not to be interchanged nor combined so that they lose their individual identification. To do otherwise was to proceed with the secularization of God's church.

> This is the duty of the church, as one has well said, not to reform in order to save, but to save in order to reform. Let Christ be preached . . . . Let the great principles of Christianity be unfolded and applied. Then, if the kingdom of Christ be set up in the hearts of men, it will leaven the whole environment of their work and activities; it will permeate and transform

their social relations and their political ideals; it will heal their wounds and remove their burdens.[46]

For the late Victorian evangelicals the coin of penal reform and all other aspects of "civic mission" had two inseparable faces, the one practical, the other spiritual.

Notes

1. S. H. Blake, "Our Faulty Gaol System: Memorandum of an Address Delivered on Behalf of the Prisoner's Aid Association, in Metropolitan Church, Toronto," pamphlet reprinted from *The Methodist Magazine and Review* (November 1896), 3.

2. This essay deals only with the last category and within that we are focussing particularly on work with the prisoners.

3. This group has received little serious study to date. D. C. Masters, "The Anglican Evangelicals in Toronto, 1870-1900," *Journal of the Canadian Church Historical Society*, 20:3-4 (September-December, 1978), 51-66, is the only published account of part of the movement in that denomination. Other denominations represented in the group included Presbyterians, Baptists, a few Methodists, and even one Quaker. For a more complete treatment of this movement see Ronald G. Sawatsky, "'Looking for That Blessed Hope': The Roots of Fundamentalism in Canada, 1878-1914" (Ph.D. Thesis, University of Toronto, 1986).

4. Ferenc Morton Szasz, *The Divided Mind of Protestant America* (University City, Alabama: University of Alabama Press, 1982); see chapter 5, "The Triumph of Evangelical America, 1901-1917: The Conservatives," 56-67.

5. Desmond Morton has published several accounts of Howland and his political career. The best known is *Mayor Howland, The Citizens' Candidate* (Toronto: A. M. Hakkert, 1973). This book focusses on the two years that Howland was mayor of Toronto and is a good study of municipal politics. Unfortunately Morton does not attempt to assess the role of religion in Howland's life and in his tenure as mayor.

Morton added to his publications on Howland with an article in *The York Pioneer*, "Mayor Howland, The Man Who Made Toronto Good," 75:2 (Fall 1980), 23-30. In this case Morton concentrates on Howland's role as a moral reformer, but again, Howland's religious beliefs are not analyzed for clues to motivations and goals.

6.   Biographical information on Blake is extensive: Henry James Morgan, *The Canadian Men and Women of the Time* (Toronto: William Briggs, 1898), 90-1; Henry James Morgan, *The Canadian Men of the Time* (Toronto: William Briggs, 1912), 111; W. Stewart Wallace, *The Macmillan Dictionary of Canadian Biography*, 3rd ed. (Toronto: Macmillan Company of Canada, 1963), 61-2; G. M. Rose, *Cyclopedia of Canadian Biography* (1886), 72-3; Henry J. Cody, "Samuel Hume Blake," *University of Toronto Monthly*, 15 (1914-15), 15-17.

7.   For the purposes of this essay we will limit our analysis to Howland and Blake. The other Canadian members of this movement were mostly middle to upper class men who represented a cross-section of the top leaders of the religious, legal, financial, political, and business interests of late nineteenth century Toronto. For more on this group see Sawatsky, especially chapter 5.

8.   See Donald G. Wetherell, "To Discipline and Train: Adult Rehabilitation Programmes in Ontario Prisons, 1874-1900," in *Histoire Sociale/Social History*, 12:23, (May 1979), 145-65, for an excellent study of Ontario's prison reform programmes and the PAA's role in them.

9.   See *The Evangelical Churchman* [hereafter *EC*], February 1883, 505.

10.   "The Toronto Mission Union," *EC*, 1 May 1884, 632.

11.   *EC*, 9 June 1887, 49.

12.   "City Missions," *EC*, 17 June 1886, 66.

13.   There were Mission Halls on Herrick, Chestnut, Hayter, and Sackville Streets.

14.   "Toronto Mission Union," *EC*, 14 May 1896, 240.

15.   For details of this see "Nursing-at-Home Mission," *EC*, 11 February 1897, 93.

16.   "Nursing-at-Home Mission," *EC*, 11 February 1897, 93.

17. The Goforths were probably the most famous missionaries of the Canadian Presbyterian church in China after 1888. See Rosalind Goforth, *Goforth of China* (Toronto: McClelland and Stewart, 1935).

18. Toronto Public Library, Baldwin Room, Henry O'Brien Papers, "Scrapbook," 21 March 1889.

19. "Scrapbook," 21 March 1889.

20. "Scrapbook," 21 March 1889.

21. "Mr. Stead on Social Reform," *EC*, 30 November 1893, 567.

22. "The Church As The Agent Of Social Reform," *EC*, 19 April, 1894, 182.

23. *EC*, 19 April 1894, 182.

24. "Prisoners' Aid Reform," *EC*, 24 January 1884, 465.

25. *EC*, 25 February 1897, 115-28. The articles dealt with the present system and prison reform, and presented extensive background material on the Childrens' Aid Society, the Industrial Schools, the Working Boys' Home (formerly the Toronto Newsboys' Lodging), the Prisoners' Aid Association, various aspects of the religious work in the jails, and other more technical treatments of subjects such as indeterminate sentences, the probation system, and the cellular system.

26. "What is Wanted," *EC*, 25 February 1897, 117.

27. See James Pitsula, "The Emergence of Social Work in Toronto," *Journal of Canadian Studies*, 14:1 (Spring 1979), 35-52. Note that this was really the time when the voluntary system of charity, sponsored primarily by private agencies or churches, broke down and was gradually replaced by government-sponsored welfare bureaucracies which used trained social workers.

28. *EC*, 25 February 1897, 118.

29. *EC*, 25 February 1897, 120.

30. See Wetherell, 156-60, for more detail on PAA Sunday Schools and night school.

31. Blake, "Our Faulty Gaol System," 6.

32. *EC*, 25 February 1897, 115-28, a series of articles on prison reform.

33. "Prison Gate Mission," *EC*, 15 August 1878, 219.

34. *EC*, 15 August 1878.
35. "The Haven--Prison Gate Mission," *EC*, 9 December 1880, 488.
36. *EC*, 9 December 1880, 488.
37. *EC*, 15 March 1883, 565.
38. *EC*, 24 May 1883, 28-9. Henry O'Brien was listed as the treasurer for the Mission; this is one indication of a close connection with the Toronto Mission Union of which O'Brien was chairman in 1906. See Morgan (1912), 860.
39. *EC*, 21 June 1888, 73.
40. *EC*, 14 September 1893, 436.
41. The final references to the Prison Gate Mission in the sources are in the *EC*, 5 December 1895 and 9 July 1896. In both cases there is no indication of closing the Mission. Rather, there is every indication that the organization was alive and working well.
42. *EC*, 7 February 1878, 616. Unfortunately the ethos of the time was such that the sources do not give sufficient details of work which was done primarily by women and thus it becomes very difficult to assess their true impact.
43. "Reports of Execution," *EC*, 20 August 1891, 187.
44. Blake, "Our Faulty Gaol System," 7.
45. "The Church and Social Reform," *EC*, 8 November 1894, 530.
46. *EC*, 8 November 1894, 530.

7

DEACONESS AS URBAN MISSIONARY

AND IDEAL WOMAN: CHURCH OF ENGLAND

INITIATIVES IN TORONTO, 1890-1895

Alison Kemper

In October 1893, the Church of England Deaconess and Missionary Training Home opened its doors in Toronto to accommodate women desiring to serve their God in domestic and foreign missions. Toronto's prominent evangelical Churchmen and women thereby signalled their commitment to the task of training women for church work. By studying the founding of the Training Home one can discover much about the process of evangelical Church of England innovation in missions. One can see as well the outline of the ideal woman that Toronto evangelicals hoped to commission to relieve the suffering of the urban poor and the distant heathen. This study will explore the founding of the home both as a case study of innovation in missions, and as the expression of a particular model of womanhood.

Since the 1830s, when Theodor Fliedner founded the first deaconess institution in Kaiserwerth, now in West Germany, Protestants throughout Europe and North America had experimented with the notion of women's ministry.[1] The model Fliedner pioneered in Kaiserwerth was of a lifelong home for a company of nurses who staffed a hospital under the control of a clergyman. Protestants who subsequently organized groups of women into bands of pious relievers of misery believed that deaconesses had clear New Testament precedents (*e.g.*, Phoebe) and generally felt safely distinct from Roman Catholics. Deaconesses often may have resembled active orders of nuns in their sombre dress and lifelong commitment, but their advocates in

the Church of England, Lutheran, Methodist, and Reformed traditions
regarded them not as an imitation of, but as a response to, Roman
Catholic forms of women's ministry.

The deaconess movement in the Protestant Episcopal Church of the
United States began in 1855 when the Bishop of Maryland created an
association of teaching and nursing deaconesses. Other foundations
followed in the 1860s and 1870s. In the Church of England, the movement
began when William Pennefather started the Missionary Training College
for Women (later known as Mildmay House) in 1860. Although Pennefather
was a Church of England priest, he did not seek any episcopal oversight in
the training of these women, nor did he see any need to present them to
a bishop for ordination in order to term them "deaconesses." In 1862, the
Bishop of London, Archibald Campbell Tait, set apart Elizabeth Ferard as
deaconess, but the bishops as a whole declined to impose canons or other
controls over the designation of deaconesses, thereby permitting a
decentralized pattern of education, ordination, and deployment to emerge.
After more than twenty years of discussion, the General Convention of the
Episcopal Church in the United States eventually passed a canon in 1889
authorizing the appointment of deaconesses. Bishops and clergy saw this as
the cue to accelerate the movement. In 1890, with his bishop's approval,
William R. Huntingdon, a parish priest, established the first American
deaconess training institution in New York which combined theology and
social work. The diocese of Pennsylvania established in Philadelphia a
similar institution in 1891. Throughout the 1890s, the Americans established
schools directly under the control of the bishop or diocese, where women
would be trained and sent out to various tasks and destinations. In the
Episcopal Church, deaconesses were trained to be nurses and to engage in
Christian education under the control of a bishop.

Deaconesses, Not Sisters or Mothers

Prior to 1893, a few Canadian women apparently went to the United
States to attend the New York institution in its early years, and at least
two trained in England at Mildmay House.[2] No deaconess house existed in
Canada. Although the bishops of Canada discussed the ministry of women

at the 1883 Provincial Synod,[3] it was not until the 1886 Provincial Synod that the bishops hammered out a compromise between Hibbert Binney, the extreme Tractarian bishop of Nova Scotia, and the evangelical Bishop William Bennett Bond of Montreal. The compromise recognized the legitimacy of both sisterhoods and deaconesses, as long as they were introduced into a diocese with the approval of the bishop.[4] Then in 1888, the Bishop of Niagara welcomed the establishment in Hamilton of a Church of England religious order of women known as the Sisters of the Church, who were related to a mother house in Kilburn, London, England. Other Kilburn Sisters functioned in Toronto and Montreal. The *Evangelical Churchman*, the leading evangelical periodical in the Church of England in Canada, was enraged. The editors felt that bishops should not under any circumstance tolerate or endorse sisterhoods, institutions which appeared to them as "Romish."[5] Over the years the *Evangelical Churchman* wrote often against all women's religious orders, and against the Kilburn Sisters in particular. As early as 1885 they had proclaimed, "We know how the Sisters of Mercy so called are relied upon by the Romanizers to pervert the young."[6] The editors mistrusted the charitable work, the mysterious discipline, the strange, Romish vows, and the habits of the female religious. They feared that the women were proselytizing for popish causes as they went about their business and believed that these women had to be rooted out. To the editors' great regret, the moderate evangelical bishop of Toronto, Arthur Sweatman, took no action against the Kilburn Sisters or their clerical friends.[7]

It was now clear that the hierarchy would not oppose the Sisters. As a consequence, evangelicals in Toronto who were aware of the American and English examples raised the possibility of employing women in the Church of England in Canada as deaconesses. *The Evangelical Churchman* cried out, "The only right answer is the establishment of a Protestant Deaconess Institution." The paper hoped that the Romish influence of the Sisters could be reduced by proving that the deaconess could surpass her monastic counterpart in the exercise of charity. The editors could count on the support of Maurice S. Baldwin, the evangelical bishop of Huron, and they were working on Bishop Sweatman to gain his support. As the voice of the Low Church party, the *Evangelical Churchman* took the lead in encouraging the deaconess movement in Toronto. The newspaper published notices of meetings for deaconess supporters. It congratulated the English Church on its ordination of three deaconesses in 1886, and it publicized news of the American canons, training institutions, and ordination.[8]

The Alumni Association of Wycliffe College, Toronto, a theological college in the evangelical tradition of the Church of England, took the initiative in founding a deaconess institution. At their third annual gathering on 8 October 1890, the Wycliffe Alumni resolved:

> THAT Messrs. March, Wrong, Hamilton, O'Meara and C. C. Owen be a committee to investigate the work carried on under the auspices of deaconesses, and to take whatever steps they deem advisable to bring the matter before the Church.

This Deaconess Committee, whose members came from the staff of Wycliffe College and local parish clergy, began to design a preliminary outline of deaconess work in Toronto.[9]

One year later, in October 1891, the Wycliffe College Alumni Association's annual meeting was dominated by the opening ceremony of the college's new building at Queen's Park. The Alumni Association did manage, however, to hear the Deaconess Committee's report. It included three notable points:

> 1. There is a need in parishes for women's work that can be done most effectively by deaconesses . . . .
> 2. There are many ladies willing and even anxious to engage in such work, (i.e., nursing the sick, visiting the sick, etc.) Their efforts are not now as effective as they would be if they were organized in a body and under systematic direction . . . .
> 3. A small beginning should be made at once.[10]

The committee was optimistic. Its members saw the church as poised, ready, and waiting for deaconesses to do relief work among the poor and sick. They saw women ready to do without pay what clergy had been paid to do but had neglected for generations. What is most remarkable, they made these recommendations without once referring to the needs of the poor or the women themselves. The Alumni Association asked the committee to go to the College Council to get further approval and then to begin to establish a deaconess institution.[11]

The Deaconness Committee reconvened on 28 January 1892, and examined various proposals before them regarding the structure of the institution. The two first proposals were to establish a home in connection with a coffee house or a hospital, proposals which reflected the interests of lay philanthropists. The clerics and academics who constituted the committee wanted the work to begin with a home and school and to add projects as it progressed. They understood theological colleges far better than philanthropic institutions; perhaps unconsciously, they had chosen the American theological and clerical model of deaconess institutions over the older continental model.[12]

The members of the Deaconess Committee recognized that they could not go far without assistance. Although they wanted to start a school for women, they had neither the backing of the bishop or the political and financial resources of the laity. They looked chiefly to Wycliffe's patrons and their wives for such support, and proposed a list of names of some influential and socially well-connected people who could be drawn into the project. Sooner or later almost all did serve the committee. Notable were Mrs. James Patterson Sheraton (wife of the Principal of Wycliffe), Margaret Blake (daughter of Bishop Benjamin Cronyn of Huron and wife of Edward Blake, sometime Chief Justice of Canada and Liberal Premier of Ontario), Mrs. Henry Grasset Baldwin (wife of the Rector of the Church of the Ascension, Toronto), Newman Wright Hoyles, Q.C. (a member of General Synod, the Lord's Day Alliance, the Wycliffe College Council, the Canadian Church Missionary Association, and director of the *Evangelical Churchman*), Georgina (Mrs. N. W.) Hoyles, Samuel H. Blake (Edward Blakes's brother, N. W. Hoyles's law partner, President of the Toronto Y.M.C.A. and the Evangelical Alliance, director of the *Evangelical Churchman*, vice-president of the Lord's Day Alliance and the Toronto City

Mission), Robert S. P. Caldecott (prominent Liberal, temperance advocate, treasurer of Wycliffe, past president of the Y.M.C.A.), and Homer Dixon (a director of the *Evangelical Churchman*).[13] This move to include lay men and women in the committee's work reflected the alliance between evangelical lay reformers and philanthropists on the one hand, and evangelical clergy on the other. Together they had campaigned on behalf of many conservative social reforms in late nineteenth century Toronto -- charities, missions, temperance, and sabbatarianism. After the election of Bishop Arthur Sweatman in Toronto in 1874, the evangelical lay reformers and clergy could count on each other for ecclesiastical and political support, co-operation in mutual projects, and building campaigns. Now the alliance was reassembling to deal with the issue of deaconesses.[14]

A new Deaconess Committee met on February 5. Its membership included two clergy from the old Committee and the College Council, G. M. Wrong and C. C. Owen, two other clergy who were also on the College Council, G. A. Kuhring and Septimus Jones, plus two laymen from the list of influencial people, Caldecott and Hoyles. The Principal of Wycliffe, James Patterson Sheraton met with the committee at first. The new committee received four guidelines from the old one. First, that the institution should be a home and school. Second, a trained deaconess should be imported to run the project for its first year. Third, the lifestyle of the deaconesses should include distinctively non-Roman dress, no vows of celibacy, poverty, or obedience, and no pay or remuneration. Fourth, the deaconesses were to work out of the Church of the Ascension in Toronto. They had to devise a job description for the women that would harmonize with the guidelines. At the meeting, the new Deaconess Committee talked of the work of Mildmay house in London, England, where there were two classes of deaconesses. There were nurses, who acted as public health officials, medical clinicians, and home care providers, and there were teachers with the task of converting women. Kuhring mentioned the deaconess institutions in Kaiserwerth, Philadelphia, and other places. Then Jones and Principal Sheraton moved and seconded the recommendation that deaconess work be organized in Toronto along the lines of Kaiserwerth, Mildmay, and Philadelphia.[15]

That motion marked the triumph of enthusiasm over knowledge. No committee members knew any more about the institutions than they had heard during their meeting. They did not realize that they had endorse three very different models: the deaconess hospital (Kaiserwerth), the extra-diocesan philanthropic team (Mildmay), and the diocesan training school (Philadelphia). They were ready to begin working with a vague notion and high hopes, rather than wait any longer for a careful study and plan. The committee, however, did define what it expected deaconesses should do:

> General assistance of clergy in parishes in district visiting (especially spiritual work). 1) Bible reading and personal evangelistic work amongst the poor and rich; 2) Care of poor and sick. Soup kitchen and making [sic] and selling old clothes; 3) Care of young women in homes; 4) Care and correction of children; 5) Creches, etc.; 6) Prison work; 7) Training church workers; 8) the fostering and development of a foreign missionary spirit.[16]

Such a list of tasks showed that the organizers readily linked together social work among the poor with evangelism and perhaps mission, and that they believed that women were the appropriate ones to do all these things. The committee also expected deaconesses to be unmarried and to serve without pay. They were to serve as staff in creches and soup kitchens run by boards of women volunteers and as female assistants to male clergy in urban parishes. They might even be sent to Asian mission fields after their education. The committee's hopes were bright. All that was needed was a highly adaptable labour force willing to do a wide range of work for no money. The committee decided to proceed to get a house and hire a trained deaconess.[17]

In order to raise public support for the project, Kuhring, the secretary of the committee, began to work with the energy and zeal which the great task demanded. Because the movement had no established place in the thought, hearts, families, institutions or pocketbooks of Canadian churchmen or women, Kuhring had to justify such a novelty. Using the medium of a letter to the editor of the *Evangelical Churchman*, Kuhring published a twenty-point question and answer tract about deaconesses.[18] The letter was an extensive apologia for deaconesses which explored such issues as the distinction between deaconesses and Roman nuns, the relative merits of the Christian vocations of wifehood and motherhood and that of the deaconess, and the funding and deployment of deaconesses. Kuhring and the committee anticipated such challenges as, Why dress women in uniforms, forbid them both marriage and independent life, and deny them remuneration? and How do they differ from nuns?

One of the most difficult challenges for the backers of deaconesses was to speak the praises of a new role for women without calling into question the virtues of traditional women's roles. Many Canadian evangelicals had espoused the prevalent ideology of what may be termed maternal feminism. It seemed to them that God created women to civilize the savage world as mothers civilized their children. Women made the world more livable, not through their professional capabilities, but through their maternal and protective instincts. God had intended women to mother the world. J. S. Howson, a mid-nineteenth century English apologist for deaconesses, resolved the ideological conflict between the vocations to motherhood and diaconate by stating that the diaconate was intended for those he called the 500,000 "surplus" women of England, by which he meant unmarried women.[19] Kuhring, who lived and wrote in Canada in the 1890s, could not use such an argument, for there was no such "surplus" of women in Canadian society. In his apologia for deaconesses, Kuhring's response to the question "Is the Deaconess calling more sacred that that of a wife and mother?" was a simple, "By no means."

Further, the committee desired to recruit women who wished no financial reward, for it had none to offer. Their work was not to be a job, but a sacred mission. The absence of remuneration assured that no gain seekers would apply. "Why do the deaconesses receive no remuneration for their work? In order that this work may remain wholly a service of love and mercy."[20] The committee saw no place in the church for the paid professional services of women. Their attitudes paralleled that of Sir

Daniel Wilson, President of the University of Toronto and an evangelical Churchman, who hoped that the women he reluctantly admitted to the University in 1884 would be able to "lift the society above the dead level of mere gain." Women were to offer their time and energy at no cost as living symbols of voluntarism, philanthropy, and Christian self-giving. They were not to become another variety of the "working girl."[21]

Their use of the model of a trained, lifelong volunteer who depends on charitable contributions was an unrealistic expectation of the women of Canada in the 1890s. There were few unmarried women with the means to support themselves without a paid position. Then, as now, single women worked outside the home for financial reasons. The unskilled found themselves in domestic service, in the garment industry, or in other manufacturing jobs. Most social reformers felt that these women had to be protected from the temptations of the city and kept safe until they had a chance to escape from the factory into marriage.[22] For them, if deaconess work had been minimally lucrative, it might have been a possible alternative. Unfortunately, working girls were considered to be a morally questionable breed, and therefore unsuitable for deaconess or missionary training.

On the other hand, large numbers of skilled women would not be attracted to the project, for the committee had rejected the possibility of offering them what most needed first -- a salary. Women with teaching, nursing, and clerical skills were to be found in growing numbers in the public schools, hospitals, and businesses of Canada. They were not generally able to forsake their annual pay, even though low, for a future with no security and less prestige than they already possessed.[23] Although the committee had expectations that the deaconesses would be skilled workers on a par with other female professionals, none of the committee so far were women and they had not designed the project with the needs of women in mind.

The model of the deaconess proposed by Kuhring and the new Deaconess Committee soon became the subject of discussion within the diocese of Toronto. Kuhring's apologetics succeeded in winning the attention and approval of the bishop of Toronto. In June, 1892, three

months after Kuhring's letter to the editor of the *Evangelical Churchman*,
Bishop Sweatman agreed to serve as honorary president of the Deaconess
Committee, and in this capacity chaired a public meeting at Wycliffe
College. The meeting named a revised committee membership and gave
them full power to carry out the work. Women joined the committee for
the first time, although none were professional women. Those named were
Newton Hoyles, president, Georgina Hoyles, treasurer, Kuhring, secretary,
Mrs. Samuel Blake, R. Gilmore, Julia Saunders, Homer Dixon, C. C. Owen,
W. W. Baldwin, and George Goulding.[24] The *Evangelical Churchman*
reported that Sweatman expressed gratitude for works already carried on
by women. The paper's report continued,

> Still he felt the need of such an institution as a deaconess'
> training home where they could receive special training for
> special work. He had no doubt that there would be an abundant
> supply, not only of means, but of women candidates. . . . He
> would venture a happy thought, i.e., that this work . . . would
> not meet with jealousy or opposition by the sisterhood already
> in existence. They had expressed their kind sympathy.[25]

Sweatman's words were carefully chosen. He had distinguished the deaconess from the active lay woman by identifying the former as specialists.
This he did while praising other women's work and rejecting any notion of
competition with the Sisters of the Church. If his guidelines were imple-
mented, he believed that the project would be a success. After Sweatman's
moderate and conciliatory remarks, others spoke in a more hostile way
against the Sisters. The Reverend Arthur Baldwin made deprecatory
remarks about vows, candles, prayers for the departed, and vestments as
he linked Church of England sisters with the "Vestal Virgins of Rome."
The Reverend Septimus Jones then stated that the sisters were antithetical
to the Church of England. The Reverend R. Moreton spoke of Mildmay, its
operations, and its finances, and its freedom from Romish influence. While
the Bishop supported the work of trained women as deaconesses, Baldwin,
Jones, and Moreton were still battling nuns.[26]

The Head Deaconess

Throughout the summer of 1893, the committee members continued to work on finding a home and a head deaconess. They hoped to obtain a Canadian woman who had been trained in England, and first approached Miss Strawburger of Portsmouth, Ontario, a Mildmay trainee. She declined their offer, but recommended another Mildmay trainee, whom the committee did not contact.[27] The committee turned instead to a married woman, Elizabeth M. Tilley, who was the Dominion Secretary of the King's Daughters, a national Church of England devotional league for women, but not a trained deaconess. She rejected their offer three times, giving as reasons her obligations to her three children and to the league. Finally, the committee turned to Sybil Wilson, the unmarried daughter of the recently deceased Sir Daniel Wilson, and a woman of high social standing.[28] She immediately accepted the offer of the position of Head Deaconess as well as the committee's suggestion that she first go to England to train at Mildmay. The committee, in an apparent reversal of its view that deaconess work should be voluntary, offered her a salary, a housekeeper, and reimbursement for her training expenses. Perhaps this indicated an assumption that the voluntary principle applied only to the rank and file. She rejected the offer of remuneration, and instead gave to the committee the use of her own home without cost as a deaconess house and her services as a volunteer, not as an employee. Wilson had, however, some reservations. Kuhring's response to her acceptance letter indicated what some of them were. He told her,

> the work will be free from bitter words and recrimination. . . .
> I assure you that we are with you in this matter for peace
> without loss of conscience and to do positive rather than
> negative work.

It appears that Wilson feared that the role of the Head Deaconess would be controversial. She may have been concerned about the extreme rhetoric of Jones, Baldwin, and others who appeared to be more interested in combatting "ritualistic sisterhoods" rather than unbelief and poverty among the women and children of Toronto. Her concerns were apparently met.[29]

The committee was understandably delighted with Sybil Wilson. Being the daughter of Sir Daniel Wilson, she came from the evangelical social elite. She was willing to do what few "ladies" would undertake: work not simply on benevolent committees and charitable boards, but *amongst* the unwashed, impure, tubercular, and hungry. She had also relieved the committee of a considerable financial burden! They had received contributions of only $36 by October 22, 1892, while the annual expenses were projected to be $3950. Sybil Wilson's generosity was the key to the project's commencement. With a home and a figurehead, the work could now advance. It was small wonder that the committee reported its success to the 1892 meeting of the Wycliffe College Alumni Association:

> The time was approaching and we saw no light, but God, who is faithful, before the allotted time expired, sent us one who suited our needs better than any one we could have desired.[30]

The sentiments were entirely appropriate.

Wilson departed for her training in England in the autumn of 1892. She may have thought she was entering into a professional position, one in which her competence and altruistic dedication would matter most of all, but the rhetoric that appeared in the committee's minutes and on the pages of the *Evangelical Churchman* had no such emphasis. The deaconess was the prototype of the new Protestant woman -- an elitist missionary in the lower school of earth preparing her pupils for the higher school of paradise. Relief work was intended to help both the corporeal needs of the poor and sick and to help prepare them for heaven. Deaconesses would not only give the unemployed and unwashed a chance at working class respectability and cleanliness, but would offer the lower reaches of the populace a chance at salvation.[31] No amount of training could help Wilson fulfill the somewhat unconventional expectations of the deaconesses' methods of salvation. Deaconesses were to be teachers of virtue and godliness, likened, ironically, to sirens attracting sailors closer and closer to the "rock of our salvation." They were to entice sinners to godly life, faith, and charity:

> Sinners must be drawn by love; nothing is so strong, nothing so powerful, nothing so attractive . . . . Let deaconesses be loving disciples that they may attract by that alluring, fascinating virtue of love.[32]

God gave single women the spiritual call to arouse, lure, and love the fallen men of the world. Sybil Wilson was the first to respond to the call in Toronto for this new kind of women.

Although the committee was attempting to build on a foundation already established by fundraisers and enthusiasts of women in foreign missions, the ideology which propelled women missionaries to foreign parts was quite different from that which the committee hoped would attract and mobilize deaconesses. One such enthusiast, Lizzie Dixon, published a tract typical of the call to foreign missions, patterned after the missionaries' home reports and appeals which were often carried in the *Evangelical Churchman*:

> As at home, so in the mission field, woman's work is very varied . . . . Amongst most nations where the knowledge of God and His Son Jesus Christ is unknown, women have been oppressed and down trodden.

A woman's foreign missionary yearnings might be roused by the realization that the intolerable conditions of child marriage, lack of education and nursing care, and ignorance of Jesus Christ demanded her active commitment abroad. Some one would have to go into the homes of the women in foreign parts who were deprived of the opportunity to hear the gospel in public. English Christian women had to come forward and use the Good News to advance and redeem their sisters in the dark places of the world. It was an exotic and attractive appeal for women volunteers, the sort of romantic challenge that would draw the devout, the adventurous, and the feminist. As an appeal for foreign missionaries, it had worked, but it was quite different from the appeal for deaconesses made by Kuhring. It remained to be seen whether the appeal for deaconesses would produce results.[33]

While Sybil Wilson was in England, the committee continued two campaigns on behalf of the deaconess home: intercessory prayers and public appeals for funds. The friends of deaconess work began to meet monthly in the board room of the Y.M.C.A., a central meeting place of Toronto's conservative reformers.[34] They prayed together, spoke publicly, and wrote articles to attract monetary support and women. To their surprise, the women of Toronto did not clamour to join a deaconess institution and the foreign missionary organizations did not come forward to divert their funds for such work.[35] A large number of prominent Churchmen would find themselves covered with embarassment if the deaconess experiment did not produce successful results.

By the time Sybil Wilson returned home in the summer of 1893, the committee's appeals had not attracted any applicants.[36] In September the committee finally worked out an application form. It asked a woman to submit two testimonials, personal statistics, background information on church and hospital work, evidence of baptism and communicant status, and essays explaining her vocation. If under thirty, she had to gain the permission of her parents. If single, she had to state the occupation of her father, or if widowed, her deceased husband's occupation. Seemingly, the new head deaconess and the committee did not anticipate attracting women whose own educational or business backgrounds were of any significance; the application did not include any questions about these topics.[37] Still no applications came forward. The committee began to think that the recruitment and application process were faulty, and decided that the remedy might be found in a simpler application form. There appeared to be an impending crisis -- the house was to open soon, but there were no eager young women to introduce as the first trainees.[38]

The Deaconess Home

On October 3, 1893, the Church of England Deaconess and Missionary

Training Home opened at 46 St. George Street in Toronto with much pomp and praise. Bishop Sweatman, in his opening address, noted the apostolic roots and noble aims of the project. The Wycliffe College Alumni Association gathered with prominent lay men and women to wish their new project every blessing. The fanfare tended to obscure the fact that no women came forward to enter the home as the first deaconess trainees. And there was almost no money -- only $155.50 to date.[39] Only Sybil Wilson sat in what was her own home which now bore a very long official name.

The work passed formally out of the hands of the Deaconess Committee that had been created in June 1892 and into the hands of the Board of Management of the new home. The expectation was that the home would flourish if the limited time, skills, and energy of the committee would be supplemented by an expanded board, in which Wycliffe alumni would retain much of their representation and control. Without trainees, however, the early months were full of much uncertainty and instability. The board realized that, in any case, it did not know where deaconesses might fit within an established system of professional male clergy and female volunteers. Demonstrating its continued dependence, the board addressed the question to the Alumni Association.[40]

In January 1894, the scene changed. A woman named Annie Rae arrived to become the first trainee, to be what would now be called a probationer. In March, Margaret Darling followed as the second probationer.[41] By the spring of 1894, only $452.76 had been collected as the expenses continued to mount. At the same time, it became clear that Sybil Wilson's health was not able to withstand the work she had undertaken. Her inability to continue dealt a nearly mortal blow to the nascent training home. The board held a series of meetings from April 5 to May 17 to search for a temporary replacement, a new home, and eventually, a permanent Head Deaconess to replace Sybil Wilson.[42] Their difficulties once again appeared nearly insurmountable. The whole project had depended entirely on the house, the money, and the expertise of one woman, assets which were no longer available.[43] Nevertheless, the board decided that the work would go on. In August, Suzanne Lucinda Sandys became a probationer, and in September, Julia Saunders, a member of the committee in 1892 and their fourth choice, agreed to serve as temporary Head Deaconess. F. H. Duvernet, a professor at Wycliffe, loaned the training home his house for a year, and two more probationers arrived. Contributions, although still meagre, began to arrive more regularly than before. The work seemed no longer doomed although it was fighting for life.[44] Fanny Cross became the new permanent Head Deaconess in January 1895. On December 26, 1895, the first two of the home's probationers received ordination as deaconesses, Annie Rae and Suzanne Lucinda Sandys. The institution thereby gained stability, a higher profile, and greater credibility.[45]

Epilogue

The Deaconess Home began to take root and grow as the board, composed mainly of lay philanthropists and reformers, turned the work in a more pragmatic direction. The institution gradually responded to the tangible needs of the Church of England in Canada. The home produced deaconesses who found paid non-clergy employment, albeit at low salaries, in the formal structures of the church -- in parishes, missions, and schools in the far north, on the Prairies, in British Columbia, in urban centres, and overseas. They helped to define the diaconate as a distinctive ministry for women in the church.[46] The home moved beyond its founding aims based on the clergy-model and modified its original vision of the deaconess as an ideal woman, second only to the mother, who selflessly gave herself as a life-long volunteer, unsullied by the workplace, in order to lure others to God.

The institution retained the name of the Church of England Deaconess and Missionary Training Home until 1956 when it officially became the Anglican Women's Training College, a title it had borne informally since the 1930s. In 1969, it combined with the United Church of Canada's Covenant College to became the Centre for Christian Studies in Toronto.

Although the aims and the ideal changed in important ways after 1895, elements of the original aims and the first picture of the ideal woman lingered into the mid-twentieth century. Only in the 1960s were women trained on a par with men within the church. Recalling the anti-Romish origins of the home, deaconesses were forbidden until the 1950s to visit the prominent Church of England sisterhood in Ontario, the Sisters of St. John the Divine.[47]

Restrospectively, the early initiatives of members of the Church of England in Canada to recruit, train, and deploy a corps of deaconesses who would serve as urban missionaries and role models of an ideal woman might be said to have succeeded only in spite of themselves. The pious and well-meaning hopes of the founders had not been matched by clarity of design or sober realism. All the good will and good intentions of the evangelicals were almost destroyed by their unreasonable demands for self-sacrifice and by lack of popular support. The work of deaconesses and the Deaconess Home survived and eventually flourished, in spite of, rather than because of, the idealism of the founders.

Notes

1. Although there are many books about the origins of the deaconess movement, the best one is Cecilia Robinson, *The Ministry of Deaconesses*, 2nd ed. (London: Methuen, 1914), from which much of the following account is taken. See also Mary Sudman Donovan, *A Different Call: Women's Ministries in the Episcopal Church, 1850-1920* (Wilton: Morehouse-Barlow, 1986).

2. Robinson, *Ministry*, 129. See the text below at note 27. Work must be done to discover the identity of these women, to find out what relationship they had to their diocesan bishops, and to determine the place and nature of their ministries. Were their talents and training used in Canada or did they choose to remain in the U.S.A., where such ministry had a more secure foothold? Did they go to the U.S.A. on the first leg of a missionary journey to China or Japan? Did Canadian bishops see the American schools as a more satisfactory solution to the deaconess problem than a Canadian school would be? All this is a puzzle.

3. See Archives of the General Synod, Anglican Church of Canada,

Journal of the Proceedings of the Synod of the Province of Canada,
1883; and Robinson, *Ministry,* 131.

4.   See Archives of the General Synod, Anglican Church of Canada,
     Journal of the Proceedings of the Synod of the Province of Canada,
     1886.

5.   *The Evangelical Churchman,* 7 June 1888 [hereafter *EC*].

6.   *EC,* 17 September 1885, 222.

7.   *EC,* 2 July 1891, 102. Almost every issue published in the summer of
     1891 is full of material condemning the Sisters of the Church.

8   *EC,* 16 October 1890, 277 and 281.

9.   Archives of the General Synod, Anglican Church of Canada, *Minute
     Book 1* (1888-1902), Wycliffe College Alumni Association, 82 (8
     October 1890), in Scrapbook I of the Anglican Women's Training
     College Collection. George MacKinnon Wrong was Professor of
     Ecclesiastical History at Wycliffe; Heber Hamilton was the Dean of
     Wycliffe College; Thomas Robert O'Meara was rector of the Church of
     the Holy Trinity, East Toronto [hereafter WCAA *Minutes*].

10. WCAA *Minutes,* 6-9 Oct. 1891.

11. WCAA *Minutes,* 6-9 Oct. 1891.

12. The College Council included the following clergy: C. C. Owen, G. A.
     Kuhring, T. R. O'Meara, Bernard Bryan, W. J. Armitage, C. J. James,
     C. H. Marsh, and G. M. Wrong. They were among the most active
     young evangelicals in the Diocese of Toronto.

13. Wycliffe College Archives, Deaconess Committee of the Wycliffe
     College Alumni Association, *Minutes,* 28 January 1892 [hereafter
     WCAA-DC *Minutes*].

14. Deaconess Committee Report to WCAA, in WCAA *Minutes,* 4-7
     October 1892.

15. WCAA-DC *Minutes,* 5 February 1892. There is some confusion about
     which house in Philadelphia was under discussion this time. Was it
     the Episcopal one that had been discussed one week earlier, or was it
     the Lutheran one, which Kuhring seems to have known more about?
     Also, although Sheraton is not listed in the minutes as a member of
     the committee, he seconds a motion.

16. WCAA-DC *Minutes*, 5 February 1892.

17. WCAA-DC *Minutes*, 5 February 1892.

18. *EC*, 3 March 1892, 108-9. It later appeared separately as a pamphlet.

19.J. S. Howson, *Deaconesses* (London: Longman, Green, 1862), 10.

20. No one asked why clergy were paid. Was theirs not a service of love and mercy?

21. Wayne Roberts, "Rocking the Cradle for the World: the New Woman and Maternal Feminism, 1877-1914," in Linda Kealey, ed., *A Not Unreasonable Claim: Women and Reform, 1880's-1920's* (Toronto: Women's Press, 1979), 28.

22. See Alice Klein and Wayne Roberts, "Beseiged Innocence: The 'Problem' and Problems of Working Women -- Toronto, 1896-1914," in Janice Acton, ed., *Women at Work: Ontario, 1850-1930* (Toronto: Women's Press, 1974), 211-59.

23. Their annual pay would be $200-$300. A good profile of the women who did volunteer to go to the mission field is David Barrett, "Women in the Canadian Church Missionary Association, 1896-1901" (Unpublished paper, 1985, available at Wycliffe College Library).

24. Deaconess Committee Report to WCAA, in WCAA *Minutes*, 4-7 October 1892.

25. *EC*, 30 June 1892, 315.

26. *EC*, 30 June 1892, 315.

27. Some file copies of the committee's correspondence have been preserved. Archives of the General Synod, Anglican Church of Canada, Francis Dobbs to G. A. Kuhring, 11 and 18 June 1892, Anglican Women's Training College Collection, File 1-A [hereafter AWTC Collection]. While it would be useful to know how many Canadians trained at English institutions, the English records are few and far between. Apparently, no enrollment records of Mildmay survived. We do not know Strawburger's first name or the name of the other Milday graduate she recommended.

28. G. A. Kuhring to Sybil Wilson, 3 September 1892, AWTC Collection, File 1-A.

29. G. A. Kuhring to Sybil Wilson, 14 September 1892, AWTC Collection, File 1-A.
30. WCAA *Minutes*, October 1892, 136.
31. *EC*, 25 August 1892, 413.
32. *EC*, 25 August 1892, 413.
33. *EC*, 10 August 1893, 383.
34. *EC*, 26 January 1893, 37.
35. Among Presbyterians, by contrast, foreign missionary money did go to support women church workers at home. See *The Story of our Missions* (Toronto: Women's Missionary Society of the Presbyterian Church in Canada, 1915), 5.
36. *EC*, 12 October 1893, 491.
37. *EC*, 28 September 1893, 462.
38. Archives of the General Synod, Anglican Church of Canada, Board of Management of the Church of England Deaconess and Missionary Training Home, *Minutes*, 18 October 1893, 21 [hereafter CEDMTH *Minutes*; used by permission of the Centre for Christian Studies, Toronto.]
39. *EC*, 12 October 1893, 491.
40. For the transition to the Board, see WCAA *Minutes*, 6 October 1893. For the total confusion of the Board, see CEMDTH *Minutes, passim.*
41. *Graduates Note Book*, AWTC Collection, File 2-D.
42. CEMDTH *Minutes*, 5 April 1894, 29-30.
43. CEMDTH *Minutes*, 5 April-17 May 1894, 29-35.
44. *EC*, 6 September 1894, 421.
45. *EC*, 2 January 1896, 3.
46. Many annual reports of the CEDMTH record the deployment of the members of its graduating classes.
47. Conversation with the Rev. Marjorie Pezzack, 1983.

8

FOR THE UPLIFT OF THE WORLD:

THE MISSION THOUGHT OF JAMES A. MACDONALD,

1890s-1915

Brian J. Fraser

The encounter between Western Christianity and other cultures is one of the themes running throughout the writings of John Webster Grant, from his earlier work on Christian missions in India to his later work on missions among the native peoples in Canada.[1] As Grant pointed out in *God's People in India*, whenever the gospel was introduced into a new culture, it came as a foreign import from a foreign culture. The foreignness of Christianity in modern times was "greatly aggravated by the close association of missions with an outward movement of European power and influence that has affected the entire world."[2] Grant recognized, however, an ambiguity in motivation among missionaries and their supporters. They were seldom conscious agents of imperialism, often being among the most outspoken critics of their own societies, but they did function as carriers of Western culture into foreign lands. In his discussion of this theme, Grant touched upon a subject taken up anew by mission historians in recent years. To examine the relationship between Christianity and culture in the mission thinking of the Rev. James A. Macdonald, a Canadian Presbyterian minister and journalist with roots in Scottish Presbyterianism, is the intent of this paper.

James A. Macdonald never was a missionary. There is no record of his serving a student mission field during his theological education at Knox College, Toronto, in the 1880s. His primary interest while a student was editing the alumni journal, *Knox College Monthly*. Following graduation, he stayed on as editor of the *Monthly* and served as librarian at the college. His first church, in St. Thomas, Ontario, was a large congregation in a prosperous urban centre. After five years in the pulpit, he returned to Toronto to establish a religious publishing house, The Westminster Company, and edit a widely-circulated series of religious newspapers. In 1903, he was appointed managing editor of the Toronto *Globe*, central Canada's leading English-language Liberal newspaper.[3] Why, then, consider the ideas of this non-missionary in a volume dedicated to exploring new trends in the history of missions in Canada?

The reason is to be found in the recent historiography of those scholars who have directed our attention to the importance of the ideas of the *senders* of missionaries. By 1910, at the end of two decades of unprecedented mission recruitment and support, and at the height of the power and influence of the Laymen's Missionary Movement among the churches of North America, Macdonald had become a popular and respected missions promoter, frequently sharing the platform with Robert Speer, J. Campbell White, and John R. Mott at international missionary conventions.[4] William R. Hutchison, introducing a symposium that constituted one stage of a larger project on 'Missionary Ideologies in the Imperialist Era, 1880-1920', focusses attention on the stated purposes, the presuppositions, and the motivations of the missionary movements in their parent nations and asks what the relationship was between the responsibility assumed by missionaries and their supporters for the spread of Christian civilization and the primary goal of evangelization.[5] Paul Jenkins argues that to be truly contextual, mission historians have to study the sending field as well as the mission field. In collaboration with social historians, they should look at the theology/ideology of the senders as a source of understanding the formation and motivation of the missionaries sent, as an aspect of the social history of the cultural aspirations of the senders and as an agent of change in the sending society.[6]

With the press and the platform as his pulpit, Macdonald preached his message, that civilization had to be Christianized for the uplift of the world, to a broad cross-section of North American Christians.[7] What

Macdonald meant by this phrase, drawn from the central ideas in the two addresses he gave to national Laymen's Missionary Movement conventions in Canada in 1909 and the United States in 1910,[8] is the focus for this paper. The result will be, I trust, a kind of topography of the mission thought of those to whom and for whom Macdonald spoke in a period roughly parallel to that examined by Hutchison and his colleagues.[9] The main features delineated will be the roots from which Macdonald came, the ideas he espoused, the media through which they were spread, and the society to which they were addressed.[10]

Macdonald's Roots

Macdonald left no doubt in the minds of the delegates at the Men's National Missionary Congress in Chicago in 1910 as to the supreme obligation of North America in the time of crisis that was upon them. They had been chosen by God to spread "the gospel of faith and love and a new life for the whole world."[11] At issue in the crisis were the millions in the heathen world "dying without God."[12] Much had been given to America -- material wealth, people, achievement, and culture -- "all that is noblest in the life of the world"[13] -- but such an inheritance from God brought with it the obligation of service to the world. At the heart of that service was the person and the work of Jesus Christ and the primary purpose of missions was evangelization. Macdonald's understanding of the forces that would uplift the world and Christianize civilization were shaped by the influences he encountered during his early years in south-western Ontario, his student years in Toronto, and a year spent in Scotland.

Macdonald was born in East Williams Township in Middlesex Country, Ontario, on January 22, 1862. His father had moved to Ontario from Pictou County, Nova Scotia, and the family traced its roots to the Scottish Highlands through North Carolina.[14] The Free Church congregation in which Macdonald was raised was under the ministry of Lachlan McPherson, who stayed out of the Presbyterian unions of 1861 and 1875 because he felt the bases of union compromised the Free Church principle of the headship of Christ over the nations. Macdonald remembered visits from John Ross of Brucefield during communion seasons at East Williams. Ross led the resistance to the union of 1875 within the Canada Presbyterian Church on the basis of the same principle of Christ's headship.[15] The insistence on the authority of Christ over all dimensions of life led to a concern for political and social matters that found expression in the Grit liberalism of George Brown and the Toronto *Globe*.[16] The same emphasis led to a spirit of missionary expansionism among south-western Ontario Presbyterians that produced more support and recruits for home and foreign missions than any other part of Canada.[17] When Macdonald began classes at the University of Toronto and Knox College in 1884, he brought a faith that was Christocentric in content, political and social in its scope, and missionary in its orientation. The religious environment in which he had been raised was conservative in its theology, but evangelical in its desire for the spread of the influence of a Christianity that stressed individual responsibility and humanitarian benevolence.[18]

The two men who impressed Macdonald most during his years at the University of Toronto and Knox College were William Caven, Principal of Knox, and George Paxton Young, Professor of Mental and Moral Philosophy at University College. After serving as minister at St. Mary's in south-western Ontario, Caven was appointed Professor of Exegetical Theology at Knox College in 1866 and became Principal in 1873. The work of evangelizing the world was the most important obligation for the church, as Macdonald remembered Caven's teaching.[19] Caven's thought focussed on the revelation of redemptive grace in the person and work of Christ. He emphasized the central themes in Paul's theology -- sin, atonement, and redemption -- and presented sin as an unbridgeable gap between God and humanity, requiring God's supernatural intervention in the person of Christ for the effecting of salvation.[20] Macdonald also recalled Caven's political activities. He was an active supporter of the Liberalism of George Brown, but was quick to criticize the Liberal Party when civil liberty or the moral purity of the country were ignored in its deliberations.[21]

If Caven influenced the core of Macdonald's evangelical faith, George Paxton Young shaped the way he thought of his role in society. Young's philosophical teaching was directed at the formation of moral character and responsible citizenship in his students. Macdonald gave Young credit for enabling his students to become in their various spheres of activity a conscience to the community.[22] The ethical idealism of T. H. Green, towards which Young moved in the 1870s and 1880s, provided a restatement of liberal social principles adapted to the more collective society emerging in Great Britain and North America in the latter part of the nineteenth century.[23] The universe was ordered according to the moral principle of self-sacrificing love for the well-being of a world society; it was best understood and governed through conscience, that innate power of moral judgement with which God had endowed each soul; and the responsibility of those with ability and education was to provide the moral leadership that would promote an harmonious social order that encompassed the world. The influence of Caven and Young reinforced and broadened the Free Church evangelicalism in which Macdonald had been raised. But his education was not yet completed. Still to make its impact was the 'Back to Christ' school of Scottish liberal theologians.

For the school term of 1888-1889, Macdonald was in Scotland with several of his classmates from Knox College. While there, according to a colleague on the *Monthly* staff:

> he fell under the influence of a certain school of theologians who were attracting a good deal of attention. On his return to Canada, it was not long before the influence of these teachers showed itself in various ways in the pages of the *Monthly*.[24]

The pages of the *Monthly* following Macdonald's return suggested that those who comprised this school were Marcus Dodds, George Adam Smith, W. G. Elmslie, Henry Drummond, and A. B. Bruce.[25] Macdonald considered Bruce the founder of the 'Back to Christ' school for the English-speaking world. Through historical and literary criticism, the spiritual consciousness and the ethical teaching of the historical Jesus were recovered and became the standard by which the doctrine and practice of the Church was evaluated. In the person of Christ was found the most effective apologetic for Christianity. Christianity was not a theory to be accepted or a system to be expounded, but a spirit perfectly manifest in the life of Christ. Its divine claims were vindicated by his divine character.[26] The Scottish evangelical liberals did not reduce Jesus' "absolutely unique metaphysical relation to God" to the ethical example of the Ritschlian school. This enabled them, in Macdonald's mind, to conserve the best of the old views as to the essentials of the faith, enrich them with an ethical emphasis, and find support for them in the most rigorous of modern scholarship.[27] This group of Scottish evangelical liberals also saw themselves as leaders in the creation of an ethical world community based on the evangelical virtues of individual responsibility and social concern. A modernized Christianity, they believed, would provide the spiritual and ethical motivation to foster the ethos of international interdependence necessary to the progress of humankind and the uplift of the world.[28]

The formation of Macdonald's faith took place during a turbulent period of change within North Atlantic Presbyterianism. As a student editor and budding journalist, Macdonald followed the shifting currents of thought more closely than many. In the evangelical liberalism of the Scottish 'Back to Christ' school, he found a new apologetic that mediated between the Christocentric and ethical faith within which he had been raised and the modern spirit of science, collectivism, and progress he encountered among his contemporaries. As he pointed out in the first issue of *The Westminster*, the magazine he founded on his return to Toronto in 1896:

> No false liberalism must be allowed to loosen our hold on the great Christian verities. No shallow rhetoric must move us away from faith in the Almighty Saviour. Standing true to the doctrine of the Cross, we open our eyes to the new light that ever breaks on the vision of those who believe in a living Christ.[29]

The new apologetic claimed to address the crisis of authority and faith experienced by many in the late nineteenth century by combining an evangelical feeling for Christ with an historical and philosophical reformulation of the essential doctrines of the Christian faith more suited to the modern mind.[30] As Macdonald noted in an editorial marking the end of the nineteenth century, "The changed conditions of life, the widened horizons of thought, the new knowledge and the new needs have made necessary a new evangelism if the old Evangel would reach men and be again, as it was of old, a recovering and redeeming power."[31] In the faith that Macdonald brought to the platforms of missionary conferences, there were three aspects he considered crucial to a new evangelism -- its spiritual uniqueness, its ethical emphasis, and its social implications.

Macdonald's Ideas

In keeping with the monism of the Idealist world-view in which he found a reasonable answer to the crisis of faith experienced by evangelical Christians in the nineteenth century, Macdonald preferred to speak of the unique quality of Christianity as 'spiritual' rather than 'supernatural'. The uniqueness of Christ lay in the perfection with which he disclosed the spiritual principle found in the character of God and determinative of the duty and destiny of humanity -- the principle of love and self-sacrifice in service to the world. Other world religions were lacking in their power to meet the spiritual needs of humanity. The study of non-Christian religions would improve the effectiveness with which missionaries presented the spirit of the gospel in their evangelizing but no science of world religions would bridge the gulf between Christ and other religious leaders.[32]

Macdonald took pains in his address in Chicago to distinguish the Christian spirit from Western civilization. He suggested that the Orient, for example, in its encounter with the spirit of Christ, might find an expression of the Christian life and a conception of the Christian faith that was nearer to the ideal of Jesus than the commercialized life and materialistic philosophies of the West. The uniqueness of Christianity lay in the spirit of Christ, not in the culture of North America. That spirit might take different forms as it sought to meet the needs of "the varieties of life, of temperament, of emotion, of aspiration of the other great peoples of the world."[33] North America's responsibility for the uplift of the world, Macdonald insisted, involved the spread of spiritual principles, not the determination of their cultural embodiment.

The most distinctive aspect of the spirit of Christ in Macdonald's mind was its ethical power and purity. "To make vital and dominant," Macdonald said in Chicago, "the reality of moral distinctions, the necessity for moral choices, the supremacy of moral obligations, the inevitableness of moral retributions is, indeed, a service urgently required by the heathen world."[34] While God's love and Christ's eternal salvation were the source of the will and power behind the moral life, the ethical elevation of the human race was the very heart of the mission of the Christian nations in North America.

To implement this vision of a Christian civilization, Macdonald relied on changed people who would change the circumstances for themselves and for others. North American civilization was as heathen in much of its life as the lands to which missionaries were being sent. If the Church was to bring home "to the heart and the conscience of the American people a vivid and more complete sense of responsibility for the uplift of the world," it would have to accept the need for its own Christianization and clearly preach the social ethics of Jesus to its society.[35]

By 1909, Macdonald assumed that his audience agreed "that Christianity has to do, not merely with individuals and with salvation into an after-world, but also with the social fabric, with the organized society of individuals, and with the institution of civilized life under which we live."[36] In the progressive evolution of understanding the spirit of Christ, the modern church was marked by the emphasis placed on the social aspects of the gospel and the social message of Jesus. Macdonald expected the family, the church, the school, democratic political institutions, and the economic system to work together to form Christian character, not only in individuals, but also in the personality of the nation. The result would be a progressive improvement in the moral quality and social effectiveness of the democratic institutions that had evolved in Canada through the struggle for responsible government during the nineteenth century. In principle, the social, political, and commercial institutions of Canada were sound, but they had to be elevated by the spirit of Christ to achieve their highest moral and social potential. A collective Christian conscience would bring Canadian civilization -- "the sum total of those institutions and conditions that gave character to our everyday life and create the atmosphere in which men live" -- under the dominance of the motive and spirit of Jesus Christ.[37]

In spite of Macdonald's protestations about the distinction between the spirit of the Gospel and the culture of North America, his ethical emphasis and its social implications made the process of evangelization dependent upon the spread of North American civilization. Granted that it was a reformed and purified North American culture that was to undertake the mission of Christianizing civilization and uplifting the world, it still had to be incarnate in a particular set of institutions and values. The Idealist philosophical framework within which Macdonald thought left little alternative. As he told the Student Volunteer Movement convention in 1914, every great nation "has, indeed, its vocation, its calling from the great world, its legacy of ideas for the service of humanity" and "embodied some special faculties, some tendencies, represents a distinct idea or aspiration, holds the germ of a common faith or tradition or purpose distinct from all the others in the world." The needs of the world had advanced beyond the age of nationalism into the age of internationalism. The distinct vocation or idea that was embodies in the experience of the nations of North America was that of cooperative nationhood. In being true to this vocation in the spirit of Christ, North America would enable the Latin American republics of the hemisphere, the emerging nationalities of Africa, and the awakening nations of the Orient to have their full chance to see the spirit of Christ and contribute to the world community.[38] William Hutchison's caution that it is too indulgent to exonerate the burgeoning social and educational ventures of missions from involvement in cultural imperialism is accurate in relation to Macdonald's views.[39] There was a degree of cultural paternalism in Macdonald's position that could not be glossed over or excused by the best intentions of enlightenment and reform. To understand the nature of the cultural paternalism that accompanied Macdonald's Christianity, however, requires a closer examination of the institutional system through which it was expressed and the society to which it was addressed.

Macdonald's Media

Macdonald's choices of career -- the editor's office, the pulpit, and the platform -- were all means of influencing the ways in which people thought and acted. Within his frame of thought, it was ideas that determined how people acted. Macdonald was a popular public moralist who sought to use the editorial, the sermon, and the speech as a means of forming a Christian consensus on the character of the Canadian nation, and later, as the crisis of culture spread to a militaristic Europe, of the North American continent.

From the very beginning of his career as a student journalist in 1885, Macdonald was attracted by the interdenominational crusade to evangelize the world in one generation.[40] His first recorded contact with this network of voluntary organizations for the spread of Christendom was through the YMCA at University College in Toronto and the Canadian Inter-Collegiate Missionary Alliance, founded in 1884 and modelled on a similar American organization begun in 1879. Dwight L. Moody played an important inspirational and coordinating role among the various organizations, and the *Monthly* carried a length report on Moody's Summer School at Northfield in 1886, where Henry Drummond and A. T. Pierson attracted most of the attention.[41] Macdonald later told his readers in *The Westminster* that the religious conventions sponsored by such groups offered the church an enthusiasm based on knowledge and guided by conscience that it badly needed.[42] Though he was reported to have attracted the attention of the Edinburgh papers with his oratorical skills while in Scotland,[43] Macdonald promoted such enthusiasm through religious journalism before he became a popular platform speaker at conventions throughout North Atlantic Christendom.

Up to one half of the space in each number of the *Monthly* was devoted to missionary topics, including articles, debates, news, and reports from home and foreign fields. The most active of the student societies during Macdonald's years was the Knox College Student Missionary Society, and Macdonald gave extensive coverage and support to their successful efforts to send Jonathan Goforth to Honan, China, as a college missionary.[44] In 1896, after five years in St. Thomas, Macdonald returned to

Toronto to establish the Westminster Company, which grew under his direction into an extensive publishing empire in the field of popular evangelical literature. At its heart was the monthly magazine, *The Westminster*, and eventually a weekly companion, *The Presbyterian*.[45] Macdonald left no doubt in the minds of his readers as to the spiritual and moral obligations that the religious press had in Canadian society. Its message was the Gospel of Christ. "Because he lived and died and rose again," Macdonald wrote, "Lord of Life and Saviour of men, there is hope for the lowest and help for the worst. In the light of the Cross, life's enigmas are to be read, and by the power of the Risen One life's burdens are to be borne." In keeping with the Free Church insistence on the headship of Christ over all things and the Idealist interpretation of this belief he had learned from George Paxton Young, Macdonald refused to limit the sphere of the religious press:

> This is its creed: All life is sacred, all interests are religious,
> all service is Christian; and this is its claim: All things are ours
> -- industry, commerce, learning, literature, politics, all are ours,
> and we are Christ's, and Christ is God's.[46]

When he left religious journalism for *The Globe* in 1903, he assured the readers of *The Presbyterian* that he would continue "to stand steadfastly for those things which to me seem first and best in the life of Canada," just as he had in the religious journals he had edited.[47]

Macdonald's position as managing editor of the most influential English-language Liberal newspaper in Canada between 1903 and 1915 increased his prestige as a conference speaker to those voluntary religious organizations that sought to mobilize the laity of the church for the uplift of the world.[48] Nevertheless, he remained convinced that the church was crucial to the well-being of a democratic society. The two great organs and agents of national life in a democracy, he argued in a pamphlet issued by the Laymen's Missionary Movement, were the church and the state. Other institutions, such as the press, the school, and social and industrial organizations, benevolent societies, clubs, leagues, unions, and associations of all sorts, were important insofar as they educated and moulded a public opinion that enriched and uplifted the life of the community. But the decisions that shaped the life of the nation ultimately found their way to the parliament to be legislated as the will of the people. The moral leadership in the formation of that will came from the church, equipped with "its agencies everywhere, its message to the heart and conscience of the individual, its ideal a regenerated social order, its emphasis on moral distinctions, moral obligations, and moral retributions, its motive the redemptive power and constraining love of a Divine Personality."[49] The only social institution that held a higher place in Macdonald's hierarchy of moral and social influence was the home.

In introducing *The Westminster* in June of 1896 as a "paper for the home," Macdonald claimed that the home was the strategic point in the moral warfare that raged in modern society. The home, in Macdonald's mind, was the root of social order because it was the first influence on the character of future citizens.[50] "The Christian ideal," he wrote, "is to prepare for larger freedom by a deeper education, and by a fuller appropriation of those spiritual forces that come from the Church and the Christian home, forces which act from within outward, and build up character which has true beauty and abiding strength."[51] To recognize the centrality of character formation in Macdonald's thought is to understand the key to his strategy for the Christianization of civilization and the uplift of the world. In the new age of democracy governed by public opinion that Macdonald saw dawning, character was the power that replaced position and privilege. People of good moral character were the key agents of change in society. Institutional structures were important, but they were powerless without good people working in them. Given enough people filled with the Christ motive of life and living according to the Christ standard of service, the redemption of the world seemed assured.[52]

The media through which Macdonald chose to work -- religious and general journalism, the pulpits of the church, and the platforms of a variety of voluntary organizations dedicated to the promotion of Christian missions and benevolence -- were designed to have a formative influence on public opinion in a democratic society and, in Macdonald's strategy, to create a collective Christian character and conscience that would determine the spiritual and moral quality of life in North America and, through its example and influence, the world. But it was Western culture, albeit the best of a purified and democraticized Western culture, that was the lens through which Macdonald perceived the spirit of Christ that was to uplift the world. Macdonald's 'Whig' assumptions about the desirability and inevitability of the triumph of liberal religion and government were the source of his cultural paternalism.

Macdonald's Society

Maurice Careless has encouraged Canadian historians to pay more attention to the "limited identities" that are found within the Canadian nation.[53] Clifford Geertz has encouraged students of religion to recognize that religious belief is a way of looking at the world, at the heart of which is the conviction that "the values one holds are grounded in the inherent structure of reality."[54] Macdonald was a member of a particular religious group within Canada, a south-western Ontario Presbyterian Liberal who reached the height of his career as Canada entered the years of economic prosperity and national optimism during the Liberal government of Prime Minister Wilfrid Laurier from 1896 to 1911. His way of looking at the world, rooted in his formative experiences and expressed in his mission addresses throughout the first decade of the twentieth century, reflected an evangelical liberal perspective that had made the transition from a rural to an urban context during the span of his career, and offered a convincing defence of Christianity in the midst of the crisis of faith that troubled many during the nineteenth century. He read history as the progressive unfolding of the values of liberty, benevolence, and prosperity, and believed that the advance of these values in the history of the nineteenth century proved the superiority of Christianity.

The Westminster welcomed the triumph of the Liberals under Laurier as the herald of the glad evangel that an upright nation had been born. The poetic talents of J. W. Bengough were called upon to express the tone

Macdonald felt the new Prime Minister brought to the Canadian people
after a year in office:

> Conscious somehow, in this leader,
> Of the ruling hand of God
>
> As the tribes of old beheld it
> On the wide Egyptian plain,
> Bringing gracious peace and union
> Out of long-borne strife and pain;
>
> Banishing old feuds and hatreds,
> Giving hope and courage new;
> Lighting up the broad horizon
> Of a future great and true.[55]

In the next issue Macdonald called on his readers to take advantage of the
new confidence and harmony Canada enjoyed and turn to the task of
fulfilling the destiny given to it by the God of the nations. "To do
something," he wrote, "to bring one's country up to the higher plane
among the nations of the world, to make one's countrymen honourable and
clean in public service as well as in private life, to help forward the day
of 'better manners, purer laws,' is not only the truest service the patriot
can render, but makes for the answering of the prayer: 'Thy kingdom
come.'"[56]

Macdonald's perspective had been shaped within a society that
embodied what British historians have called "the Nonconformist Conscience"[57] and what American historians have seen as the drive to create
"the Righteous Empire."[58] The signs of progress that marked the advance
of God's kingdom in the nineteenth century for Macdonald were the
increasing subjugation of the powers of nature to the use of humanity, the
extension of the liberties and rights of the individual person, and the
expansion of benevolent and reform movements which increasingly brought
human conduct and institutions into conformity with the will of God.[59]

This ideology of prosperity, progress, and purity functioned as a protest among the rising middle classes of the nineteenth century against the power and privilege of the old order of landed wealth and established position in church and state. Liberals regarded an aristocracy of education and ability to be preferable to the one of wealth and inherited authority that had ruled Europe and that, liberals believed, Tories and Churchmen had attempted to replicate in the Canadas. Social improvement in society and social advancement in the lives of individuals depended on an earnest and strenuous application of time and talents in order to promote the spread of an Anglo-Saxon evangelical Protestant culture and the glory of God.[60] During the last half of the nineteenth century, a revision of this liberalism took place, largely within the university community and among intellectuals,[61] that adapted its basic values to a more collectivist society emerging with the spread of industrialization and urbanization. Liberals invested communities with the personalities that they had previously reserved for individuals. They valued the liberalism of the Enlightenment for its destruction of the old order, but looked to a new liberalism grounded in Romanticism and Hegelianism as an essential step forward in the construction of a new organic social order that reflected more accurately the unity all things enjoyed as expressions of the mind of God.[62]

Macdonald's efforts in both the religious and the general press, modelled to some extent on the new journalism pioneered by W. T. Stead and dedicated to the exposure of corruption and immorality and the promotion of reform and uplift,[63] were an attempt to preserve and propagate this evangelical liberal ideology as the guiding spirit of the North American continent. Within this framework, he endeavoured to extend the individual earnestness of the old evangelicalism to the collective morality of the nation, and he extended the role of responsible citizenship played by the individuals within the nation to nations within the world community.

By 1910, however, Macdonald's perspective was beginning to encounter realities that did not conform readily to the spiritual and moral values he was convinced formed the central dynamic of human progress. Macdo-

nald could still look back on a relatively successful history of his version
of progress in Canada itself. The prosperity of the Laurier years, in
Ontario at least, was still a reality. The Liberal rule in Ottawa had
maintained a semblance of national unity, seemed open to more serious
discussions of reciprocity with the United States, and had passed legislation protecting Sunday as a day of rest. Laurier himself appeared to be
steering a cautious course in the uncertain waters of Canadian nationalism,
imperial ties, and relations with the United States, at least a course that
Macdonald could appreciate and support. But his insistence at the Toronto
mission conference that the spirit of Jesus could be seen permeating the
life of people in business, in industry, in politics and in international
affairs had a hollow ring, even when presented with his immense oratorical
skills. Dreadnoughts were not being built for defence alone. Capital and
labour were not moving toward a consensus. The movement in Canada for
the unification of the churches was encountering stiffening opposition
within Macdonald's own denomination. The world was proving far more
resistant to uplift and Christianization than Macdonald's rhetoric assumed.[64] Since the vindication of God's power was immanent to the course
of historical events, the history of liberal progress throughout the
nineteenth century that Macdonald had been able to evoke in support of
his enthusiasm for missions was seriously threatened by the collapse of
prosperity in Canada and the growth of militarism in Europe.

The ethos of Macdonald's world view, that evangelical liberal belief
in progress that gave it birth and sustained it, was cracking by August of
1914 under the weight of militarism, economic recession and political
failures. Short months earlier, Macdonald had continued to call on North
Americans to stand firm by their obligation for the uplift of the world in
the midst of its crisis. In the world's new civilization, prefigured by the
neighbourhood of nations in North America, Macdonald insisted "the
strength of any nation is not in its armed battalions, not in its dread-
naughts, but in the spirit of its people, in their ideals of freedom, in the
integrity of their national life and in the high and serious purpose of their
international affairs."

The secret of this new civilization in Canada and the United States, Macdonald assured the Student Volunteer Movement gathered over Christmas 1914 in Kansas City, was that both nations had learned something of true national greatness from the spirit of Jesus Christ. For the nation as well as the individual, the standard of greatness is service and the inspiration is unselfish sacrifice for others.[65] One of the ironies of the First World War was that the vast majority of Macdonald's colleagues in the Canadian churches used precisely this rhetoric to endorse enthusiastically Canadian participation in the war, seen as a global struggle for freedom, honour, and international law.[66] Macdonald, on the other hand, lost his job with the Toronto *Globe* because of his refusal to distinguish sharply enough between German and British militarism in speeches to peace conferences in the United States.[67] His health broke, and with it his spirit, in the confrontation between the idealism of his evangelical culture and the realities of the twentieth century.

Summation

In his studies of Canadian church history, John Webster Grant concluded that during the fifty years following Confederation churches had been the nursemaids of Canadian culture, through their influence over education, the press, and the pulpit. Few Canadians embodied this fact more fully than James A. Macdonald. The evangelical culture he nurtured aspired to bring human civilization into closer approximation to the spirit and ideals he associated with the Kingdom of God as revealed in the person and teachings of Christ. This would bring uplift to the world. Macdonald's vision of the ideal culture to foster liberty, progress and prosperity in the world community was formed within the ethos of Scottish Presbyterianism in south-western Ontario. He remained true to the religious and political ideals of that community, though their shape and scope expanded to accommodate the transformed society that emerged in Canada in the early twentieth century. His goal was to impose the values of an evangelical liberal culture on the world for its Christianization and uplift. Evangelization and acculturation were inextricably linked in Macdonald's mission thought.

Notes

1. John Webster Grant, *God's People in India* (Toronto: Ryerson Press, 1959), and *Moon of Wintertime: Missionaries and the Indians of Canada in Encounter since 1534* (Toronto: University of Toronto Press, 1984).

2. Grant, *God's People*, 3.

3. No biography of James A. Macdonald exists. The details of his life in this paper have been drawn from reminiscences by his contemporaries and colleagues, extensive readings in the journals and papers he edited and from some of his obituary notices. See *Globe* (Toronto), 15 May 1923; J. M. Duncan, "The Late Managing Editor," *Knox College Monthly*, 16 (May 1892), 25-6; and A. Shortt, "A Personality in Journalism," *The Canadian Magazine*, 29 (October 1907), 520-4.

4. On the Laymen's Missionary Movement in Canada, see J. S. Moir, "'On the King's Business': the Rise and Fall of the Laymen's Missionary Movement in Canada," *Miscellanea Historiae Ecclesiasticae*, 7, Bibliotheque de la Revue d'Histoire Ecclésiastique, Fasicule 71, Congrés de Bucarest, août 1980, 321-33, and M. Prang, *N. W. Rowell: Ontario Nationalist* (Toronto: University of Toronto Press, 1975), 64-9. Rowell was instrumental in bringing the Laymen's Missionary Movement to Canada and was a close colleague of Macdonald's in both religious and political matters.

5. William R. Hutchison, "Evangelization and Civilization: Protestant Missionary Motivation in the Imperialist Era: Introduction," *International Bulletin of Missionary Research*, 6 (April 1982), 50-1. The symposium was held at the 1980 meetings of the American Society of Church History and included papers by Charles W. Forman on the Americans, Hans-Werner Gensichen on the Germans, Torben Christensen on the Scandinavians, and Andrew F. Walls on the British. See Torben Christensen and William R. Hutchinson, *Missionary Ideologies in the Imperialist Era, 1880-1920* (Aarhus: Aros Publishing, 1984). Similar issues are addressed by: Stuart Piggin, "Assessing Nineteenth-Century Missionary Motivation: Some Considerations of Theory and

Methods," D. Baker, ed., *Religious Motivation: Biographical and Sociological Problems for the Church Historian* (Oxford: Blackwell, 1978), 327-37; Wilbert R. Shenk, "The 'Great Century' Reconsidered," *Missiology*, 12 (April 1984), 133-46; R. P. Beaver, "Missionary Motivation through Three Centuries," J. C. Brauer, ed., *Reinterpretation in American Church History* (Chicago: University of Chicago Press, 1968), 113-51; Max Warren, *The Missionary Movement from Britain in Modern History* (London: SCM, 1965), 9-77.

6.   Paul Jenkins, "Mission History -- A Manifesto," *Missiology*, 10 (April 1982), 199-210.

7.   An obituary in *The Outlook* (New York), 30 May 1923, noted that it was said of Macdonald that he "met more people, appeared on more public platforms, and spoke before larger audiences outside of his own country than any other Canadian of his day."

8.   James A. Macdonald, "The Christianization of Our Civilization," in *Canada's Missionary Congress* (Toronto: Canadian Council, Laymen's Missionary Movement, 1909), 115-21, and "America's World-Responsibility," in *Proceedings of the Men's National Missionary Congress of the United States of America* (New York: Laymen's Missionary Movement, 1910), 43-51.

9.   One of the primary concentrations for Hutchison and the others involved in the project on "Evangelization and Civilization" is on comparative history. My intention in this paper is to concentrate on the Canadian context, with some indication of the international connections that shaped Macdonald's ideas. Hopefully, it will make a small contribution to the variety of national studies that will make comparison possible. See Hutchison, 50-1 and 64-5.

10. This approach to intellectual history was suggested by T. W. Heyck, *The Transformation of Intellectual Life in Victorian England* (London: Croom Helm, 1982), 21-2.

11. Macdonald, "America's World Responsibility," 50.

12. Macdonald, "America's World Responsibility," 45. Macdonald's view of the crisis in missions had its roots in A. T. Pierson's classic statement of the claims missions had upon the North American churches,

The Crisis of Missions; or the Voice out of the Cloud (1886). He called the book "the best survey of the field" and in a review he quoted Pierson on the meaning of a crisis: "It is a combination of grand opportunity and great responsibility; the hour when the chance of glorious success and the risk of awful failure confront each other; the turning-point of history and destiny." See the *Knox College Monthly*, 5 (January 1887), 182-3. Macdonald also reprinted Pierson's article, "Our Opportunity and Our Risk," in the *Monthly*, 6 (May 1887), 36-41. In 1887, Pierson became editor of the *Missionary Review of the World*, hailed by Macdonald as "one of the best missionary magazines ever published." In 1888, the *Monthly* offered the *Missionary Review* to its readers in a combined subscription offer and received a very favourable response. See the *Knox College Monthly*, 7 (February 1888), 249, and (March 1888) 314. On Pierson's place in the missionary movement, see Dana L. Robert, "The Legacy of Arthur Tappan Pierson," *International Bulletin of Missionary Research*, 8 (July 1984), 120-5.

13.   Macdonald, "America's World Responsibility," 45. Macdonald, in common with most other evangelical liberals of the age, believed that each of the great historical civilizations had embodied particular ideas or values that he synthesized in his Hegelian world view. These ideas then contributed to the opportunity and obligation that Anglo-Saxon civilization faced in the latter part of the nineteenth century. In this article Macdonald claimed that Greece gave the world culture, Rome gave law and military prowess, Israel gave religion, Russia gave authority, Germany gave industrial organization, and Britain gave colonizing genius. America's destiny was "to exemplify before the world a nation of loyalty to the standards of service set up by Jesus, the Master of all." 50.

14.   *Globe*, 15 May 1923. Much was made by both Macdonald and those who admired his oratory of his Gaelic background. He joined the Gaelic Society in Toronto during his student years and was commended by Professor Adam Shortt of Queen's University for "his Celtic

fervour and enthusiasm for whatever enlisted his sympathies." Shortt, 520.

15. Macdonald's reminiscences of his boyhood were recorded in *The Westminster* (Toronto), 20 November 1897. On these Presbyterian unions, see John S. Moir, *Enduring Witness: A History of the Presbyterian Church in Canada* (Toronto: Presbyterian Publications, n.d. [1974]), 128-45.

16. On the relationship between Brown's religion and his politics, see John S. Moir, "George Brown," in W. S. Reid, ed., *Called to Witness*, 2 (Toronto: Presbyterian Publications, 1980), 39-46. In *Enduring Witness*, Moir noted that the Free Church spirit, with its crusades for moral and social purity and democratic principles in the affairs of both church and state, came to dominate the new united church after 1875. See Moir, *Enduring Witness*, 144.

17. On the expansionist spirit of the region in other matters and the inter-relationship between commercial, humanitarian, and religious motivation in the minds of expansionists like George Brown, see D. Owram, *Promise of Eden: The Canadian Expansionist Movement and the Idea of the West, 1856-1900* (Toronto: University of Toronto Press, 1980), 38-58.

18. The characteristic blending of individual obligation and disinterested benevolence in the wake of the religious revivals of the eighteenth century in Great Britain and the United States has been noted by Warren, *The Missionary Movement*, 33-5, and C. W. Forman, "A History of Foreign Mission Theory," in R. Pierce Beaver, ed., *American Missions in Bicentennial Perspective* (South Pasadena: William Carey Library, 1977), 69-140.

19. Macdonald, "Rev. Principal Caven, D.D.," *Knox College Monthly*, 15 (November 1891), 9.

20. Macdonald, "A Biographical Sketch," in William Caven, *Christ's Teaching Concerning the Last Things and Other Papers* (Toronto: The Westminster Company, 1908), xvii-xix. In addition to the articles collected in the posthumous volume, Caven's basic approach to the theological issues of the nineteenth century can be found in William

Caven, "Progress in Theology," *The Catholic Presbyterian*, 8 (October 1882), 273-82, and "Clerical Conservatism and Scientific Radicalism," *Knox College Monthly*, 15 (October 1891), 285-95.

21. In his biographical sketch, Macdonald detailed the political positions of Caven that had impressed him. See Macdonald, "Sketch," xxiv-xxv.

22. *The Westminster*, 18 December 1897 and 5 March 1898. Macdonald recalled that Henry Calderwood's *Handbook of Moral Philosophy* was used as a textbook, and noted in a review that R. L. Dabney's *The Practical Philsophy* adopted an approach similar to that of Young in its emphasis on conscience as the centre of human life and the importance of applied ethics in the personal, social, and civic dimensions of life. See *The Westminster*, 22 January 1898.

23. On Green, see Melvin Richter, *The Politics of Conscience: T. H. Green and His Age* (Cambridge: Harvard University Press, 1964). On Young's philosophical thought, see L. Armour and E. Trott, *The Faces of Reason: An Essay on Philosophy and Culture in English Canada, 1850-1950* (Waterloo: Wilfrid Laurier University Press, 1981), 85-104.

24. J. M. Duncan, "The Late Managing Editor," *Knox College Monthly*, 16 (May 1892) 26.

25. On the impact of this group on Scottish Presbyterianism, see A. L. Drummond and J. Bulloch, *The Church in late Victorian Scotland* (Edinburgh: St. Andrew Press, 1978), 215-91.

26. Macdonald's new perspective on Christian apologetics was evident in comments on the different approaches represented by F. R. Beattie, a Canadian teaching at Columbia, South Carolina, and R. Y. Thomson, the new professor of apologetics at Knox, in the fall of 1890. Macdonald argued that Thomson's Christocentrism avoided the intellectual skirmishes surrounding Beattie's theism. See "The Editor's Book Shelf," *Knox College Monthly*, 12 (September 1890), 286-7. See also R. Y. Thomson, "The Evolution in the Manifestation of the Supernatural," *Knox College Monthly*, 12 (October 1890), 293-318.

27. Macdonald found this perspective represented in Canada by T. B. Kilpatrick, a student of the Scottish evangelical liberals who came to teach at Manitoba College in 1899. His views on the 'Back to Christ'

movement were best expressed in an article on a series of lectures on the person of Christ that Kilpatrick delivered in Toronto in 1900. See *The Westminster*, 17 November 1900.

28. Bernard Aspinwall, "The Scottish Religious Identity in the Atlantic World. 1880-1914," in D. Baker, ed., *Religion and National Identity* (Oxford: Basil Blackwell, 1982), 505-18. Aspinwall made special mention of A. B. Bruce's journal, *The Modern Church*, as an important vehicle for the Christian reformism of the era and of Henry Drummond as an influential religious reformer in Glasgow, a city regarded by the likes of Jane Addams and Washington Gladden as a model of civic patriotism. Macdonald commended Bruce's publication to his readers in the *Monthly*, 15 (November 1891) 46.

29. *The Westminster*, 1 (June, 1896), 5. The preachers of the Cross, Macdonald had argued earlier in the *Monthly*, were "the tide-markers of Christian progress." He listed Paul, Origen, Chrysostom, Ambrose, Augustine, Luther, Knox, Whitefield, and Chalmers in the category. See Macdonald, "The History of Preaching," *Knox College Monthly*, 8 (May 1888), 30-7.

30. Macdonald's reactions to the various trends and debates of these years can be traced in two regular features of the *Knox College Monthly* during his years as editor -- "The Editor's Book Shelf" and "Here and Away". See also, Macdonald, "Pietism in Germany and Evangelism in Canada," *Knox College Monthly*, 8 (June 1888), 90-6). On the Scottish situation during this age of change, see A. C. Cheyne, *The Transforming of the Kirk: Victorian Scotland's Religious Revolution* (Edinburgh: St. Andrew Press, 1983).

31. *The Westminster*, 16 December 1899.

32. Macdonald, "The Study of Non-Christian Religions," *Knox College Monthly*, 9 (January 1889), 165-7. The article commented on lectures Macdonald heard in Scotland from Max Muller and A. B. Bruce. His position on the relation of Christianity to other religions was similar to that of George M. Grant, *The Religions of the World* (London: Adam and Charles Black, 1895). A more negative attitude to other religions, reflective of the exclusiveness of the older Calvinism, was

expressed by S. H. Kellogg, an American missionary and a teaching
colleague of B. B. Warfield at Alleghany, who was called to the
Toronto congregation that Macdonald and many of the faculty and
students at Knox attended in 1887. See S. H. Kellogg, "The Exclusiveness of Christianity," *The Presbyterian Review*, 1 (April 1880), 340-65.
Macdonald was also critical of the premillenialism that Kellogg shared
with mission leaders such as A. T. Pierson, although this difference
of opinion on eschatology did not prevent him from commending their
efforts in the promotion of mission work. See S. H. Kellogg, "Is the
Advent Pre-millenial?," *The Presbyterian Review*, 3 (July 1882), 475-
502, and Macdonald's comments on premillenialism in "The Editor's
Book Shelf," *Knox College Monthly*, 10 (June 1889), 117, and 13
(December 1890), 110.

33. Macdonald, "America's World-Responsibility," 47-8. George Leslie
Mackay, the Canadian Presbyterian missionary to Formosa whose
autobiography Macdonald edited and in large part wrote for publication, adopted many features of the Formosan culture as he worked
there. Kellogg warned that such an approach led to "the heathenizing
of Christianity." See S. H. Kellogg, "Mission Salaries in the Foreign
Field," *Knox College Monthly*, 9 (January 1889), 159.

34. Macdonald, "America's World-Responsibility," 49.

35. Macdonald, "America's World-Responsibility," 44.

36. Macdonald, "Christianization," 116.

37. Macdonald, "Christianization," 116. I have discussed this version of
the Social Gospel among Canadian Presbyterians in my doctoral thesis.
See B. J. Fraser, "The Christianization of our Civilization: Presbyterian Reformers and their Defence of a Protestant Canada, 1875-
1914" (Ph.D. thesis, York University, 1982).

38. Macdonald, "Vocation," 166.

39. Hutchison, "Evangelization and Civilization: Protestant Missionary
Motivation in the Imperialist Era: Comment," *International Bulletin of
Missionary Research*, 6 (April 1982), 64. In his comment on the
comparative insights offered by the four papers in the symposium,
Hutchison noted something that bears further investigation in the

Canadian context -- the difference between societies where the commitment to empire was new and accelerating, such as the United States, and those where imperialists were wearying of the civilizing business, such as Britain. A much broader sample of missionary promoters would be necessary to hazard any conclusions regarding the Canadian situation, influenced as it was by both cultures.

40. For overviews of the development of and dynamics within the benevolent empire of mainline American Protestantism, see Robert T. Handy, *A Christian America: Protestant Hopes and Historical Realities* (New York: Oxford University Press, 1971), and Martin E. Marty, *Righteous Empire: The Protestant Experience in America* (New York: Dial, 1970).

41. A. H. Young, "The Summer School at Northfield," *Knox College Monthly*, 6 (August 1887), 230-7. On Moody's role among these voluntary societies, see J. F. Findlay, Jr., *Dwight L. Moody: American Evangelist, 1838-1899* (Chicago: University of Chicago Press, 1969), especially, 339-55. For Macdonald's positive assessment of Moody and his work, see *The Westminster*, 28 August 1897, and 30 October 1897.

42. Macdonald, "Great Religious Conventions," *The Westminster*, 3 (August 1897), 53.

43. Macdonald, "Here and Away," *Knox College Monthly*, 9 (February 1894), 229.

44. For a history of the missionary society, see J. S. Mackay, "Knox College Student's Missionary Society," *Knox College Monthly*, 1 (February 1883), 17-21, and D. McGillivray, "History of the Knox College Students' Missionary Society," *Knox College Monthly*, 5 (January 1887), 158-62, and (February 1887), 227-32. The foreign missionary scheme was approved by the society in the fall of 1886 and its rapid progress can be traced in the pages of almost every subsequent issue of the *Monthly*.

45. On the growth of this empire, see Lorne Pierce, ed., *The Chronicle of a Century* (Toronto: Ryerson Press, 1929), 176-83.

46. *The Westminster*, 6 November 1897. On Protestant religious journalism in Canada, see T. R. Millman, "Canadian Anglican Journalism in the

Nineteenth Century," *Journal of the Canadian Church Historical Society*, 3 (March 1959), 1-19, and Steven Chambers, "The Canadian Methodist Magazine: A Victorian Forum for New Scientific and Theological Ideas," *The Bulletin*, 30 (1983-1984), 61-80. In Patrick Scott, "Victorian Religious Periodicals: Fragments That Remain," in D. Baker, ed., *The Materials, Sources and Methods of Ecclesiastical History* (Oxford: Blackwell, 1975), 325-40, the growth and function of the religious press in the context of the world's "first journalising society" is examined. The secular press in Canada is examined in Paul Rutherford, *A Victorian Authority: The Daily Press in Late Nineteenth-Century Canada* (Toronto: University of Toronto Press, 1982).

47.   *The Presbyterian*, 10 January 1903.

48.   One such organization that Macdonald, together with his friend C. W. Gordon, brought to Canada from the United States was the Presbyterian Brotherhood. It sought to recruit the leading men in all walks of life to conduct their work according to "sure principles of the Kingdom" and make the church "a leavening and purifying force in the life of the nation." See *The Presbyterian*, 29 November 1906, 21 February 1907, 7 April 1907, 7 November 1907, and 18 March 1909.

49.   Macdonald, *The Interests of the Nation in the Missions of the Church* (Toronto: Canadian Council, Laymen's Missionary Movement, n.d.), 6. Another expression of his views on the centrality of the church was found in an early editorial by him in the *Globe*, 22 January 1903.

50.   The centrality of the home in Macdonald's concern for social progress was his expressed reason for caution with respect to the women's movement at the turn of the century. The home, he assured the Women's Home Missions Society, was far more powerful than politics or parliament in shaping the character of the nation. *The Presbyterian*, 1 April 1909. Macdonald had also been supportive of women going overseas to the mission field to extend the influence of the home, as well as reach a section of the foreign population that in many cultures was closed to male contact. See "A Trained Nurse for Honan," *Knox College Monthly*, 8 (July-August 1888), 177-81. Mac-

donald served as Principal of the Presbyterian Ladies' College in Toronto from 1896 until 1901.

51. *The Presbyterian*, 1 January 1898.

52. Macdonald did not hesitate to specify the number of people needed. In Toronto in 1909, he claimed that "Four thousand Christ-men could redeem Canadian civilization in this generation." Macdonald, "Christianize," 119. Speaking to the student Volunteer Movement in 1914, he seemed convinced that "Five thousand students should revolutionize North America." Macdonald, "Vocation," 168.

53. J. M. S. Careless, "'Limited Identities' in Canada," *Canadian Historical Review*, 50 (March 1969), 1-10.

54. Clifford Geertz, *Islam Observed* (New Haven: Yale University Press, 1968), 95-7.

55. *The Westminster*, 16 October 1897.

56. *The Westminster*, 6 November 1897.

57. See, for example, D. W. Bebbington, *The Nonconformist Conscience: Chapel and Politics, 1870 - 1914* (London: George Allen and Unwin, 1982).

58. See Marty, *Righteous Empire*.

59. D. H. Meyer, *The Instructed Conscience: The Shaping of the American National Ethic* (Philadelphia: University of Pennsylvania Press, 1972), 124-5. Meyer analyzed the way in which these assumptions shaped the dominant Protestant morality of the United States in the nineteenth century.

60. "Evangelical religion," Stuart Piggin concluded, "sanctioned the climb to respectability and power of new classes against the resistance of older elites because progress for all was given the force of divine command. In an age of transition, to work for the glory of God was a more effective way to self-improvement than blatant forms of self-glorification. Hence the achievement motive released in new aspiring classes and sublimated by evangelical religion expressed itself in unprecedented evangelistic aggression. Between the rational age of Descartes (*cogito, ergo sum*) which appealed to few and today's sensuous world (*sentio, ergo sum*) which appeals to all, lay the great

age of mission (*actio, ergo sum*) which appealed to many." Piggin, 336-7.

61. The university liberals were studied in C. Harvie, *The Lights of Liberalism: University Liberals and the Challenge of Democracy, 1860-1886* (London: Allen Lane, 1976), and the intellectuals who wrote for the journals of Victorian Britain were examined in Heyck, *The Transformation of Intellectual Life in Victorian England*. Both groups in Canada were included in A. B. McKillop, *A Disciplined Intelligence: Critical Inquiry and Canadian Thought in the Victorian Era* (Montreal: McGill-Queen's University Press, 1979), and Ramsay Cook, *The Regenerators: Social Criticism in Late Victorian English Canada* (Toronto: University of Toronto Press, 1985).

62. This argument was expressed by T. B. Kilpatrick, "Pessimism and the Religious Consciousness," in A. Seth and R. B. Haldane, eds., *Essays in Philosophical Criticism* (Glasgow: Maclehose, 1883), 256-77.

63. Macdonald, "The Peace Message of W. T. Stead," in *Messages of the Men and Religion Movement, 1: Congress Addresses* (New York: Funk and Wagnalls, 1912), 104-24. On Stead, see J. O. Baylen, "W. T. Stead and the 'New Journalism'," *Emory University Quarterly*, 21 (1965), 196-206. J. E. Mennell, "William T. Stead: Social Politics and the New Journalism" (Ph.D. thesis, University of Iowa, 1967), noted that in the new journalism the reader was approached emotionally rather than intellectually. While Macdonald would have insisted that his writing encompassed both, he consistently referred to the heart and the conscience as those aspects of human perception to which he appealed.

64. For a survey of this period in Canadian history, see R. Craig Brown and Ramsay Cook, *Canada: 1896-1921: A Nation Transformed* (Toronto: McClelland and Stewart, 1974).

65. Macdonald, "Vocation," 165-8.

66. One of the starkest and most poignant contrasts within Macdonald's circle of friends was between himself and C. W. Gordon, a classmate at Knox College whose writing career as Ralph Connor Macdonald had launched. Gordon had no doubts whatsoever as to the rightness of

the war nor Canada's duty to give unquestioning loyalty to the British cause. See C. W. Gordon, *Postscript to Adventure: The Autobiography of Ralph Connor* (Toronto: McClelland and Stewart, 1975), 201-356.

67.   For a contemporary, though unsympathetic, account of Macdonald's views on peace and the issues surrounding his departure from the *Globe*, see J. C. Hopkins, *The Canadian Annual Review of Public Affairs, 1915* (Toronto: The Annual Review Publishing Co., 1916), 348-53.

9

A WATCHFUL EYE:

THE CATHOLIC CHURCH EXTENSION SOCIETY

AND UKRAINIAN CATHOLIC IMMIGRANTS,

1908-1930

Mark George McGowan

The two great waves of European immigration to Canada from 1900 to 1930 provided Canadian churches with an opportunity to evangelize and extend their control in the urban centres and on the Prairie frontiers. In these new mission fields Protestants and Catholics clashed, intrepidly struggling for the spiritual allegiance of the new Canadians. Much has been written on the role of the churches among the immigrants, but the quality and quantity of scholarly research on English-speaking Roman Catholic endeavours pales in comparison to that on Protestant churches and French-Canadian Catholics. Normally, this could leave the uninitiated with the impression that J. S. Woodsworth was correct when he commented, "The Catholic Church has, so far, done comparatively little for these peoples [immigrants]."[1] Recent exploration, however, suggests that English-speaking Catholics in the early twentieth century were enfused with a missionary zeal similar to that of Protestants, and inspired by Pope Pius X's pledge, *instaurare omnia in Christo* -- to establish all things in Christ.[2] Despite the shortage of clergy and the reluctance of available anglophone priests to serve under French-Canadian prelates in the West, several Anglo-Celtic Catholic programmes for immigrants existed between 1900 and 1930. Archbishop Neil McNeil's Catholic Immigration Office in

Vancouver, the Knights of Columbus Immigration and Welfare Bureau, the Sisters of Service and the Catholic Women's League immigrant hostel project, all established between 1912 and 1924, provided the main thrust of Catholic immigrant aid.[3]

Perhaps the most persistent, yet most overlooked of the English-speaking Catholic responses to immigration was the Catholic Church Extension Society. In 1905, an expatriot Canadian, Monsignor Francis C. Kelley, founded the first Extension Society in Lapeer, Michigan. Three years later, a Canadian group headed by Archbishop Fergus P. McEvay of Toronto and Apostolic Delegate Donatus Sbaretti established an independent Society in Toronto. Motivated by charity, Catholicism, and a modicum of patriotism, the C.C.E.S. announced its purposes:

> To foster and extend the Catholic faith. To develope [sic] the missionary spirit in the clergy and the people. To assist in the erection of parish buildings . . . . To extend the comforts of religion to pioneer localities. To supply altar plate and vestments to the poor missions. To encourage the circulation of Catholic literature. To found a seminary for the education of missionaries. To direct colonists to suitable localities. In a word, to preserve the Faith of Jesus Christ to thousands of scattered Catholics . . . especially in country districts and among immigrants.[4]

Moreover, the Society sought to achieve these objectives as a fund-raising body of clergy and laity, and not as a missionary order of priests in the field.

Such aspirations attracted some of the wealthiest and most prominent Canadian Catholics. Early governors of the C.C.E.S. included brewer Eugene O'Keefe, President Thomas Shaughnessy of the Canadian Pacific Railway, and Chief Justice Sir Charles Fitzpatrick. In addition, the Society reached a wide Catholic public by means of its control and ownership of *The Catholic Register and Canadian Extension*, one of the largest Catholic weekly newspapers in Canada. Archbishop Neil McNeil of Toronto referred to the C.C.E.S. as "the only organization in which our home missions can be regularly and effectively aided by the Catholic laity."[5] Consequently, it is no surprise that Pius X, delighted by the Society's aims and ideals, granted it a pontifical constitution in 1910.

John Webster Grant, in his paper, "The Reaction of WASP Churches to Non-Wasp Immigrants," asserted that Protestant responses to immigrants were characterized by three elements: threat, call, and challenge. Newcomers were perceived as a threat to the social order, and therefore Protestants felt called upon to save the foreigners from irreligion and 'popery', and challenged to assimilate them for the good of Canada.[6] Grant's three-point motif, with variations, may be applied to the Extension Society. The real threat in the eyes of the Society were Protestant missionaries who might lure Catholic immigrants away from the 'true Faith'.

Ukrainian Catholics of the Byzantine or Ruthenian Greek Rite were of particular concern to the Society because they lacked both clergy and chapels in Canada. The call for the Society was clear: preserve the Catholic faith in the Ukrainians and forge a strong Catholic presence from 'sea-to-sea'. Concurrently, C.C.E.S. leaders cultivated a national vision, maintaining that their "religious duties and patriotic endeavours" would not work at cross purposes.[7] The examination of the Extension Society's efforts to solve the Ukrainian "problem" offers an opportunity to encounter the spiritual and nationalistic aspirations of English-speaking Catholics in early twentieth century Canada. In their attempt to aid Ukrainian Catholics, the Society's leaders charted a course through dangerous waters between their French-Canadian co-religionists with whom they shared their faith on the one hand, and Canadian Protestants from whom they adapted a patriotic Anglo-conformism on the other.

Catholicize and Canadianize

The foundation of the society's philosophy and practice was laid by Monsignor Alfred E. Burke, president of the C.C.E.S. from 1908 to 1915. A native of Prince Edward Island, Burke was an eclectic figure who dabbled in Island politics, local agricultural societies and bee-keeping, and once campaigned for a tunnel to be built under the Northumberland Strait. Known thereafter as "tunnel Burke," he gained a reputation as a vociferous imperialist, Catholic crusader, and temperance advocate. As a Catholic leader at a time of racial tension within the Canadian church, Burke's uncompromising support for more extensive use of the English language in the church angered many of his co-religionists in Quebec. His lifelong friend Francis Kelley commented, "His opinions were like dogmas of Faith. No wonder Canada split over him. Half of his world swore by him and the other half at him."[8]

In 1908, Burke and his fellow governors of the Society began a vigorous programme of charity, evangelization, and English-language instruction, principally directed at immigrants in the Canadian West. The Society gave first priority to Ukrainian Catholics -- known to contemporaries as Ruthenians -- who hailed from Galicia in the Austro-Hungarian Empire. Two thirds of the Ukrainians in Canada were members of the Byzantine Rite Church, and therefore were in union with Rome. By 1911, Ukrainian Catholics numbered close to 150,000, comprising one of the largest non-English and non-French speaking groups in the Canadian Catholic Church.[9] Burke described them as a people, who by merit of their Catholic faith, were "thrifty, intelligent, energetic and ambitious" and thereby were "raw materials for the best type of Canadian citizenship."[10] It was important to Society leaders that the Ukrainian Church be strengthened in order to defend against ambitious Protestant missionaries.

In terms of Extension Society policy towards the Ukrainians and other groups, this threat of Protestant intrusion and the call to Catholicize were inextricably linked. There is little doubt that such developments as the rise of the Protestant Laymen's Missionary Movement, the successes of Methodists among Italians, and the work of Presbyterians among the Hungarians and Ukrainians provided the impetus needed to frighten Canadian Catholics into forging ahead with the challenge of the Society's programme of Catholicization.[11] Such fears were reiterated frequently by Society members and *The Catholic Register*. The Society's Chancellor, Archbishop Fergus McEvay wrote:

It is our bounden duty . . . to have a watchful eye for all these strangers. This is necessary from the standpoint of the welfare of the Church and especially because of the spiritual needs of the newcomers. You are aware that gigantic efforts are being put forward by the missionary societies of the sects, not only to maintain their own adherents, but to draw away the faithful who so rightly belong to our Church. That they have only been too successful is a matter which we must admit with feelings of compunction.[12]

In the public forum, Mary Hoskins, president of the Society's Women's Auxiliary, and Burke, who also served as editor of *The Catholic Register*, referred to the Protestant threat by reassuring Catholics that, "the Extension Society was founded to prevent wolves from ravaging the sheepfold."[13]

This Dominion-wide call for a "watchful eye" in the face of Protestant proselytizing was often accompanied by more extreme views. In his speech to the Second American Catholic Missionary Congress in 1914, for example, Bishop Michael Fallon of London, Ontario, an ardent Society supporter, expressed his long-term goal: " . . . we propose to make this North American continent Catholic; to bring America to Jesus Christ through the divine doctrines of the Catholic Church."[14] Similarly, in the pages of *The Catholic Register*, Burke proclaimed that Canada should be Catholic since "the Catholic Church alone can make it what God seems to have intended . . . , the home of a great race destined to achieve the highest ideals in religion and civicism."[15] Thus, certain leaders of the Society set the call to Catholicize on a higher plane, which can perhaps be describes as Catholic imperialism.

Rhetoric aside, the major task for the Society was to supply the Ukrainians with badly needed clergy, chapels, and schools. Utilizing the pulpit and the pages of *The Catholic Register*, Burke initiated a massive public campaign to resolve the Ukrainian "crisis." When speaking at the First American Catholic Missionary Congress in 1908, he warned that if Catholics failed to act quickly and meet the needs of Ukrainians in

Canada, the church would lose its Byzantine Rite brethren to Protestantism:

> We can afford no longer to resist the cry . . . of the strange
> peoples of our Faith -- Catholics and submitted to the Holy See
> -- which are pouring into our country without any pastor of
> their own. Within the last few weeks an earnest appeal on
> behalf of ONE HUNDRED AND FIFTY THOUSAND RUTHENIANS
> of this class has been made to the church of Canada . . . .
> These people have been victims of religious and political
> proselytizers to an incredible extent since they reached America,
> and through the agency largely of missionary societies. Just
> think of what the perversion of such a body of people would
> mean to us: . . . . And all this time we stand idly, and let me
> add criminally, negligently by, and permit them to do their work
> unquestioned.[16]

A similar appeal to the First Canadian Catholic Plenary Council in 1909, with the help of supporting documentation from Bishop Emile Légal of St. Albert and Father Achille Delaere, netted a pledge of $5,000 per Canadian diocese for the struggling Ukrainian Catholics.

The Society bolstered this education programme by sending two priests to the Prairies to assess the needs of the Ukrainian Catholic Church and investigate rumours of a Presbyterian attempt to establish a schismatic Ukrainian sect. Upon their return to Toronto in 1909, Fathers Nicholas Roche and H. J. Canning, armed with the testimony of bishops, missionaries, and the immigrants themselves, reported that Ukrainian Catholics were being drawn to a new Independent Greek Church, which was supported financially and spiritually by the Presbyterian Home Mission Board.[17] Moreover, it appeared that the Presbyterians were educating clergy for the new church at Manitoba College, and had founded an anti-Catholic Ukrainian newspaper, the *Ranok* ("Dawn").[18] Armed with this information, Burke mounted a fierce attack in *The Catholic Register* against the Presbyterian Home Mission Board, its chairman Dr. E. D.

McLaren, and Ivan Bodrug, the leader of the Ukrainian schismatics. Referring to the Presbyterians and their Ukrainian converts as "wolves in sheep's clothing" and a "hireling gang of missionary Hessians,"[19] Burke berated McLaren for his acts of "treachery":

> The Independent Church still retain their crucifixes, their altars, their confessionals, their pictures of the Blessed Virgin and saints, and what is more to the point, 'the bogus' priests supported by Presbyterian money, still try to make the people believe that they are Catholics in the true sense of the term. It is this deception of a simple people, this trickery, this fraud against which we protest . . . . We know that the ultimate purpose is to win them away from their allegiance to the Catholic Church. Is this necessary for a higher Canadian citizenship?[20]

Later, Burke even accused the Presbyterians of luring the Ukrainians away from the Catholic Church with gifts of whisky, "which they love."[21] As his campaign continued, however, the circulation of *The Catholic Register* rose from 3,000 in 1909 to 17,000 in 1913, and the coffers of the Society began to fill.

By 1912, Francis Kelley credited Burke and the Extension Society's campaign with having caused the demise of the Independent Greek Church and the subsequent resignation of McLaren from the Presbyterian Home Missions Board. More likely the Independent Greek Church died because of Ukrainian contempt for Protestant influences in the churches' administrative structure and liturgy.[22] In any case, when the Presbyterians ceased financing the venture, the Independents proved unable to survive on their own.

The Extension Society found it far easier to assail the Protestant home mission efforts that to re-create a viable church structure among Ukrainian Catholics. Liturgical, historical, and cultural differences between Society supporters and the Byzantine Rite Ukrainians were a constant source of contention. The problem of recruiting clergy was one case in point. Byzantine Rite priests were permitted to marry, but due to protests from the Latin Rite hierarchy in America, the Vatican in 1894 prohibited the further immigration of married priests to North America. In Canada, existing non-celibate clergy were objects of scorn, and on several occasions the Extension Society received letters from Latin Rite clergy protesting any effort to recruit married priests for the Ukrainians.[23] In conjunction with Archbishop Langevin of St. Boniface, the Society tried several methods of recruiting celibate clergy, all of which met with little success. Ukrainian celibates were few in number, and efforts to entice members of this small minority to Canada proved difficult. As one observer commented, the celibate Basilian monks who were enlisted earned little respect from the Ukrainian people, because such monks were usually drawn from among those considered to be the lowest ranks of Ukrainian society.[24] Other efforts to instruct French, Belgian, and Canadian priests for the purposes of transferring them to the Byzantine Rite met with mixed results. A few French-Canadians and Belgians were eventually sent to the West, but again many Ukrainians reacted to them, refusing to attend mass or confessions, afraid that these former Roman clergy were merely agents of Latinization.[25] Subsequently, the Society opened up schools in order to train second generation Ukrainian Canadians for religious life, and by World War I, the C.C.E.S. paid the tuition for the few Byzantine Rite candidates at St. Augustine's Seminary in Toronto.

The numbers of Byzantine Rite clergy in Canada, however, remained small. In 1917, there were only twenty-nine clergy for nineteen parishes and 139 missions, and most of these priests were non-Ukrainian. Such figures are astonishing, considering that in 1912 twenty-seven priests administered to a smaller flock.[26] The only noteworthy success in the clergy question came in 1912, when the Society was ably to finance the trans-Atlantic passage of Nicetas Budka, the first Ukrainian Catholic Bishop of Canada.

The building of the Ukrainian missions involved far more than the allocation of clergy and the construction of chapels. The Society had promised to be "purely and simply Canadian and Patriotic as well as religious," and as such its works would "singly uplift Canadian civilization."[27] With a double edged sword of Catholicization and Canadianization, the Extension Society leaders sought English-speaking missionaries for the West who would introduce the immigrant to Canadian life and thereby ensure both the newcomer's survival and the betterment of Canadian society. Monsignor Francis Kelley proclaimed publicly that the English-speaking priest would be "the backbone of the future," and likewise Burke had selected anglophone St. Dunstan's Seminary in Price Edward Island, his alma mater, as the Society's missionary college. Perhaps it was Archbishop Fergus McEvay who best asserted the Canadianizing and Catholicizing aims of the Society in a letter to Archbishop Louis Bégin of Quebec:

> . . . as to the Society's means of action, there may be ground for an honest difference of opinion. We have been striving to do our best in a most disinterested and, what appeared to be the most practical way. The foreign element, the main object of our solicitude can in the opinion of some of us at least, be reached in only one of two ways, either through the medium of men who speak their on language, or through the offices of those who speak the English language which is that of the majority in the West and which is the language the foreigners must learn of necessity if they are successfully to procure a livelihood in the places in which they live. You know how difficult it is to get good priests who speak the languages of the Poles, Ruthenians [and] Hungarians . . . .[28]

Bilingual schools, funded by the C.C.E.S. and operated by clergy, became an important vehicle for this language policy.

Ukrainian Catholics viewed the Society's implicit anglicization programme with mixed emotions. While many were hostile to anything that might threaten their mother tongue and culture, some Ukrainian leaders did encourage the use of English as a second language. In February 1910, for instance, Ivan Komarinzki, President of the Ruthenian Educational Society, informed *The Edmonton Capital* that Ukrainians "have to adapt themselves to Canadian customs, to learn the English language and to work at whatever their hands will do . . . . They have come to Canada to stay."[29] In fact, his one-hundred-twenty member society was busy translating classics of English literature into Ukrainian. Similarly, during the First World War, the *Kanadyskyi Rusyn*, the Ukrainian Catholic weekly funded in part by the C.C.E.S., printed the imperialist Rudyard Kipling's *The Jungle Book* in Ukrainian in serial form. Finally, letters to the editor appearing in *The Catholic Register* revealed that the C.C.E.S.-sponsored schools in Ukrainian settlements were zealously engaged in the teaching of the English language to immigrant children with noticeable success.[30]

By the time the First World War began, the Extension Society had established itself as an immigrant and frontier aid organization whose spiritual and national policies were firmly entrenched. In terms of direct aid to Ukrainian Catholics, the Society and its Women's Auxiliary had provided chapels, hundreds of priests' vestments, altar plate, Catholic literature, urban hostels for women, school funds, medical facilities, and money for the education of clergy.[31] An examination of the Society's financial records, however, reveals that the small successes of its first seven years were essentially cosmetic, and the Society never reached its potential. From 1908 to 1915, its average annual collections of nearly $17,000 were meagre when compared to the hundreds of thousands being raised by Protestant churches.[32] Archbishop Neil McNeil, the Society's second chancellor, from 1912 to 1934, lamented that while the Presbyterians in 1915 raised $402,399.34 for home missions, the Extension Society managed only $17,434.26.[33] Having examined the Society's financial records and operational practices, McNeil blamed deep seated problems in the Canadian Catholic Church and the Society's own methods for its unfulfilled potential in the immigrant missions.

The lukewarm attitude of many English-speaking Catholics toward the work of the C.C.E.S. McNeil also attributed to inadequacies in the Society's methods. In 1913, after weeks of investigation, McNeil stated that low collections resulted, in part, from the fact that five other English Catholic weeklies ignored the Society because of the threat to circulation posed by *The Catholic Register*.[34] Other Anglo-Celtic prelates blamed

Catholic apathy on Burke's poor relations with the hierarchy, his opiniona-
ted and overbearing manner, and the "rough and quite too belligerent" tone
of *The Catholic Register*.[35] The outbreak of war in Europe and the
subsequent drop in immigration levels also had a negative bearing on the
attention given the Society of Catholics. When McNeil attempted to reform
the Society, in light of these problems, the Board of Governors split into
two hostile camps: one group supported McNeil and the other vociferously
defended the Burke record.[36]

Coupled with the internal problems of the Society and English-
speaking Catholic apathy, was the inability of the C.C.E.S. to speak with a
national voice. From the Society's inception, many French Canadians had
regarded it as an anglicizing institution that threatened the traditional
French-Canadian role as missionary to the West and its peoples, and
thereby imperilled the linguistic balance in the church. Several factors
accentuated these French suspicions: the Society's preference for English-
speaking missionaries, the use of St. Dunstan's as the missionary college,
the dominance of anglophones on the Board of Governors, and the
imperialistic and pro-English attitudes held by Burke. Patrick T. Ryan, the
Auxiliary Bishop of Pembroke, noted that Burke's pleas on behalf of the
Ukrainians fell on deaf ears in Quebec because, "he was regarded as simply
trying to discredit the work of the French bishops and priests in the
West."[37] Eventually, at the height of the bilingual schools crisis in
Ontario, and the subsequent French-English split in the hierarchy,
Archbishops Bégin and Archambault quit the Board of Governors. By 1911,
the Society lost all of its French-speaking governors, except Bishop Légal,
and *The Catholic Register*'s continued opposition to bilingual schools
reinforced French-Canadian alienation from the Society.[38] Finally, the
external and internal problems of the C.C.E.S. caused Burke and Justice
Fitzpatrick to resign from the Board in May 1915.

Social Catholicism and Education

The new leaders of the Society, Archbishop McNeil and presidents
Father Thomas O'Donnell, from 1915 to 1924, and Father J. J. Blair from
1924 to 1941 did not shift the C.C.E.S. significantly from its Canadianizing

and Catholicizing ideals. The threat, call and challenge motif remains applicable for the period 1915 to 1930. The only important change was the Society's adoption of the social action principles of Pope Leo XIII's *Rerum Novarum*. As a bishop and former editor of both *The Casket* and *The Aurora*, McNeil had long been a respected advocate of social Catholicism. Accordingly, he restructured *The Catholic Register* by appointing J. A. Wall of Antigonish as editor, and by enlisting the services of Henry Somerville, a young Catholic writer and founder of the Catholic Socialist Society in his native England. Somerville's "Life and Labour" column helped to transform *The Catholic Register* into an articulate Catholic weekly with a profound social conscience.[39] In addition, the editorial comments were toned down, and the triumphalist photographs of Extension leaders which had regularly appeared on the front page, were eliminated. McNeil hoped that a reformed *Register* would precipitate a general improvement in the fortunes of the Society.

The Society's new president, Father O'Donnell, focussed his attention on the plight of the immigrants and retreated from unnecessary melées between Protestants and French-Canadian Catholics. Immediately following his accession to office. O'Donnell initiated a three-month campaign on behalf of the Ukrainian Church, requesting that all Catholics set aside their past differences and join in a triple alliance of bishops, clergy, and laity. From April to June 1916, O'Donnell's programme raised $16,754.91, a sum that surpassed all previous annual collections by the Society, save one. By the end of his tenure in 1924, O'Donnell's fund-raising expertise helped to increase the Society's annual revenue from an average of $17,000 under Burke to yearly sums in excess of $125,000. Moreover, the Ukrainians received the highest priority when these funds were allocated.[40] In addition to regular fund raising, O'Donnell instituted a bursary programme that netted over $45,000 for the Ukrainian Church and the education of missionaries. The Society's higher revenues also permitted the building of medical facilities and the erection of new Ukrainian schools in the West.[41]

Society projects were not restricted to the Prairies. In Toronto, for example, McNeil honoured Archbishop McEvay's earlier commitments to Ukrainian Catholics by helping to found St. Josaphat's Church in 1914.

Previously, the Ukrainians had worshipped in "Old" St. Helen's Church, and had used St. Peter's Parish Hall for their entertainment. Father Charles Yermy, pastor of the Ukrainians, praised the English-speaking Catholics of Toronto and the Extension Society for their help and hospitality. He was particularly grateful for the linguistic instruction offered by the C.C.E.S Women's Auxiliary:

> There was another need which confronted us; viz., the inability
> of our Ruthenian people to talk the English language. This was
> a great drawback and when the matter was brought to the
> notice of the Women's Auxiliary . . . the convenor of the
> teaching committee . . . graciously gave up her home two
> evenings a week during the winter months for the foreigner's
> classes. The young ladies of the Auxiliary gave their services as
> teachers and were at their posts punctually every teaching
> night, in spite of rain or storm . . . .[42]

It appears that even in its urban mission field, the Extension Society included the introduction of the English language to immigrants within its religious mandate.

As its programmes accelerated and its revenues increased, the Society remained imbued with the call to Catholicize and preserve the Faith, although there were fewer exhortations regarding the wholesale conversion of all Canadians. Similarly, the Society's leaders still considered the Protestant threat as acute, and by 1917, the new staff at *The Catholic Register* returned to the "ravenous wolves" rhetoric when referring to Protestant missionaries. The following report from the *Register* in 1917 indicates both the sense of urgency felt by the Society and the apparent insufficiency of its programmes:

> Foul birds have fattened upon her [Church's] harvest fields and
> because the harvesters were few, have in many cases ruined
> portions of the crop. The non-Catholic sects with coffers filled
> with the wages for the nasty work of proselytism have sent

forth among the poor foreigners well paid missionaries . . .
seemingly for the Canadianizing of the 'Strangers Within Our
Gates' but in reality to destroy them in the Faith of Jesus
Christ and to lessen the power of good in this Canada of ours,
of the Catholic Church, the civilizer of nations.[43]

Later McNeil added that in the event of a church union among Protestants, Catholic efforts would crumble in the face of potential Protestant
mission funds totalling eleven million dollars.[44] His sense of urgency about
the home missions never waned, and between 1916 and 1926 he addressed
Canadian Catholics on several occasions, imploring them to put the faith
ahead of all other concerns and to rally behind the Society's banner.
Despite numerous reforms and changes in the Society, this perpetual sense
of emergency indicates that the C.C.E.S. had failed to solve the Ukrainian
problem and was unable to rally many of Canada's 3.9 million Catholics.[45]

The internal problems of the Burke era had been solved, but new
obstacles and the ghosts of linguistic conflicts haunted the Society in the
post-war period. Renewed interest in foreign missions and the enormous
support given by *The Catholic Record* to the China Missions Society,
diverted the attention of Catholics away from less romantic mission
projects.[46] More important, however, McNeil and O'Donnell, despite
petitions and copious letters of appeal for *rapprochement*, failed to repair
the damage between the Society and the French-Canadian hierarchy in
Quebec. The French bishops retained their belief that the C.C.E.S. was an
anglicizing institution, and consequently, they preferred to aid the
Ukrainians and others by means of independent diocesan collections.[47]
Their suspicions were sustained by the comments of Society supporter
George Dale c.ss.r. who advocated a healthy and tolerant assimilation of
immigrants into English-Canadian society.[48] Such assertions only widened
the breach between English and French-speaking Catholics over home
missions.

The founding of St. Joseph's College, in Yorkton, Saskatchewan, for
Ukrainian boys was further evidence of the heightened drive for Canadianization and Catholicization that typified the efforts of Society members

such as Daly. In 1920, the C.C.E.S. announced the opening of this, their latest school, with lofty expectations:

It [the Church] hopes there to recruit those who in future will look after the faith and education of these Ukrainian people, and it's doing its best to bring these people in touch with our ordinary Canadian customs. These boys are thoroughly instructed in English and taught the value of the various institutions we have. They are taught loyalty to the faith and to the country into which they have come to build up a future for them-selves.[49]

Bishop Budka was fully aware of this effort to familiarize his flock with Canadian ways; in an attempt to show both his approval and his loyalty to Canada, he submitted letters to *The Catholic Register* and *Kanadyskyi Rusyn* praising the "benefits of an English education."[50] Such developments illustrate how *rapprochement* between the Society and French Canada failed, and with it the Society's hope to speak with a "national" Catholic voice.

The problems experienced by the Society within the Canadian Catholic community at large were compounded by the difficulties plaguing Bishop Budka. Budka's pro-Austrian stance before the First World War cast a shadow over his loyalty in the eyes of many Canadians. This suspicion persisted despite Budka's open proclamation of the loyalty of the Ukrainian people, and their desire to serve the British Crown.[51] After the war, however, Budka's administrative abilities were questioned by several Latin Rite bishops and by his own attorney, who complained of the bishop's loss of esteem among the Ukrainian clergy and people.[52] Furthermore, the post-war rise in Ukrainian nationalism, resulting from the creation of the Republic of Ukraine, and the birth of the Ukrainian Orthodox Church in Canada (1918), challenged the loyalties of many Ukrainian Catholics and provoked increased leakage from the church. This crisis was compounded by an inability to attract large numbers of new clergy and by the exodus of many serving clergy to the United States.

In the face of these problems of the early 1920s, many Canadian Catholics were unwilling to support what seemed to be a dying Byzantine Rite in Canada. In 1928, a confidential report submitted to the Canadian Catholic hierarchy concluded that the establishment of the Byzantine Rite in Canada had been a failure. Furthermore, it argued that since young Ukrainians were "eager" to be assimilated into Canadian society, the best remedy was "the *Gradual, Prudent, Systematic Absorption* of *Ruthenian Catholics* into the *Latin Church*."[53] Neither the Latin Rite bishops nor the C.C.E.S. mentioned or acted upon the report, even though by 1928 the Ukrainian Church was highly vulnerable: the *Kanadyskyi Ukrainiets (Rusyn)* had collapsed and Bishop Budka was recalled to Europe.

Despite the on-going crisis in the Catholic home missions after World War I, the Extension Society provided the Ukrainian Catholic Church with over $250,000 between 1920 and 1927. By the late 1920s however, Ukrainians took greater control over their church's financial affairs, and the new bishop, Basil Ladyka, rapidly recruited fresh clergy and re-established a Ukrainian Catholic newspaper. Between 1908 and 1930 the combined efforts of Ukrainians, the Extension Society, and some Canadian bishops provided the parish and ecclesiastical structure for a Byzantine Rite church into which future Ukrainian immigrants could settle with some familiarity. Consequently, with the Ukrainian Catholic Church proceeding on its own, the Extension Society shifted its attention to Amerindian missions in the Canadian West and North. When the Great Depression of the 1930s created an awesome demand for the relief of the rural and urban poor, the Society's focus altered accordingly: its interest in new Canadians would never regain prominence.

The Maturing Vision and Clash of Visions

In the final analysis, J. S. Woodsworth's comments regarding Catholic inactivity among immigrant groups cannot be considered definitive. English-speaking Catholics through the agency of the Catholic Church Extension Society attempted a vigorous immigrant-aid programme. When examined in terms of John Webster Grant's motif of threat, call, and challenge, these Catholic efforts bore striking similarities to contemporary Protestant developments. Extension Society projects were marked by a profound sympathy for the plight of the newcomer, a determined effort to extend and preserve the Catholic faith, and a firm conviction that Catholic immigrants must be integrated into English Canadian society, for their own good and the greater good of Canada. Ukrainian Catholics provided the Society with its greatest challenge, and helped reveal more fully the C.C.E.S.'s dual aspirations to Catholicize and Canadianize the newcomer. Despite clashes between the religious cultures of the Latin and Byzantine Rites, by 1930 the Ukrainians still retained their distinctiveness and independence, although English-language education was advancing successfully among Canadian-born Ukrainians.

The Ukrainian "question" and the concurrent rise of the Extension Society gave English-speaking Catholics the opportunity to exercise their belief that the extension of Catholicism and the building of a better Canada were two sides of the same coin. In his book *The Sense of Power*, Carl Berger has identified "many types of Canadian nationalism," each with its own understanding of history, the national character, and national mission.[54] Between 1908 and 1930, the English-speaking Catholics of Canada were by no means exempt from this phenomenon; they had begun to identify more readily with certain cultural, social, economic, and patriotic features of English Canadian life. As the product of a "double minority"[55] -- a linguistic minority in Canadian Catholicism and a religious minority in English Canada -- they were able to incorporate some of the characteristics of each majority without being fully assimilated into either. In time, they evolved a national vision which fused zealous Catholicism with many of the social and patriotic traditions of English Canadians. The fact that they survived as a double minority and perhaps their familiarity with "Americanists," such as Bishop John Ireland and James Cardinal Gibbons, provided English-speaking Catholics in Canada with confidence that Catholicism and patriotic citizenship were compatable. In this sense, the "watchful eye" of the C.C.E.S. over Ukrainian Catholics reveals the maturation of an English-speaking Catholic vision of Canada.

Such a vision had serious implications for both the immigrants and the Canadian Catholic Church as a whole. The Society and the Anglo-

Celtic hierarchy erred when it believed that French-Canadian Catholics would rally to their side in the fight against Protestant missionary efforts on the frontier. The vision of the C.C.E.S., and the Catholics it represented, threatened the "Gestae dei per Francos"[56] -- the French-Canadian belief that God had chosen the French as His stewards of the faith in the West. French Canadians, for whom Frenchness and Catholicity were intrinsic, inseparable, and almost mutually inclusive could never support the Extension Society as long as it exposed immigrants to a Roman Catholicism within a ciborium of English language culture. Subsequently, the Society failed to win the solid allegiance of the entire Canadian Roman Catholic Church, an institution plagued by its own inadequacy to quell the war of visions that swelled in its heart. Caught in the crossfire, Catholic immigrants received only a portion of the bounty that might have flowed from a church united.

Notes

1. J. S. Woodsworth, *Strangers Within Our Gates* (Toronto: The Missionary Society of the Methodist Church, 1911), 306.
2. "Opening Address," in F. C. Kelley, ed., *The First American Catholic Missionary Congress* (Chicago: J. S. Hyland, 1909), 4.
3. John Webster Grant, *The Church in the Canadian Era* (Toronto: McGraw-Hill Ryerson, 1972), 93-4; George Boyle, *Pioneer in Purple* (Montreal: Palm, 1951), 114; Jean Hullinger, *L'Enseignment Social des Evêques Canadiens de 1891 à 1950* (Montreal: Fides, 1957), 70; Ella Zinck, s.o.s. "The Sisters of Service--1920-1930," Canadian Catholic Historical Association, *Study Sessions*, 43 (1976), 23-38.
4. Archives of the Archdiocese of Toronto [hereafter AAT], Catholic Church Extension Society, *Minutes of Meetings*, 2.
5. AAT, Neil McNeil Papers, "Bulletin on the Ruthenian Situation," 1916.
6. John Webster Grant, "The Reaction of WASP Churches to Non-WASP Immigrants," Canadian Society of Church History, *Papers* (1968), 1-4.
7. George Daly, *Catholic Problems in Western Canada* (Toronto: Macmillan, 1921), 85; similar statements can be found in *The Catholic*

Register [hereafter *CR*], 12 November 1908, 18 February 1909 and 26 February 1920.

8. Francis C. Kelley, *The Bishop Jots It Down: An Autobiographical Strain on Memories by Francis Kelley* (New York: Harper, 1939), 149; AAT, A. E. Burke Papers, "Fact Sheet on Alfred E. Burke," by James McGivern, sj.

9. This paper will avoid the term Ruthenian -- now considered pejorative -- and will use "Ukrainian" throughout except where Ruthenian is used in direct quotations. Establishing an exact figure on the numbers of Ukrainians in Canada before 1921 is difficult due to the numerous ethnic identities -- Austrian, Galician, Bukovynian, Ruthenian, Ukrainian -- given by Ukrainians to the census takers. Ethnic and religious sources tend to be too liberal in their estimates. See Vladimir J. Kaye, "Settlement and Colonization," and Paul Yuzyk, "Religious Life," in Manoly Lupul, ed., *A Heritage in Transition: Essays in the History of Ukrainians in Canada* (Toronto: McClelland and Stewart, 1982), or AAT, Ruthenian and Ukrainian Papers, "Fact Sheet Submitted by Bishop Budka," 1919; or Alexis Barbizieux, *L'Eglise Catholique au Canada* (Quebec: L'Action Sociale Catholique, 1923), 72-8.

10. *CR*, 5 September 1912.

11. John Zucchi, "The Church and Clergy, and the Religious Life of Toronto's Italian Immigrants, 1900-1940," Canadian Catholic Historical Association, *50th Anniversary Edition, Study Sessions*, 2 (1983), 533-548; Zoriana Sokolsky, "The Beginnings of Ukrainian Settlement in Toronto, 1891-1939," in Robert Harney, ed., *Gathering Place: Peoples and Neighborhoods of Toronto, 1834-1945* (Toronto: Multicultural History Society of Ontario, 1985), 287-9.

12. Public Archives of Canada [hereafter PAC], Sir Charles Fitzpatrick Papers, 13:5815, Archbishop Fergus McEvay to Sir Charles Fitzpatrick, 29 December 1910.

13. Speech by Mary Hoskin in Francis Kelley, ed. *Official Report of the Second American Catholic Missionary Congress* (Chicago: J. S. Hyland, 1914), 282; *CR*, 16 September 1909.

14. "Sermon by Michael Fallon," *Official Report of Second . . .*, 33-4.
15. *CR*, 18 February 1909.
16. Alfred E. Burke, "The Need of a Missionary College," *The First American Catholic . . .*, 83.
17. Francis C. Kelley, *The Story of Extension* (Chicago: Extension Society Press, 1922), 163; *CR*, 24 February 1910, and 16 September 1909; R. P. A. Delaere, *Mémoire sur les tentatives de schisme et d'herésie au milieu des Ruthènes de l'Ouest Canadien* (Quebec: L'Action Sociale Ltée, 1908).
18. Reprinted in Toronto *Telegram*, 20 September 1909.
19. *CR*, 23 February 1911 and 17 August 1911.
20. *Telegram*, 20 September 1909.
21. *CR*, 7 April 1911.
22. Pauly Yuzyk, *The Ukrainians in Manitoba* (Toronto: University of Toronto Press, 1953), 73; *CR*, 16 March 1911; Kelley, *The Story of Extension . . .*, 164.
23. AAT, Catholic Church Extension Society Papers [hereafter CCES], Archbishop Paul Bruchési to Fergus McEvay, 13 June 1910; Achille Delaere to Paul Bruchési, 7 June 1910.
24. CCES, Memorandum of Leo Sembratowicz, 22 October 1909.
25. AAT, CCES, Memorandum of Leo . . . ; Josaphat Jean, "S. E. Adélard Langevin, Archévêque de St. Boniface et les Ukrainiens," Canadian Catholic Historical Association, *Reports* (1944-45), 103; Paul Yuzyk, "Religious Life," 149; AAT, CCES, Father Boels to Archbishop Fergus McEvay, 13 October 1909.
26. *CR*, 31 May 1917; AAT, Ruthenian and Ukrainian Papers, "Fact Sheet Submitted by Bishop Budka," 1919.
27. *CR*, 12 November 1908.
28. PAC, Fitzpatrick Papers, 12:5816, Archbishop McEvay to Archbishop Louis N. Bégin of Quebec, 27 September 1910. For more information on the Extension Society's relationship with French Canada see Mark G. McGowan, "Religious Duties and Patriotic Endeavours: The Catholic Church Extension Society, French Canada and the Prairie West, 1908-

1914," Canadian Catholic Historical Association, *Historical Studies*, 50 (1984), 107-120.

29. *CR*, 3 February 1910.

30. *CR*, 28 April 1910.

31. AAT, CCES, *Minutes of Meetings*, 17 April 1912, 25 and 4 April 1915, 47-51; *CR*, 16 January 1910, 28 April 1910, and 17 August 1911.

32. "Report of the Committee on Statistics," in *Canada's Missionary Congress* (Toronto: Canadian Council of Laymen's Missionary Movement, 1909) 323; John S. Moir, "'On the King's Business': The Rise and Fall of the Laymen's Missionary Movement in Canada," *Miscellanea Historiae Ecclesiasticae*, 7, Bibliothèque de la Revue d'Histoire Ecclésiastique, Fascicule 71, Congrès de Bucharést, août 1980, 329.

33. AAT, McNeil Papers, "Bulletin to Clergy," 8 April 1916.

34. AAT, CCES, *Minutes,* 2 April 1913, 28-30; PAC, Fitzpatrick Papers, 15, 6540, Archbishop McNeil to Fitzpatrick, 8 November 1913.

35. AAT, McNeil Papers, Bishop James Morrison to McNeil, 29 January 1913; Bishop David Scollard to McNeil, 4 February 1913; Auxiliary Bishop P. T. Ryan to McNeil, 26 February 1913.

36. AAT, CCES, *Minutes,* 2 and 22 April 1913; PAC, Fitzpatrick Papers, XV, 6540, McNeil to Fitzpatrick, 8 November 1913.

37. AAT, McNeil Papers, Bishop Ryan to McNeil, 26 February 1913; further evidence found in PAC, Fitzpatrick Papers, 82:45453-4, "Memorandum from A. E. Burke to the Duke of Norfolk," 6 April 1909, and 82:45458, Burke to Fitzpatrick, 9 April 1909. The French-Canadian objections are clearly articulated by Archbishop Langevin of St. Boniface: Archdiocesan Archives of St. Boniface, Langevin to Arthur Beliveau, 20 September 1909, Langevin Papers, 34286-91, and Langevin to Archbishop Begin, 21 August 1908, Langevin Papers, 34269-71. In the former Langevin exclaims: La conclusion est que l'idée de la "Church Extension Society" de bàtir un Petit Seminaire, à Toronto, pour recruter le clergé de l'ouest devient un ineffabilité, un fiasco, en face du nouveau Petit Seminaire de St. Boniface. Les ruthènes seront aidés par la 'Church Extension Society'; mais nous resterons maîtres du terrain et nous leur [sic] conservons la foi en

leur conservant leur [sic] langue qui est le rempart les idées ambitieuses des irlandais des Etats-Unis et du Canada, j'allais dire d'Ontario surtout . . . n'auront guères de réalisation j'espère. * * * Dieu nous préserve de ce nationalisme étroit et provocateur qui croit tout conquerir avec de l'argent et de beaux discours.

38. AAT, CCES, *Minutes*, 19 November 1910, 23. See also AASB, Father A. Husson, OMI to Langevin, 7 March 1910, Langevin Papers, 34297.

39. Jeanne Beck, "Henry Somerville and Social Reform," Canadian Catholic Historical Association, *Study Sessions*, 42 (1975), 96-103; Boyle, *Pioneer in Purple*, 125-38.

40. *CR*, 6 April 1916, and 6 July 1916; AAT, CCES, "Financial Reports, 1918-1929;" AAT, McNeil Papers, "Record of Donations Sent to the Ukrainian Diocese." Only in 1919 were Ukrainian missions given less than third highest priority. From 1921 to 1927 they were first.

41. *CR*, 9 March 1922, 11 March 1922, 25 March 1926, and 15 December 1927.

42. *CR*, 25 May 1911. See also Sokolsky, 284.

43. *CR*, 4 January 1917.

44. AAT, CCES Papers, CCES Annual Reports, 1922-23; *CR*, 15 January 1920.

45. AAT, McNeil Papers, "Bulletin to Clergy," 8 April 1916; "Can We Defend the Church?" 11 July 1920; "Circular Letter," 1 October 1924; "Circular Letter," 15 January 1926.

46. Grant Maxwell, *Assignment in Chekiang* (Toronto: Scarborough Foreign Mission Society, 1982), 57.

47. PAC, Fitzpatrick Papers, 28:15197-8, Bishop Roy to Fitzpatrick, 20 January 1920.

48. Daly, *Catholic Problems*, 85; *CR*, 4 March 1920; AAT, McNeil Papers, Speech by Bishop Henry O'Leary, "One of Our Needs for the Church in Canada," 2 January 1926.

49. *CR*, 4 December 1919.

50. *CR*, 25 July 1918; *Kanadyskyi Rusyn*, 29 January 1919.

51. Stella Hryniuk, "The Bishop Budka Controversy: A New Perspective," *Canadian Slavonic Papers*, 33 (1981), 162.

52. AAT, Ruthenian and Ukrainian Papers, Thomas Murray to McNeil, 21 May 1921.
53. AAT, Ruthenian and Ukrainian Papers, "Confidential Report on the Ruthenian Problem in Canada," 1923.
54. Carl Berger, *The Sense of Power* (Toronto: University of Toronto Press, 1972), 9.
55. John S. Moir, "The Problem of 'Double Minority': Some Reflections on the Development of the English-Speaking Catholic Church in Canada in the Nineteenth Century," *Histoire Social/Social History*, 4 (April 1971), 53-67.
56. Raymond Huel, "*Gestae Dei Per Francos*: The French Catholic Experience in Western Canada," in Benjamin Smillie, ed., *Visions of the New Jerusalem* (Edmonton: Newest Press, 1983), 39-54.

10

FROM JEWISH MISSION TO INNER CITY MISSION:

THE SCOTT MISSION AND ITS ANTECEDENTS

IN TORONTO, 1908 TO 1964

Paul R. Dekar

In a volume honouring John Webster Grant and his pioneer work in the history of Christian missions in Canada, it is fitting to examine the formative years of one of Canada's most remarkable "inner city" missions, the Scott Mission in Toronto.[1] At a time when thousands of hungry and lonely people continue to rely on hostels and food banks, the Scott Mission exemplifies an important, century-old approach to ministry by Christians in Canada's cities. Such missions emerged after 1880 as part of a general urban reform movement which accompanied the rapid development of modern Canadian cities. Canadian Christians came to believe that some special "home mission" effort should be undertaken to meet the needs of those living in poorer districts of Canada's burgeoning urban centres. The home mission concept was not new, but earlier it had been applied primarily to work in the west and among native people. In the 1880s new missions began to look after the physical health and spiritual welfare of "neglected and friendless" persons in Toronto and other cities.[2]

The Scott Mission is one of the oldest missions of this kind. Visiting it on any given day, one observes homeless people seeking respite from the loneliness of the streets; a line-up of skid row men and a few women filing in for free meals; families "shopping" in the free clothing and grocery stores; children arriving for day care or summer camps; people gathering for non-denominational services, Alcoholics Anonymous, first aid classes, family enrichment programmes, or other public meetings; and individuals departing for foster homes, with meals on wheels, or for myriad other purposes. Such ministry is characteristic of inner city missions and settlement houses found in every Canadian city. In most respects, The Scott Mission differs very little from other such missions.

The Scott Mission, however, does differ from others in one important respect. It originated as a mission to Jews. From its early years as the Christian Synagogue, until the death of its longest-serving superintendent, Morris Zeidman (1896-1964, superintendent 1926-1964), it had, as its primary purpose, to minister to Jewish people and to foster understanding of Jewish culture. Some of the main features of the mission, for example, its comprehensive programme of social ministries and its absence of denominational affiliation, can best be understood as a consequence of the need to develop a unique approach to ministry among Jews.

The opening in 1908 of a mission to Jews represented the culmination of a half-century effort by a few Canadian Presbyterians to respond to Saint Paul's affirmation that the Gospel "is the power of God for salvation to every one who has faith, to the Jew first . . . ." (Rom. 1:16). Interest in missions to Jews among Canadian Presbyterians received formal expression in the 1840s when funds were raised to aid missioners among Jews in Scotland and the Holy Land. A few years later, in 1859, the Presbytery of Kingston ordained Ephraim Menachem Epstein, a converted Jew trained in medicine and theology, to missionary service in the Holy Land. In 1892, another Canadian Presbyterian similarly trained in medicine and theology, Charles A. Webster, went to the Holy Land.[3] During the 1890s several missionary agencies organized the first mission to Jews in Canada, including a short-lived (1892-1895) Presbyterian mission in Montreal and the Toronto Jewish Mission, founded in 1893. These early ventures suffered from lack of financial support, dearth of interest among Christians generally, and organized opposition by Jews.[4] Only with the establishment of what was to become The Scott Mission did any mission to Canadian Jews achieve a measure of success and security within Canadian Protestant church life.

From Jewish Mission and Christian Synagogue to Scott Institute

In 1886, an overture was presented to the General Assembly of the Presbyterian Church in Canada under the signature of fourteen names, seeking "a Scheme of Missions to the Jews" and declaring as the reason for undertaking such an endeavour "that it was dutiful for the Canadian Presbyterian Church to co-operate in fulfilling the Gospel injunction, 'To the Jew first . . . .'" The General Assembly adopted a resolution by which it received the overture, agreed that Jewish Missions should have a place in the denomination and authorized the foreign mission board to establish a mechanism by which funds might be given to this purpose.[5] Two initial undertakings resulted which have already been mentioned -- the appointment of the Reverend Charles Webster as a missionary in the Holy Land, and the creation of a mission to Jews in Montreal from 1892-1895. A third undertaking was envisioned -- the opening of a mission in Toronto -- but the Presbytery of Toronto found it "difficult to support." Practically this meant that the Presbytery encountered the same two problems that the struggling interdenominational Toronto Jewish Mission confronted, namely, lack of staff and funds.[6]

An upsurge in Jewish immigration from Eastern Europe after 1905 resulted in the growth of the Toronto Jewish community to a population of 15,000 by 1907. Some Toronto Presbyterians expressed fresh concern to undertake a mission to Jews. In 1907, a resolution was placed before the General Assembly of the Presbyterian Church in Canada calling for a mission to Jews. The resolution passed, authorizing the Board of Foreign Missions "to commence a mission to the Hebrew people in Toronto, with the privilege of extending the work elsewhere in Canada as the circumstances may warrant."[7] The pastor of St. John's Presbyterian Church and a former moderator of Toronto Presbytery, the Reverend John McPherson Scott, was appointed to chair a subcommittee of the board to establish the Toronto mission to Jews.[8] The newly-formed "Jewish Mission Committee" in turn called Shabbetai Benjamin Rohold (1876-1931) to supervise the work.[9]

The choice of Rohold was significant because of his background, personal character, and leadership abilities. Son of a Jerusalem rabbi, Rohold received the best rabbinical education available in Jerusalem. He became a respected Talmudic scholar and went to England to continue his education. There, at the age of twenty-three he was converted to Christianity after a period of spiritual crisis concerning Biblical passages which refer to the promised Messiah. His personality was such that, unlike many Jewish converts to Christianity, he maintained friendly relations with Jews. He received further training in geography and Christian theology, became a missionary among immigrant Jews in Scotland, served in Toronto from 1908-1921 and, returning to the Holy Land, directed the British Society mission on Mt. Carmel until his death in 1931. His wife, Belle Petrie, whom he met as a volunteer worker at the Toronto mission, continued this work until 1960.[10]

Upon Rohold's arrival in Canada, the new Jewish mission officially opened at its first premises at 156 Terrauley Street (now Bay Street) on April 6, 1908. During the first year the mission launched a wide range of organizations, facilities and services including reading rooms, Gospel services, night school for men and women, sewing classes for women and girls, Sabbath School and Bible classes, boys' and girls' choirs and clubs, scouting and camping programmes, a nursery, tracts and Scriptures distribution available in English, Hebrew, and Yiddish, prayer meetings, systematic visitation of homes, a free dispensary, and poor relief.[11]

Such activity was not unique to home missions, but Rohold provided a rationale specific to the needs of a Christian mission to Jews. Rohold recognized that centuries of Christian persecution of Jews made Jews wary of overt proselytism. This led him to emphasize, as an essential approach to evangelism, "unconditional, whole-hearted, sincere love without interest."[12] Observing the conditions of sickness and poverty among immigrant Jews arriving from Eastern Europe, he argued that it was necessary to provide social services to those in need, quite apart from whether or not they ever expressed interest in the more purely spiritual or Christian dimension of the work. Understanding the former as a means to the latter, he clearly thought of mission in a "holistic" manner characteristic of many missiologists today. In this view, social concerns and sensitivity to people of other religious traditions are as significant as evangelism in the mission of the church.

The early records of the mission, summarized annually in detailed reports to the denomination, indicate that Jews availed themselves of the social services in considerable numbers. As an example, in 1910, 8234 Jews visited the reading room, 292 enrolled in English-language classes, a weekly average of fifty-eight girls attended sewing classes, 3,142 cases were treated in the dispensary, some 9000 tracts were distributed, and 5243 attended services of worship. Eight years later, Rohold compiled statistics for the first ten years of missionary effort. They included 10,610 Gospel meetings and 485 open air meetings, 21,000 cases treated in the free dispensary, including provision of medicine, vaccinations, operations and confinements, 40,500 visits to homes, shops and other institutions, and distribution of over 60,000 tracts and 5500 New Testaments.[13]

Such an ambitious range of activity necessitated a substantial staff. The first requirement was pastoral oversight. Rohold had not been ordained before coming to Canada. Because of the status of the work under the Board of Foreign Missions, special provision for Rohold's ordination had to be arranged. In 1909, the General Assembly of the Presbyterian Church authorized the board subcommittee to proceed with Rohold's ordination. This took place in the Presbytery of Toronto on September 28, 1909. Rohold also received special permission to participate in Presbytery affairs.[14]

Medical personnel, women to lead the girls' programmes, English-language instructors and others -- in all, a paid staff of ten -- had to be recruited. From the start, such numbers of qualified people, especially staff with sensitivity to the particular difficulties of ministering among Jews, could not be recruited. As a result the mission had to rely upon volunteer workers. While rooted positively in the voluntary principle of North American church life, the use of volunteers was not problem-free. In the case of the Toronto mission, funding and staffing became sources of tension with the denominations.[15]

By 1913 several administrative changes were necessary. The mission outgrew its original quarters at 156 Terrauley Street and moved to a new building constructed specifically for the mission in an area of Jewish settlement at 165 Elizabeth Street on the corner of Elm. The work was transferred from the Board of Foreign Missions to the Board of Home Missions and the Women's Home Missionary Society. This shift reflected the reality that the mission functioned within the Canadian context, the need to coordinate the Toronto work with other Presbyterian missions to Jews, including one opened in Winnipeg in 1910 and a new work begun in Montreal in 1914, and the growing recognition that "non-Anglo Saxons" constituted a special category in *home*, rather than *foreign* mission work.[16]

The most significant change was the formal organization of a Hebrew-Christian congregation. After three years of missionary activity in Toronto, seventeen Jews openly confessed Christ and petitioned to form an autonomous congregation. Rohold claimed that this was an important development which would render the work more accessible to other potential Jewish converts than most Presbyterian congregations. There were, he reported, many "secret" believers who feared open identification with the Christian church. Such fear was grounded in Jewish protests against Christian proselytism, including court cases, street-fighting, and the organization of an Anti-Missionary League.[17]

Under these circumstances, it is not surprising that Toronto Presbytery acceded to the request of the Jewish Christian petitioners and unanimously authorized the establishment of a congregation, which took as its name The Christian Synagogue.[18] This fitted the historic pattern by which, for over a century, Jewish missions generally permitted Jewish converts to Christianity to develop their own patterns of church life, including worship, outreach, and structure, within autonomous congregations. While this traditional pattern conflicted with the desire among English-speaking Protestants to assimilate non-Anglo-Saxons to Anglo-Saxon ways, Rohold argued that converts should be permitted to form their own congregation with its own unique qualities. From Rohold's perspective the fact that seventeen Jews formed the core of the new congregation was an unmistakable sign of momentous and imminent changes in the history of the people of Israel. There is no evidence that any debate took place at the time as to whether or not this was the best way to integrate Jewish converts to Christianity into the main body of the church.[19]

During the period of Rohold's capable leadership, he cautioned that it would be wrong to calculate success in statistical terms alone. The experience of missions to Jews generally was that conversions did not occur *en masse*. Nonetheless, he professed to be satisfied with the progress of the work that he did see. He summarized the accomplishments as of 1918:

> It has pleased God to show us some visible fruit of our labors. We have been privileged to listen to the testimony of hundreds of Jews confessing faith in Christ and to witness the baptism of forty-two adults and children . . . .
>
> We gratefully put on record the fact that our missionaries have won the hearts and confidence of hundreds of the Jewish people. Certainly there is not now the bitter opposition that we experienced ten years ago. An appetite has been created for the Word of God. The person of Jesus and His character are no more reviled, but are held in reverence by those Jews who come in contact with the Christian Synagogue. Of course, occasionally there is an outburst and agitation . . . . This is painful to the missionary, because he sees how Israel has fallen, and a greater compassion is awakened because Israel's deepest needs are made bare.[20]

Given the historic absence of numerical success in winning Jewish converts to Christianity, Rohold's satisfaction was certainly warranted. He appears not to have perceived that such factors as anti-semitism, the strength of Jewish traditions, the growing impact of the Zionist movement, and the development of Jewish philanthropic and educational institutions providing parallel services were insurmountable obstacles to greater success of the mission. Rather, he believed that the main stumbling block to further growth stemmed from another factor, inadequate funding and staffing. This viewpoint was formulated in a mission policy statement prepared in 1920. The statement stressed, among other things, the urgent need to recruit Hebrew Christian workers who knew both Yiddish and

Hebrew, who were saturated with Jewish worship, and who had an attractive personality.[21]

In a sense, this "job description" for a missioner among Jews fitted Rohold and few others. Candidates with such qualifications simply were not widely available. As well, however, there were growing doubts about the wisdom of sponsoring specific missions to Jews. Evidence for this is suggested by the shifting focus of the mission from work directed specifically to Jews, to an effort to reach "all peoples," by which was understood all the non Anglo-Saxon immigrants to Canada. The all-peoples approach, associated with J. S. Woodsworth, superintendent of All Peoples' Mission in Winnipeg, had gained general acceptance. According to this approach, mission should touch all phases of community life and become "the centre of social and religious influence for the neighborhood in the complex life of the Non-Anglo-Saxon quarter in the city." Mission was not only an activity of the church in response to the Gospel, but also a means of assimilating immigrants to Anglo-Saxon life. Activities such as language classes, Canadian Girls in Training, and Scouting were available to all new-comers, whether Jew or Gentile.[22]

As a result of the wide acceptance of these ideas of missions, it is understandable that the departure of Rohold for the Holy Land in 1921 created an enormous vacuum in leadership for the specifically Jewish focus of the mission. With no successor in view who possessed the qualifications identified by the 1920 policy statement, the home mission board named the Reverend J. I. Mackay, a non-Hebrew Christian, to succeed Rohold as superintendent of the Toronto home mission. It also reconceived the mission and reorganized it under a new name, the Scott Institute. This move reflected a measure of continuity with the work as it had existed since 1908, in that it commemorated John McPherson Scott who had long supported the cause of missions to Jews. It also reflected, however, an abrupt shift from the contextual approach of Rohold.[23]

The work continued on this basis for the next five years. In the minds of some, the diminution of the specifically Jewish character of the work posed no problem, for the institute had, as its principal aim, provision of social services which would enable all racial groups to adapt fully to the Canadian scene. Annual reports highlighted the efficiency of the mission in terms of providing services to new Canadians. This permitted the staff to do "more substantial work than ever before, even for the Hebrew population."[24] Given the premises, and the general circumstances of the period which included the debate over church union with Methodists, and the comprehensive vision of social reform among advocates of a social gospel, it is understandable that outreach to Jews received scant attention. Although the Jewish core of the worshipping congregation did not disperse, these Jewish Christians very much wanted for themselves an autonomous congregation and a pastor of Jewish origin.

From Scott Institute to Scott Mission

This hope was realized with the appointment of Morris Zeidman as superintendent of the Scott Institute in 1926. A Jew born near Czestochowa, Poland, Zeidman immigrated to Canada in 1912 at age sixteen. A year later he was drawn to the Christian Synagogue by a Yiddish sign describing it as The House of Good Tidings of the Messiah of the Children of Israel. Zeidman became first an inquirer and, subsequently, a Christian. He began volunteer work with the mission. In 1919, Rohold urged that he be given a staff position. Rohold praised Zeidman:

> Mr. Zeidman has done wonderfully well since I am away. He is sound in his message and as a young man, is remarkably good in ability, earnestness and zeal, and we ought to encourage him in every way possible.[25]

Fortunately for the future of the Jewish mission, Zeidman received the recommended encouragement. He went on for theological studies at Knox College, Toronto. Upon his graduation, ordination and marriage to Annie Aitken Martin, Zeidman took a small Maritime Presbyterian church for a year. He returned to Toronto in 1926 and, for the remainder of his life, provided a dynamic leadership for the Scott Institute.[26]

At the time of his appointment, Zeidman found the Jewish work of the Scott Institute at a low ebb. The all-people's approach had destroyed the corporate sense of identity of the Jewish congregation. Moreover, it had failed to generate an influx, in significant numbers, of adherents from other traditions or ethnic groups. In addition, disputes surrounding the union of most Presbyterians with Methodists and others to create the United Church of Canada in 1925 resulted in administrative delays in determining the future of the work. Finally, in 1926 the building which housed the Scott Institute was awarded by the civil court to the continuing Presbyterian Church in Canada.[27]

Newly named to head the mission, Zeidman moved to restore it to its original purpose as a mission to Jews. As a first step, he won approval to organize the congregation on a self-supporting basis as part of the Presbytery of Toronto rather than under the home mission board. As another step, he sought to secure a sounder financial base for the work. This he won in 1928, when, after receiving an invitation to take up another appointment in St. Louis, Missouri, the Presbytery of Toronto expressed its appreciation of his work, urged him to remain in Toronto, increased his salary, and provided for new quarters at 307 Palmerston Avenue where his family and the specifically Jewish activities of the mission could be housed adequately.[28]

Within a few months Zeidman reported with considerable satisfaction that the Scott Institute had been restored to its earlier state of health as a mission to Jews. As a mechanism to win support among Presbyterians for the cause of Jewish missions, in 1930 he launched the "first Hebrew Christian magazine in the Dominion of Canada," the *Presbyterian Good News and Good Will to the Jews* (renamed in 1942 the *Hebrew Evangelist*, and in 1948 the *Scott Mission Review*). In myriad articles published in this periodical and elsewhere, Zeidman articulated an approach to missionary work among the Jewish people similar to that of Rohold before him. Two essential elements of this approach were the need to minister to Jews intentionally and on an exclusive basis; and the need to demonstrate Christian love through meeting essential human needs.

Zeidman expressed these views in an important address, "Relationship of the Jewish Convert to the Christian Church," delivered to a special convocation of the International Missionary Council in 1931. Zeidman condemned the tendency to discredit missions to Jews and insisted that missions to Jews should attend to the spiritual *and* physical needs of people. Jews, he argued, would especially be responsive to a ministry of love. While this point should have been obvious, he observed that Christian-Jewish relationships were not always characterized by love. As an example, he cited the experience of his sister, Gertrude Manson, like himself a Christian, who had been denied membership in the Willard Hall W.C.T.U. in Toronto because of her Jewish background. Zeidman criticized the all-peoples approach then dominant in mission circles. Like Rohold before him, Zeidman argued that Jewish Christians wanted to worship with Jewish Christians, not with Italians, Poles or Anglo-Saxons. He urged that there still existed a place for autonomous congregations with a uniquely Jewish flavour, and he called for the creation of "a strong and virile Hebrew-Christian Church that will be self-supporting, self-governing, and self-propogating: a Hebrew-Christian Church that will give a newer and fuller meaning of the Church of Christ to the Western world, and interpret Him in the terms of the primitive Jewish disciples who walked and talked with Jesus on the Judean road." He believed that, in becoming Christian, a Jew did not ceased to be Jewish; rather, "free, independent and happy . . . rejoicing in the Lord Jesus Christ," he or she becomes "a better and more loyal Jew."[29]

Zeidman recognized that any Christian missionary to Jews had to break down old barriers and prejudices. Zeidman believed that the poor immigrant Jews to whom he was attempting to reach out would respond at a human level to anyone assisting them by providing needed food, clothing, and medicine. It was imperative that the church meet these needs. This did not exclude proclamation of the Gospel aimed at winning converts to Christianity. Zeidman believed that Jews were experiencing a time of spiritual awakening, and he gave considerable attention to street-preaching, house-to-house evangelism, and devotional meetings. Summarizing the interrelationship between evangelism and social concern as an approach to reaching the last wave of Jewish immigrants to Canada before the doors closed in the mid-1930s, Zeidman wrote:

These new-comers came to missions seeking advice, help and anxious to learn the English language . . . . There was great opportunity for work, but even then the missionary work was conducted on a very small scale. Jewish residents, who had lived in the city for a long period of years, were very seldom touched with the gospel message.

To back up these views, Zeidman pointed to statistics which showed that hundreds of Jews availed themselves regularly of the services of the mission and, during the 1930s, an average of fifty Jews participated weekly in religious meetings.[30]

There can be no question that Zeidman's appointment and approach contributed to the renewed vitality and growth of the Jewish work of the Scott Institute. This, however, was not the only factor. The mission also owed its surge of activity to the economic depression which began in the winter of 1929-1930. First, the social ministry of the Scott Institute to impoverished Jews was needed more than ever, for the immigrant community was harder hit than others by the Depression. Second, the mission was inundated by non-Jews, whose needs Zeidman and the mission staff could not ignore. Finally, already scarce sources of funding became even more scarce. Appeals for funds and bitterness about the penury of the denomination became major themes in Zeidman's relationship to the Presbyterian Church over the next few years.[31]

An official response by the Presbyterian Church in Canada to the Depression was little in evidence. Exhausted by the church union debate of the previous decade, and leery of the social gospel movement, church members were reluctant to support social action programmes, especially those sponsored on an ecumenical basis by several denominations, for example, the Social Service Council of Canada. Alleviation of the misery of the period was left to individual institutions such as the Scott Institute.[32]

Because he had always understood that responding to human need was integral to the mission of the church, Zeidman did not share the hostility of other church members towards feeding the poor and clothing the hungry. Zeidman proposed expanding this sort of ministry in response to the Depression. At its regular meeting on November 4, 1930, Toronto Presbytery authorized Zeidman "to organize a soup kitchen . . . for the relief of those suffering from hunger and poverty; and . . . to collect money for that purpose." A few days later, on November 7, one hundred and forty people received a hot meal at the "Royal York Soup Kitchen," which opened at the mission's older address, 165 Elizabeth Street.[33]

Zeidman explained the rationale for providing this service as follows:

> Every day we were interrupted at breakfast, dinner and supper
> by men looking for work. It was impossible for us to refuse a
> bite to those hungry men when they approached us when we,
> ourselves were eating.

Within a short time the mission was providing food for over 600 persons daily, for a total of 150,000 meals in 1931. That year as well, the mission distributed over 30,000 articles of clothing, supplied over 600 emergency baskets of groceries to poor and destitute families, and provided over 2000 beds for homeless unemployed young men. By the end of 1931, the work of the mission was gaining fresh support and increased attention. The Toronto *Telegram* of November 3 1931, in an article headlined "Church Again Feeds the Hungry," credited Zeidman for his excellent work and noted his willingness to lay out his own money if sufficient funds were not forthcoming from other sources.[34]

Zeidman acknowledged such recognition with satisfaction, as when he concluded his 1932 report with these words:

> The work of the Scott Institute is being noted by the press,
> broadcasted over the radio, and talked of in lodges, clubs,
> bridge parties, offices, shops and factories. It will go down in
> history as the contribution of the Presbyterian Church in
> Canada to the relief of the people at a time of world-wide and
> national crisis, unemployment and distress.

As the work continued Zeidman believed that it was responsible for "an epic of evangelistic and social welfare work the volume of which can be matched by few Church institutions in Canada." Describing the figures with a flair for exaggeration, Zeidman reported "almost staggering and unbelievable" growth not only in attendance by Jews at service and prayer meetings, but also in the quantity of programmes and participants in them.[35]

With the great increase in the social ministry of the mission, Jews as well as non-Jews were served on an equal basis at the soup kitchen at the corner of Elizabeth and Elm. Zeidman understood his own calling primarily in terms of his outreach to Jews. Throughout the 1930s he reported progress to the church in breaking down ancient barriers and prejudices between Christians and Jews. He could not claim great numbers of converts, but he believed that he was making significant inroads into the Jewish community. Among the evidence which he cited was the fact that contributions for the mission were received from Jews.[36]

Two dimensions of the Scott Institute's ministry -- mission to Jews and relief work -- remained inextricably bound together in Zeidman's thinking even as his ministry, or at least that of the mission, was inundated by needs of non-Jews. During the 1930s, as the storm clouds of anti-semitism gathered in both Europe and Canada, and as Canada virtually suspended Jewish immigration, Zeidman warned that talk of good will had to be matched in practice to be believed. He never wavered in his conviction that the only way to reach Jews with the Gospel of Jesus Christ was to break down the traditional stereotype of Christians among Jews through relief work, friendly personal relationships, compassion, and love. In an article on "Evangelizing the Jews," published in 1941, Zeidman argued that his approach had demonstrated accomplishments:

> Two factors have contributed to the breaking down of the enmity between the people and your missionaries: (1st,) The Scott Institute Relief Work. The Jewish people have a very high regard for charity. In spite of many vaudeville jokes about Jewish stinginess and miserliness, they are really a most

generous and compassionate people. They usually refer to themselves as 'The Merciful Children of the Merciful.' The charitable work of the Scott Institute has provoked the admiration of the whole community. During the dark days of the economic depression, we distributed aid to all, irrespective of colour, race or creed. Naturally the Jewish people are also helped, and that contributed a great deal toward removing misunderstanding and prejudice . . . . That brings us to the *second reason* for the success of our work. The Jewish people today no longer look on the Presbyterian missionary as an intruder, but as a friend, to whom they come in times of trouble and distress for counsel; and in times of joy, they in turn invite us to their homes to visit them as friends and neighbours. It is quite a common thing for me to be invited to the festive table of Jewish homes on Passover, and there, during the ritual recitation of prayers, I have been asked to lead in devotions, and have preached Christ as Israel's promised Messiah. No longer do we need police protection. On the contrary, our work is being appreciated, and practically all opposition has disappeared.[37]

This lengthy quotation prompts comment on at least two points. First, it is clear that social relief or welfare was central to the work of the mission. While some Jews took advantage of the resources of the mission and others contributed financially to it, the generous availability of food, clothing, health care, day camps, and other programmes was not directed exclusively to Jews. Already by the late 1930s the work had lost its exclusively Jewish character. Correspondence from the mission was on two letterheads, one from 165 Elizabeth Street, which had ceased to be a centre of Jewish occupancy but which was very much "inner city," and the other from 307 Palmerston Boulevard, which now housed the evangelistic services for Jews.

Second, while the transformation of the Scott Institute from a mission to Jews to a more typical inner city mission was well under way by the end of the 1930s, Zeidman himself continued to devote most of his energy to ministry among Jews. Zeidman never abandoned his own Jewishness, and he put his mission principles, summarized earlier, into practice. He conducted services in Yiddish, and he did not stress the Christian ordinances or sacraments of baptism and communion. He preached on distinctive themes which would serve to explain to Jews the essence of the Gospel of Jesus Christ in terms readily understood by Jews. He anticipated some of the theological discussions which have arisen in the Jewish-Christian dialogue, for example, by asking "Are Christian Gentiles Spiritual Jews?" and by refuting the deicide charge. Such practices and theological distinctives were not necessarily understood in the church at large, and therefore contributed to the tensions which culminated in Zeidman's move to sever the ties of the mission with the Presbyterian Church in Canada, but they undoubtedly contributed to the respect he gained among some Jews.[38]

From the start of his ministry in Toronto Zeidman encountered difficult in recruiting adequate staffing and raising sufficient funds from Presbyterian sources to support his ministry. Finally, in 1941, he resolved to continue the work of the Scott Institute as a non-denominational mission. Naturally there were other issues than staffing and funding involved in this decision. Especially, Zeidman believed that the difficulties he encountered were due primarily to the fact that he was promoting two causes of marginal interest to the church at large, mission to Jews and social ministry. In fairness to the Presbyterian Church it should be noted that the "divorce" was not a one-sided affair. Elements in Zeidman's mode of operation -- his willingness to ignore some of the financial controls placed upon him by the denomination, his highly contextualized approach to Hebrew Christianity, and his tendency to promote himself and the work of the mission above all other matters -- contributed to disaffection with the mission in the Presbyterian community.[39]

In the end the separation was of mutual benefit. For its part, the Presbyterian Church no longer had to contend with a rather independent minister and an unconventional, irregular ministry. For his part, Zeidman was free to continue his ministry without the oversight of those unsympathetic to his cause. The mission secured new and greater funding than had ever been the case, and Zeidman was no longer encumbered with a denominational structure that did not really support his ministry. Zeidman did not sever all his ties with the Presbyterian Church in Canada. He remained on its rolls as one of its ordained ministers, and he was subsequently honoured by his alma mater, Knox College, which awarded him a Doctor of Divinity degree on April 30, 1963.[40]

In late 1941 the Scott Institute ceased operating under Presbyterian auspices. As a non-denominational mission, renamed the Scott Mission, it reopened in new quarters at 724-726 Bay Street. A newspaper advertisement headline "'The Scott' Carries On" and noted that the ministry of service to the poor of downtown Toronto was available to "all needy, irrespective of race, colour or creed." The Scott Mission moved to its present address at 502 Spadina in 1948, at a time when the College and Spadina area was still largely a Jewish neighbourhood. Zeidman never abandoned his work among Jews.[41]

Another aspect of Zeidman's work remains to be emphasized, namely, his support for Jewish causes. During the 1930s he urged that Canada's doors be open to Jews fleeing persecution in Europe, and he unequivocally condemned anti-semitism, for example, by denouncing the lies and slanders contained in the notorious writing known as "Protocols of Zion." He defended his work on the grounds that "radical discrimination" festered in the Christian churches, thus necessitating activities such as his services of worship and out-door camp specifically designed for Jews.[42] After the Second World War he returned to his native Poland and undertook relief work for survivors of the Holocaust.[43] He supported Zionism and visited the State of Israel, maintaining cordial relations with relatives and friends who settled in the new state.[44] Although not himself greatly influenced by dispensational theology, which interprets events surrounding the re-emergence of a Jewish commonwealth as fulfillment of prophecy, Zeidman and his work were supported by dispensationalists. Members of his board, including its long-time chairperson J. H. Hunter, did use the dispensational method to interpret the Bible prophecy, thus interpreting the establishment of a Jewish state as a sign of the nearing end of this age.[45]

During the 1940s and 1950s the dual work of evangelism in Jews and alleviation of human suffering continued to dominate Morris Zeidman's ministry. Nevertheless the relief work of the mission came to be quite independent of missionary outreach to Jews. This was due in some measure to the success of the Canadian Jewish community in responding to the needs which the Scott Mission had long laboured to meet. Ultimately, the social ministry of the mission, initially developed as a means of reaching Jews, ceased to be needed by Jews. The need for a Christian mission of compassion did not, however, cease to exist. As a result, the work continued to grow. The mission had to enlarge its present site at 509 Spadina Avenue and, in 1959, Alex Zeidman, Morris' son joined the staff, preparing the way for the transition which took place with Morris Zeidman's death in 1964. Although not unconcerned with ministry to Jews, the younger Zeidman had the social ministry of The Scott Mission as his primary interest. In October of 1964 the last service of the old Hebrew-Christian congregation took place. The few remaining Jewish Christians thereafter joined various congregations around the city. The transformation of The Scott Mission from mission to Jews to an inner city mission was now complete.

Notes

1.   There is no comprehensive study available on Canadian Protestant missions to Jews or The Scott Mission. The best treatment of the early years is provided by Stephen Speisman, *The Jews of Toronto: A History to 1937* (Toronto: McClelland and Steward, 1979), chapter 9. See also, T. M. Bailey, *The Covenant in Canada: Four Hundred Years History of the Presbyterian Church in Canada* (Hamilton: MacNab Circle, 1975); Marilyn Felcher Nefsky, "The Cry That Silence Heaves," The Canadian Society of Presbyterian History, *Papers* (1983); John S. Moir, *Enduring Witness: a History of the Presbyterian Church in Canada* (Toronto: Presbyterian Publications, n.d. [1974]); Alex Zeidman, "Mission Work," in *Spirit of Toronto*, ed. Margaret Lindsay Holton (Toronto: Image, 1983), 208-15. An important paper is Ben Volman, "The Gospel of Hope To All: Morris Zeidman and the Relief

Work of The Scott Institute 1930-1941" (Unpublished paper, Knox College, 1980).

I wish to acknowledge the cooperation of several people: Mrs. Annie Zeidman, widow of Dr. Zeidman and an important staff member of the mission; the late Dr. Alex Zeidman, son of Morris and Annie Zeidman, head of The Scott Mission until his death in 1986; and Ben Volman interim pastor The Hamilton Friends of Israel. All expressed interest in the preparation of this paper and were generous in terms of time and documentation.

2. For background, Richard Allen, *The Social Passion: Religion and Social Reform in Canada, 1914-28* (Toronto: University of Toronto Press, 1973); William T. Gunn, *His Dominion* (Toronto: Canadian Council of the Missionary Education Movement, 1917); Paul Rutherford, "Tomorrow's Metropolis: The Urban Reform Movement in Canada, 1880-1920," Canadian Historical Association, *Historical Papers* (1971), 203-224; Paul Rutherford, ed., *Saving the Canadian City: The First Phase, 1880-1920* (Toronto: University of Toronto Press, 1974); E. A. Christie, "The Presbyterian Church in Canada and Its Official Attitudes towards Public Affairs and Social Problems, 1875-1925" (Ph.D. thesis, University of Toronto, 1955).

3. S. B. Rohold, *Historical Sketch. The Story of Our Church's Interest in Israel* (Toronto: Christian Synagogue, 1918), 4-6.

4. Hugh J. Schonfield, *The History of Jewish Christianity from the First to the Twentieth Century* (London: Duckworth, 1926), 209-10; A. E. Thompson, *A Century of Jewish Missions* (Chicago: Fleming H. Revell, 1902), 236-45. As an example of anti-mission polemic see Lewis A. Hart, *A Jewish Reply to Christian Evangelists* (New York: Bloch, 1906).

5. *Acts and Proceedings of the General Assembly of the Presbyterian Church in Canada* [hereafter *A and P*], 1886, cited in the Correspondence files on "The Mission to the Jews in Palestine 1892-1895," and United Church of Canada Archives, Toronto [hereafter UCA], "Presbyterian Jewish Mission in Montreal."

6. Speisman, 131-2.

7.   *A and P*, 1907, 70.

8.   Presbyterian Church of Canada Archives [hereafter PCA], *Minutes of the Presbytery of Toronto*, 1906; Rohold, 7.

9.   A brief biographical sketch is found in Jacob Gartenhaus, *Famous Hebrew Christians* (Grand Rapids: Baker, 1979), 153-9, and also, memorial notes in the *A and P*, 1931, and in *Christians and Jews: A Report of the Conference on the Christian Approach to the Jews, Atlantic City, New Jersey, May 12-15, 1931* (New York: International Missionary Council, 1931). A few other documents are available in the biographical files, PCA. In addition to his routine missionary work, Rohold was influential in the formation of the Hebrew Christian Alliance in 1914, serving as its first president and as editor of *The Hebrew Christian Alliance Quarterly*. He also was the author of three short books on Jewish history.

10. Gartenhaus, 158, concludes, "a missionary among the Jews for thirty-three years, he was the means of winning many Jewish souls for Christ. He was zealous in his activities to disseminate the good tidings among his fellow Jews. Yet he was always unassuming in his manner, courteous, and gentlemanly in all his relationships with his fellow men."

11. Rohold, 8-11.

12. Rohold, 10.

13. Rohold, 18-20; *A and P*, 1910, Appendix, "Jewish Work," 141-3.

14. *Minutes of the Presbytery of Toronto*, October 5, 1909, 89.

15. Volman, 19-23.

16. *A and P*, 1913, Appendix, "Our Mission to the Jews," 4-6.

17. *A and P*, 1912, Appendix, "Jewish Work," 149; Speisman, 134-9; Rohold, 21.

18. Rohold, 14; *A and P*, 1914, Appendix, "Mission to Jews," 4.

19. Rohold, 10, discussion of "How to reach the Jews." For a fuller treatment of the debate in missiological circles regarding missions to Jews, Morris Zeidman, "Relationship of the Jewish Convert to the Christian Church," in *Christians and Jews. A Report of the Conference on the Christian Approach to the Jews, Atlantic City, New*

Jersey, May 12-15, 1931 (New York: International Missionary Council, 1931).

20. Rohold, 20-21. A more frank discussion of the realistic limits of the accomplishments is provided by Morris Zeidman, "The Place of the Mission in the Scheme of Jewish Evangelizaion," *Good News and Good Will to the Jews,* 5:1 (November 1932), 1-5.

21. UCA, "Policy: Work amongst the Jews," 1920, Presbyterian Church in Canada, Board of Foreign Missions, Box 1, file 39. Also Speisman, 140-1.

22. For a general treatment, see Gunn, *His Dominion,* and J. S. Woodsworth, *Strangers within Our Gates* (1909; reprint edition, Toronto: University of Toronto Press, 1972). Also, N. Keith Clifford, "His Dominion: A Vision in Crisis," in Peter Slater, ed., *Religion and Culture in Canada* (Kitchener: Canadian Corporation for Studies in Religion, 1977); Margaret Prang, "'The Girl God Would Have Me Be': The Canadian Girls in Training, 1915-39," *Canadian Historical Review,* 54 (1985), 154-84; *A and P,* 1922, 52-4.

23. *A and P,* 1923, Appendix, "Work among Non-Anglo-Saxons," 13.

24. *A and P,* 1923, 12-13; 1924, 10-12.

25. UCA, 1919 Report, Presbyterian Church in Canada, Board of Foreign Missions, Box 1, file 38. Rohold was frequently absent from the mission, visiting other Canadian cities to promote the work of the mission and to explore opening other missions.

26. A brief summary of Zeidman's life is provided in his obituary, *A and P,* 1965, 690-1.

27. *A and P,* 1929, Appendix, "Report of the Missionary Work at the Scott Institute," 38.

28. *Minutes of the Presbytery of Toronto,* 6 March 1928, 8; PCA, M. Zeidman to George Geare, Convenor of the Home Missions' Sub-Committee on Jewish Work, 19 February 1941.

29. M. Zeidman, "Relationship of the Jewish Convert to the Christian Church," in *Christians and Jews,* 88-91.

30. *A and P,* 1933, 29; 1935, 41.

31. This is summarized from the paper by Volman and from interviews of Alec Zeidman and Ben Volman. Zeidman's reports (see, for example, *A and P*, 1936, Appendix, 28; *A and P*, 1939, Appendix, 24-5) reveal his financial concerns.

32. Moir, 237; G. Rienks, "Social Concerns within the Presbyterian Church in Canada" (Th.M. thesis, Knox College, 1966).

33. Minutes, Toronto Presbytery, November 4, 1930, 5. M. Zeidman, "The Soup Kitchen," *Presbyterian Good News and Good Will to the Jews*, 1:2 (February 1930), 2, cited by Volman, 11.

34. Volman, 13.

35. *A and P*, 1932, 35; 1939, 23.

36. *A and P*, 1932, 35.

37. *A and P*, 1941, 30-1.

38. See Zeidman's myriad pamphlets (undated but probably originating as articles in his periodical), including *Who Crucified Jesus?*, *Are Christian Gentiles Spiritual Jews?*, *Major Hebrew Feasts*, *Passover Appeal to the Hebrews*, and *Jewish Belief in Mediatorship between God and Man*.

41. For circumstances leading to the rupture, see: PCA, W. A. Cameron to Ross K. Cameron, 9 July 1941; George Beare to Ross K. Cameron 29 August 1941; and M. Zeidman to Ross K. Cameron, 19 June 1941.

40. *A and P*, 1965, 690-1.

41. Volman, 17; PCA, clipping from an unidentified newspaper, 1941, in The Scott Mission records; pamphlet, *Who? When? Where? A Brief History of the Scott Mission* (n.d.).

42. M. Zeidman, *Evangelizing the Jews* (c. 1934); for general background, see the paper by Nefsky, above, note 1.

43. M. Zeidman, *Report of Missionary Journey to Poland* (c. 1948).

44. M. Zeidman, "Report of Missionary Journey," *Scott Mission Review*, 10 (February 1954), on his visit to Israel.

45. J. H. Hunter, *Palestine, the Jew, and Peace* (1944); interviews with Alex Zeidman and Ben Volman provided some information on the background of supporters of the mission.